THE *RUNNER'S WORLD*
COMPLETE BOOK OF RUNNING
FOR BEGINNERS

THE *RUNNER'S WORLD*
COMPLETE BOOK OF RUNNING
FOR BEGINNERS

EDITED BY **AMBY BURFOOT** EXECUTIVE EDITOR, *RUNNER'S WORLD*

Everything You Need to Know to Begin Running for Pleasure, for Health – for Life!

RODALE

This edition first published in 2005 by
Rodale International Ltd
7–10 Chandos Street
London WIG 9AD
www.rodale.co.uk

© 2005 Rodale International Ltd

Illustrations © 1997 by Robert Frawley. Originally published in
Runner's World Complete Book of Running by Rodale Inc. Adapted and
revised in 2004 by Claire Moore for *Runner's World Complete Book of
Running for Beginners.*
Text and cover design by Studio Cactus

Printed and bound in China.

1 3 5 7 9 8 6 4 2

A CIP record for this book is available from the British Library
ISBN 1–4050–7741–7

**This paperback edition distributed to the book trade by Pan
Macmillan Ltd.**

Visit us on the Web at *www.runnersworld.co.uk*

RODALE

WE **INSPIRE** AND **ENABLE** PEOPLE TO IMPROVE
THEIR LIVES AND THE WORLD AROUND THEM

Contents

Introduction

Welcome to *The* Runner's World *Complete Book of Running for Beginners,* a book that I hope will change your life. It certainly has the potential. Running is the simplest and most effective exercise in the world. It can help you lose weight, live longer, gain confidence, improve your vitality, build stronger bones and much, much more.

But the question isn't really what running can do for you, to paraphrase John F. Kennedy's famous remark. Running has already proven its value millions of times with millions of ordinary people – people just like you.

The question is whether you're ready for running. If you are – if your mind is set, and you won't be sidetracked – then this book can lead you in the right direction. It can establish the foundation, point you down the right path and help you avoid the most common mistakes.

But it all begins with you.

GETTING TO KNOW YOU

A year or more before you started reading these words, I tried to work out who you are. I wanted to say, 'Hello. Please make yourself at home'. I wanted you to know that I recognize and understand you, even though we've probably never met. I decided that if we could develop a personal relationship from the very beginning, you'd be more likely to embrace the message of this book. So who do I think you are?

I think you might be overweight and have finally decided to do something about the excess kilos. Or you might be overstressed and have decided you need some get-away-from-it-all exercise time for yourself. You might be depressed; you might have heard that exercise can help you deal with depression. You might be a parent who has decided to begin exercising with the kids. You might be a one-time athlete, even a former runner, who got out of the habit, and now you want to start over again with a simple, effective running and walking programme.

You might be a card-carrying older person who wants to keep fit, active and energetic as long as you can. Many of you will be women who have seen and heard about other women's running success stories; now you want to join the party. Some of you will be men who have recently noticed a disturbing bulge around your midriff; you want to take action right now, before things get out of control.

So let's do that. Let's get going. Here are the 10 key principles behind every successful running programme. The rest of this book will then spell them out in fuller detail.

1. Start today. Procrastination gets you nowhere, whereas action creates boldness and more action. It's also true, for all of us, that today is the first day of the rest of our lives. If we don't get started today, we might not get started tomorrow . . . or ever.

You no doubt have a million reasons why you can't get started on a run/walk programme today. You're too tired, too busy and don't have the right pair of shoes. But forget about the excuses. Open the front door and get going. Don't look back, and don't turn back. You'll always be thankful that you got started today. (OK, that excuse about the shoes is a fairly decent one, but not good enough. You can walk 30 minutes today in whatever comfortable pair of shoes you own. Then get the new shoes tomorrow.)

2. Remember the child within. Maybe you think you don't know how to run, but that's not true either. You first learned to run when you were a child. No one had to give you any lessons. Learning to run was as simple as learning to say 'Mummy' and 'Daddy'. You simply mimicked what you saw others doing and found that running came to you easily and naturally.

You still know how to run today, because the child within you remembers. Unless you have a serious health issue of some sort, you can *still* run today. Of course, you might not be able to go very far, but that's OK. When you were a child, you ran and rested, catching your breath. Then you ran and rested again. The training programmes in this book (parts 9 and 10) follow exactly the same system. You'll soon be running and walking as happily as you were in your childhood.

3. Accept no barriers. Runners come in all shapes, sizes and ages. It makes no difference whether you are male or female, tall or short, plump or skinny, young or old. Whatever you imagine your limitations to be, they aren't. Others just like you have become fit, successful runners. Remember: celebrities such as Oprah Winfrey, Al Gore,

P Diddy, Gordon Ramsay, Sir Ranulph Fiennes and Lorraine Kelly have actually completed marathons. If they can do it, so can you.

Some of you will think that you are too overweight and out of shape to begin running. OK, so you might be right. But you're not too far gone to begin walking, and then to transition into the simple, progressive run/walk programme presented in part 10. The human body is an incredible machine. Set it in motion, and it will begin getting in to shape. Automatically.

4. Keep it simple. Running and walking are the oldest, simplest and most effective exercises on the planet. Your Paleolithic ancestors were running and walking six million years ago, and before long they were regularly covering up to 10 miles a day. Today, we don't, which is one of the primary reasons (along with a bad diet) why we have developed so many so-called 'lifestyle diseases'.

To reverse these diseases and get healthy again, you have to get moving. It's that simple. And this book has just one basic goal: to get you to the point where you can run for 30 minutes at a time. The first 30 minutes is the hardest (and the most productive). If you choose to go further, fine. The next 30 minutes, and everything beyond, will be easier than the first 30. If you choose to go faster, be my guest. I'll be cheering for you.

The training programmes in parts 9 and 10 gradually build you up to 30 minutes of running, four times a week. (I like 4 days a week because it puts you over the 50 per cent mark in a 7-day week.) Just start them, and stick to them. You'll soon feel better than you ever imagined possible.

5. Be a tortoise. Don't be a hare. More runners fail in their beginning training programmes by trying to go too fast than for any other reason. Avoid the speed trap. Relax. Take it easy. There's no hurry.

Any time you run, no matter how slowly, you are doing an exercise that physiologists term 'vigorous'. In other words, you're working hard enough to push your heart into the 'aerobic training zone' that produces dozens of health and psychological benefits. That's all you need to do. Be happy. And be satisfied with your pace.

6. Never, never, never quit. Prime minister Sir Winston Churchill made those words famous during the German bombing of London during World War II, and they work in running and many other areas of daily life. Running is tough. You *will* get tired. You *will* develop aches and pains. You probably *won't* experience the vaunted but mostly mystical 'runner's high'.

But none of these are sufficient reasons to give up your training programme. In fact, virtually no reason is sufficient. You'll miss days, you'll catch a cold, you'll have a long plane flight, your father will be taken into hospital and so on. Life is full of events we can't control, and these events will temporarily derail you from your best-laid plans. But don't give up. Get back on track as soon as you can. The lost time won't hurt you. Only giving up can do that.

7. Eat well. Beginning a training programme is only half the battle. The other half is making sure you follow – and stick to – a healthy diet. One without the other is really no good. The two belong together. Fortunately, many studies have shown that people who are successful with exercise programmes are also successful at improving their diets.

There's no secret diet for runners. You need basically the same foods as everyone else, beginning with copious amounts of fruits, vegetables, whole grains and low-calorie drinks. Runners don't need extra protein – almost all Westerners get more than enough as it is – and most try to include modest amounts of monounsaturated fats, like olive oil and rapeseed oil. You can even succeed on a moderate low-carb diet, as long as you are getting enough carbs to fuel your workouts.

8. Find a training partner or several. Nothing will help you succeed more than a training partner – a friend, family member, colleague or neighbour who agrees to meet you regularly for workouts together. You don't have to run together every day. Once or twice a week is fine. But having a regular exercise partner gives you someone to meet at the local street corner, someone to count on for motivation and someone to talk to on the run (about everything from your sore knees to your recent promotion). You need to be good enough partners to slow down and run the same pace, and to constantly remind each other exactly why you're out on the roads breathing and sweating so hard.

9. Maintain a balance in your life. It's great to begin a running programme and to create a whole new you. But it's equally important to continue supporting the old you, including family, work and community responsibilities. Running can become a consuming passion once you get into it. And that's good, particularly if it helps you achieve your goals. But you need to keep glancing over your shoulder to make sure you're taking care of the rest of your life, too.

The vast majority of regular runners have what is sometimes called a positive addiction. That means they start to feel twitchy when they miss a run, just as alcoholics get twitchy when they can't have a drink. But it's a good feeling in this case, because running produces so many positive health benefits (while alcoholism obviously does not). However, a few runners develop a genuine 'negative addiction' – they keep running while the rest of their life falls apart. You don't want to fall into this group. And I'm sure you won't.

10. Run for your life. Running and fitness should be lifelong pursuits. It's easy to be fit and healthy when you're in your twenties. It begins to take more effort when you're in your forties. And it can get downright challenging when you move into your sixties and beyond.

Here's the way I look at it. I'm getting older and slower every day (I happen to be in my mid-fifties). I can either continue fighting the good fight and staying in the best shape possible for me, which will somewhat diminish my ageing and slowing. Or I can give up and get older and slower at an ever-faster rate.

I choose the former for many reasons. Primary among them: running doesn't just keep me from ageing physiologically. It also helps me feel better and gives me more energy every single day of my life. You can't ask for much more than that.

But you also can't have it unless you make a commitment to regular exercise for the rest of your days. The payoff is worth the investment, I can assure you. And I hope you'll decide to invest in your personal health and fitness for life.

Amby Burfoot

1
WHY
RUN?

CHAPTER 1

Reasons to Run

All the Motivation You Need to Get Running

There are dozens and dozens of great reasons to run, ranging from weight loss to enhanced creativity. Coming up is a list of reasons that will inspire and motivate your running programme.

You are reading these pages because you have decided to begin a running programme. Or perhaps you are returning to one after a long break. You might want to lose weight. You might want to lower your blood pressure. Or you simply might want to begin feeling better than you have, which is one of the best reasons of all.

Only one problem: you're worried that running might be hard. And I'm not going to lie – I'm not going to tell you that running is easy. But I will guarantee you this: there is no shortage of good reasons to begin running, all of which are best understood and appreciated by each of us individually. In other words, I know what the benefits are, but only *you* can decide which ones are most important and most rewarding for you.

Recently, the *Runner's World* magazine editors decided to celebrate all the many reasons why we love running. We gathered in our conference room, surrounded by giant, autographed photos of the great ones – from Roger Bannister to Carl Lewis, Grete Waitz to Joan Samuelson – and we let our thoughts tumble out. Pretty quickly, we came up with more than 200 reasons why we love running. When we ended the brainstorm, we were still going strong. Over the page is the distilled list – the essence.

I hope you'll find the list inspiring and motivating. I'm sure you'll find many benefits that you would like to make a regular part of your life. So read on, and go for a little run. You'll be glad you did.

1. Running is the oldest, purest, simplest sport. Adam and Eve chased each other around the Garden of Eden. More than a million years ago, early African hunter-gatherers logged 10 miles a day on the high East African plains. The ancient Greeks staged running events in their original Olympic Games, and it was the marathon that stole the show at the first modern Games of 1896 in Athens. Running is the biggest worldwide fitness activity. And the best. OK, I'm biased. But trust me – I know what I'm talking about.

2. It makes you feel better every day. This doesn't mean that running will totally immunize you against depression, heart disease or diabetes. Or any of the other illnesses from which running does, in fact, offer protection. But I can guarantee that you will always feel better after a run. And that's powerful medicine.

3. The running community is so inclusive. One of the leading writers/speakers/personalities in running is a bloke named The Penguin. Another, Jeff Galloway, is a one-time Olympian who tells us to go ahead and walk during workouts and races. And nutrition wizard Dr Liz Applegate says it's OK to eat chocolate. Is this a great sport or what?

4. You can go for the burn. Running offers endless competitive opportunities, from sprints to ultramarathons. We human beings love to challenge ourselves. It's coded somewhere deep in our DNA. Which explains why we're always trying to shrink the size of the silicon chip, build solar-powered vehicles, develop protein-packed strains of rice and run new marathon Personal Bests (PBs).

5. Or you can go nice and easy. You don't have to run fast to have a great run, and you don't have to set a PB to enjoy a race. You get as many mental and physical benefits from a

Running offers endless competitive opportunities, from sprints to ultramarathons. It's coded somewhere deep in our DNA.

slow mile as you do from a fast mile. I have a friend who likes to say, 'I've never had a bad run. Every run is its own reward.' Good attitude. I heartily recommend it.

6. Running gives you great legs. One of the women staff members at *Runner's World* admits that she doesn't have the same overall shape as most glamour models. 'But I've got much nicer calf muscles,' she says. I've run with her. And I have to agree.

7. You don't need an instruction manual. If you can walk, you can run. If you run a little bit more, you can enter a 5-K. A little more, and you're heading for a half-marathon. It's as easy as that. This and other books about running are filled with useful stuff. But you know what I like best about running? It's so blessedly simple. The books are merely for reassurance and inspiration.

8. It's the world's best weight-loss exercise. Full stop. End of discussion. Every single weight-loss expert advises two things: exercise and sound nutrition. Running is the king of the calorie-burning exercises, and it's easy to do, any time, any place, any season.

9. You can run errands while you're running (and exercise the dog, too). Have a goal in mind when you set out to run – a target destination. I know someone who returns videos to Blockbuster and books to the library on an every-other-day jaunt that also takes her to the post office for pickups and deliveries. And every dog owner I know takes Fido to the park for frequent runs.

10. Running gives you more energy. This is one of my favourite things about running, and one of the more difficult to explain. I call it the energy paradox, because most people assume that running tires you out. Which seems a logical assumption. But it's wrong. In fact, runners report having more energy than non-exercisers. No one knows why, but it's as if the oxygen coursing through your veins reinvigorates your body, powering-up your physical capabilities.

THE BEST WAY

Q : What's the single best reason for beginning a running programme?

A : The best reason is the one that's most compelling to you. It could be that you just had your first child, and you want to make sure you stay healthy and vibrant enough to enjoy a long life with your child. It could be that your doctor has told you that you need to lose weight. It could be that you have just lost your job, and you need to begin a positive, active routine to ward off depression. Don't worry about anyone else's reasons for running. Find the ones that have the most meaning in *your* life.

Eat yourself fit

Running improves your diet. It's true: when you begin to exercise regularly, you eat fewer harmful fats and more of the recommended nutrients, according to a 7-year, 10,000-person study published in a major medical journal. Exercise and diet: the one-two punch that can help you knock out any weight problem.

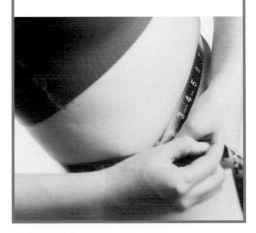

11. Running gives you a little quiet, reflective time to yourself. At *Runner's World,* we hear this all the time from our readers. For every proponent of social running, there's someone else who favours 'time out' to be alone with his or her thoughts. I see no reason to pick sides. As far as I'm concerned, both solo running and group running are great activities.

12. Running helps you reach creative breakthroughs. Writers, musicians, artists, chief executives, software engineers and many others use running to solve mental blocks and make must-do-it-today decisions. As prolific author Joyce Carol Oates wrote: 'Running! If there's any activity happier, more exhilarating, more nourishing to the imagination, I can't think what it might be.' The Greek mathematician Archimedes reached his 'Eureka!' moment in a warm bath. Many of us reach it in a warm sweat.

13. Oprah runs. US chat-show legend Oprah Winfrey finished the 1994 Marine Corps Marathon in Washington D.C. in 4:29:15 and made the cover of *Runner's World* the following April. It was our best-selling issue ever, and inspired untold thousands

'In a world so crowded with activities and responsibilities that it's difficult to make time for anything, running gives you a terrific workout in just 20 to 30 minutes.'

Running is like a best friend – always there, always dependable. It always comes through.

of people (especially women) to begin running. One of her producers, Lisa Erspamer, followed Oprah's example, lost more than 40 kg (6¼ st), and has finished several marathons. If Oprah can do it, so can you.

14. It's a positive addiction. The expression was first made popular by Dr William Glasser in his 1976 book *Positive Addiction*. Dr. Glasser wrote that you can replace a harmful addiction – such as smoking, alcoholism or overeating – with a positive one like running. Result: you're a happier, healthier person. And at *Runner's World* we've heard from thousands of runners who have followed this precise path.

15. Running gives you another excuse to relax in a hot bath. First, you ice any sore leg muscles for maybe 10 minutes. Then you slide into the steaming, frothy waters. Ahh, the perfect therapy. Just be sure to have a chilled bottle of your favourite sports drink nearby.

Running is a family affair. Many races have events for everyone in the family, and it's easy to plan an exercise activity for the whole family.

16. Running is a family affair. It's all-inclusive. Many races have events for everyone in the family, ranging from a family fun run to a 5-K race to a walk event. And it's easy to plan an exercise activity for the whole family. The smallest tot can clamber into his baby buggy, fit parents and grandparents can take turns pushing, and big brother can follow along on his new two-wheeler.

17. Running is like a best friend – always there, always dependable. We all go through phases in our lives – times when we run more, times when we run less. Your job gets too busy. Maybe you go on holiday. That's fine. Running adapts itself easily to your ebbs and flows. Best of all, when you need it more, it's always there for you. It always comes through.

18. Running improves your time management. Whether loosely lodged in your mental schedule or typed into your Palm Pilot, your daily workout is a focal point to your day. It helps you organize everything else you need to do. Often into B.R. (Before Run) and A.R. (After Run) time frames. Whatever works for you.

19. Running is honest. The distance and the stopwatch don't lie. The winner isn't determined by a group of nationalistic judges assigning point scores for form, skill and style. You get back what you put into it. In today's complex, political world, that's a refreshing thing.

20. You can use running to help others. Some runners collect coins they find on the side of the road. The super-fast win prize money to support their families. But many more runners turn their health, fitness and determination into fund-raising efforts for the less fortunate. In the UK, Race for Life has raised £50 million for Cancer Research since 1994, while in the last decade, the Team In Training programme in the US has raised $350 million for leukaemia and lymphoma research.

21. Running increases your appreciation for the environment. You crave fresh, clean air when you run. You long for soft trails, towering trees, pure water. You have plenty of time to ponder the big questions. You resolve: save the Earth. It's a lovely place.

22. Running lets you set new goals (and reach them). It's so easy to measure. Last month you could only run a mile at a time. Now, 2 miles. Progress like this leads to great satisfaction – and the desire to set and reach another goal. Some runners set distance goals. There are those who aim for faster times. Some want to run in other countries. Others want to lose weight or live long enough to see the grandchildren graduate. My recommendation: pick any goal, no matter how small, as long as it has meaning for you. Then go for it.

23. It's a great way to explore new places – cities or countryside. I know lots of runners who go out for a run as soon as they arrive in a distant city. This energizes you after a long drive or flight, helps reset your biological clock to a new time zone and gives you a great way to get familiar with the city's basic layout. Same goes for a country trail.

24. Running makes you look younger. I can't prove this, as the government refuses to fund vanity research. But go to

When you run, you crave fresh, clean air. You long for soft trails, towering trees, pure water.

any road race and look around at the vigorous, well-toned runners. As Roberta Gibb, the first woman to run the Boston Marathon (in 1966), recently said, 'People look at me and think I'm in my thirties or forties. My doctor says I have the physiology of a 30-year-old.' Gibb was 59 when she said this.

25. Running gives you a legal high. And a healthy one, too. After all these years, the 'runner's high' remains a fairly elusive subject, at least to scientists. No one is quite sure what causes it or why, and most runners would admit they don't feel a high on every run. Just often enough to make it very rewarding.

26. Running teaches discipline. And that's a good thing. It will serve you well in almost everything you do. In field after field, research has shown that the most successful people are the ones with a modest amount of talent and a tremendous amount of discipline. Practice makes perfect, both in running and in life.

Use running to help you explore new places. For example, it's a great way to find your way around a distant city after a long drive or flight.

27. Running has been fair to women. It embraced them long before equal opportunities legislation came on the scene. Of course, women runners had to stage a few sit-down strikes, but they had far more problems with officials and anachronistic rules than with their fellow runners. In fact, the men were happy to be surrounded by women in shorts. This receptiveness has encouraged tens of millions of women to begin running.

28. Women rule, genetically speaking. The late Dr George Sheehan counselled runners interested in fast performances to 'choose your parents carefully'. It turns out he was half right. The mitochondria in your muscle cells are known as the cells' 'powerhouses' because they control energy production. And all your mitochondrial DNA came from your mother. Dad didn't contribute. So if you want to run fast, choose your mother carefully.

29. Running will build your daughter's confidence and self-esteem. She'll be more in control of her life. Healthy

' Running is the king of the calorie-burning exercises, and it's easy to do, any time, any place, any season.'

result: she'll be less likely to have sex or to get pregnant at an early age. The US Women's Sports Foundation announced these study results in 1998, and they apply to girls in all sports. Especially lifetime sports like running.

30. Running is sweaty. And sweat is sexy. And that's all we're going to say on this subject.

31. Running improves your bowels! This is why the portable-toilet industry loves runners. But it's a good thing for you, too, as it may be one of the primary reasons why runners have a low risk of colon cancer.

32. The last-place finisher gets the biggest cheer. And deserves it. It makes perfect sense. After all, he or she has been running longer than anyone else in the race. We like the way spectators and other runners applaud the back-of-the-packers. Hundreds of well-wishers lined the streets to see brain-damaged ex-boxer Michael Watson complete the London Marathon, six days after he set out, despite being partially paralysed. He raised over a quarter of a million pounds for charity.

33. Size doesn't matter. In fact, small guys and girls may have an advantage, thank you. In a sports world too often dominated by steroids, 7-footers and heavyweights, it's nice to turn the tables now and again.

34. You can do it with your significant other. Running is a great activity to share with a partner. Even if your paces aren't perfectly matched, you can make time for those runs when one of you slows down and both of you simply enjoy each other's company. Lately, I've been hearing more about couples who make one or two running 'dates' a week, and I've been seeing proof of this in my own workouts in a local park. That's the romance of running.

35. Running is efficient. In a world so crowded with activities and responsibilities that it's difficult to make time for anything, running gives you a terrific workout in just 20 to 30

> *'Every run is a journey. You never know what you'll find.'*

WEBWISE

For information on all running-related topics, you can't beat *Runner's World*'s extensive website and running forums (including a Beginners' Forum). The best all-around running website.
www.runnersworld.co.uk

minutes. If presidents and prime ministers can make time to run, the rest of us can, too.

36. Running doesn't require much equipment besides shoes, shorts and a shirt. Everyone's got them, and that pretty much completes the equipment list. Throw on another layer when it gets chilly. Strip down somewhat when it gets warmer. Run barefoot on the beach. Count the waves. Feel yourself slip into the 'zone'. With no equipment weighing you down, it's easy.

37. Running is child's play. Every child runs, then stops, then runs again. It's not a workout. It's play. And when you run, you can return to this kind of play. As running's philosopher-king Sheehan wrote: 'There are as many reasons for running as there are days in the year. But I run because I am an animal and a child, an artist and a saint. Find your own play, and you will become the person you are meant to be.'

38. It's OK to walk. Just like the child. Run for a while. Then walk for a while. Smell the roses. Look for the blackbird's nest. Feel the soft earth compress beneath each footfall. Run some more. Keep at it for 30 minutes. Call it a workout. Call it being alive.

39. Running helps you sleep better. Recent national health statistics show an alarming downward trend in the average amount of sleep we're all getting. Alarming, because this can only lead to lower productivity, more accidents and more disease. You can ignore the statistics though – running helps you get a good night's rest.

40. Running makes you more brainy. I first started to notice this line of research more than a decade ago. At the time, frankly, I barely believed it myself. But the first study has produced a steady stream of follow-ups, all concluding that running is good for the brain. The most recent update: Japanese researchers found that a 12-week running programme significantly improved the reaction times and memory skills of their subjects.

Sleep better

Having problems getting your head down at night? Relax. A 1998 study concluded that exercise could be used to help people with sleep disorders. Hit the roads regularly, and also try to hit your pillow for 8 hours a night.

'Today's run could change your life in a way that you could never have imagined when you were lacing up your shoes.'

41. Running makes your baby brainier. We know – sounds amazing, doesn't it? But this was the conclusion of a study conducted a few years ago. Researchers found that the five-year-old children of women who had exercised during pregnancy scored significantly higher in an IQ test than the children of women who had remained sedentary through their pregnancy. So be a generous mum – go for a run.

42. Running gives you several recycling outlets. You can donate your old T-shirts and shoes to an organization that collects them. One group collects and sends shoes to Africa. Nike grinds up old shoes and reuses the rubber from their outsoles to build new running tracks. Or make your T-shirts into a quilt that commemorates races you've run.

43. Running shoes make your feet happy. Running shoes are about the most comfortable and healthiest footwear you can buy. Your feet are the foundation of your body. As they go, so goes the rest of you. So be kind to your feet. Wear running shoes on and off the roads.

44. Running is the core fitness activity for just about every other sport. Whether you want to climb Mount Everest or simply enjoy playing football for your local team, running

Studies have shown that running makes your baby brainier. Pregnant women who run are more likely to give birth to children with higher IQs.

To your health

Here's a short list of medical risks that have been shown to decrease with regular aerobic exercise like running.

1. Anxiety attacks (*Journal of Sport and Exercise Psychology*, 2001)
2. Arthritis disability (*Archives of Internal Medicine*, 2001)
3. Blood clots (*Arteriosclerosis, Thrombosis and Vascular Biology*, 2000)
4. Breast cancer (*Epidemiology*, 2001)
5. Cognitive disabilities with ageing (*Journal of Aging and Physical Activities*, 2001)
6. Colon cancer (*Medicine and Science in Sports and Exercise*, 2001)
7. Daily-life disabilities (*Journal of Gerontology*, 2001)
8. Depression (*Psychosomatic Medicine*, 2000)
9. Diabetes (*New England Journal of Medicine*, 2000)
10. Erectile dysfunction (*Urology*, 2000)
11. Gallstones (*American Journal of Gastroenterology*, 2000)
12. Heart disease (*Medicine and Science in Sports and Exercise*, 2001)
13. High blood pressure (*Archives of Internal Medicine*, 2001)
14. Hospital visits (*American Journal of Public Health*, 1999)
15. Immunity impairment (*Exercise Immunology Review*, 1997)
16. Mortality (*Medicine and Science in Sports and Exercise*, 2001)
17. Obesity (*Medicine and Science in Sports and Exercise*, 2001)
18. Osteoporosis (*American Journal of Epidemiology*, 1995)
19. Ovarian cancer (*Obstetrics and Gynecology*, 2000)

THE FINISH LINE

Three things to remember about this chapter:
1. Running is an Everyman sport. It doesn't matter who you are, or what you look like, or how much you weigh. You can become a runner, just as thousands of others have.
2. Running has multiple health benefits, all of which have been proven by medical studies.

It can improve your heart health, extend your life, lower your blood pressure and prevent diabetes, among many others.
3. Even more important, running is good for your state of mind. It decreases depression and increases energy and creativity.

is the place to begin. A recent medical study from Norway was entitled 'Aerobic endurance training improves soccer performance'. You get the picture. Running makes you better at other sports.

45. Running is full of great quotes from the Bible, great poets and thinkers, modern-day rockers and plenty of others. The all-time greatest running quote, according to Mark Will-Weber, editor of *The Quotable Runner:* 'Bid me run, and I will strive with things impossible.' (Shakespeare, *Julius Caesar.*)

46. Every run is a journey. You never know what you'll find. You don't know whom or what you'll see. Or, even more interesting, what thoughts might flash into your mind. Today's run could change your life in a way that you could never have imagined when you were lacing up your shoes.

Running shoes are about the most comfortable and healthiest footwear you can buy.

CHAPTER 2

No More Excuses

Discover Why You Were Always Destined to Run

Running is a simple sport, but not an easy one. Particularly not if you're totally out of shape when you begin, as Tawni Gomes and John Bingham were. But they succeeded, and you can too.

It's often the most unlikely people who make the best running-success stories. After all, it's one thing if you're whippet-thin, start running at school and keep running thereafter. It's quite another if you've led an unhealthy lifestyle for 20 to 50 years but are brave enough to launch yourself into a fitness way of living and exercising.

Tawni Gomes and John Bingham fell into this second category. No one would have ever expected that they could get themselves into shape and eventually run marathons. But they did.

Gomes is the founder of the Connectors (*www.connectingconnectors.com*), an Internet group of women committed to running and fitness. She weighed 125 kg (over 19½ st) when she began her running career. Today she weighs much less, has run a number of marathons and half-marathons, and has been featured several times on the *Oprah Winfrey Show,* along with her fellow Connectors. She is also author of the book *No More Excuses!*

Bingham, a.k.a. The Penguin, writes 'No Need for Speed', a monthly column that appears in *Runner's World* magazine. He currently tours the US and UK giving inspirational running talks at races and running clubs. He has broken 5 hours in the marathon but prefers to run more slowly so he can enjoy the moving celebration. Bingham operates the website *www.waddleon.com.*

You've put off running again and again. Now it's time to face up to it, get out there – and run.

In this chapter Gomes and Bingham share their words of wisdom with you. You can be sure they know what they're talking about, because they started at the very bottom of the fitness continuum and had to work long and hard to get in shape. No matter what your current condition, it could hardly be worse than the shape they found themselves in a few years ago. But they succeeded, and there's no reason why you can't join them.

TAWNI GOMES

It's OK for a 10-week beginning programme to take 20 weeks. Give yourself permission to progress at your own pace. Everyone has bad days and struggles to reach the next level. When I was making the transition from walking to running, I had to repeat weeks 1 and 5 on my schedule. I developed sore calves and tight hamstrings. But I kept on moving and I reached my goal. It just takes time.

Consistency is the key. Everyone has bad days, even Olympic champions. But you can't let bad days stand in your way. (If you're ill or injured, of course, you should rest.) Feeling sluggish? Bad luck. If you've planned a workout, stick to the plan. It's OK to run slower or walk more, but it's not OK to skip the workout. Remember this: you'll almost always feel better after the workout. Your energy level and your spirits will rise, and you'll be glad you did the run.

Drink water before, during and after your workout. In fact, it's a good idea to carry water with you all the time. When you launch into a beginning programme, you're going to sweat quite a bit, particularly if you're overweight. Water and sports drinks keep you fully hydrated, which prevents the kind of muscle fatigue that can disrupt your training. I've made it a habit to carry a water bottle with me on all my runs longer than 6 miles, and I can tell that the extra fluid improves my overall energy. I can run further and more easily.

Set big goals and baby goals. I started out as an overweight woman who'd recently been hit by a car and could barely walk. A year later, I finished my first marathon. How? By

Look the part

'Treat yourself to new running clothes,' says Tawni Gomes. *'It's a confidence thing. When I bought my first "real" running clothes, made from high-tech fabrics, I felt like an athlete for the first time. When you're making big changes in your life, such as beginning a running and fitness programme, it's important to reward yourself from time to time. I've bought myself gifts as small as new running socks with a fun pattern on them. It's the idea that counts. So be positive, and make it fun.'*

setting a big goal – the marathon – and many little goals to keep me motivated. You're never too fat or out of shape or time-pressured to begin a running programme. If I did it, anyone can. And along the way, you'll discover that you can accomplish much more than you first imagined.

There are no marathon police; you can't get arrested for going too slowly. Lots of runners would like to enter a marathon, but they're afraid they'll be embarrassed. They might not finish, the other runners might make fun of them or they might finish in last place. Well, of course, somebody's going to finish last, but it probably won't be you. These days, marathons are filled with plenty of slow runners who are simply trying to improve their lives just as I have and you can.

JOHN BINGHAM

Three steps forward, two steps back. I thought that once I started running regularly, I'd get better and better all the time. I thought my progress would be linear. For a while, it worked that way – I became faster with nearly every run. But suddenly the progress stopped. From that point on, I experienced a cycle of improving, hitting a plateau, slipping backwards, regrouping and moving on. It took a while, but now I'm fine with this.

Rubbish in, rubbish out. At first I had no idea how food worked inside my body. I didn't understand the correlation between what I was asking my body to process and what I was asking my body to perform. As I began to view food as fuel rather than as comfort or recreation, I discovered that the foods I wanted and the foods I needed were often the same. Of course, I still give in to an occasional craving, but at least I don't ignore the effect of food on my performance.

Sometimes less is more. I never considered myself the brightest person in the world. But I knew I had a great capacity to work hard. I applied that attitude to my running. When I read that one day of speedwork was good, I thought that three days would be better. If everyone else increased their mileage by 10 per cent per week, then I'd increase mine by 20 per cent. Eventually I learnt that improvement comes

'Consistency is the key. Everyone has bad days, even Olympic champions.'

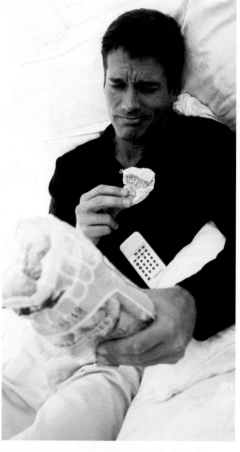

Everything in moderation: eating 'bad foods' once in a while won't affect your running performance.

THE FINISH LINE

Three things to remember about this chapter:

1. Be good to yourself. As you work on your fitness, you're going to have good days and bad days. Some very bad days – days when you wish you had never got up off the sofa. But don't beat yourself up. Instead, reward yourself. Everyone has bad days, but everyone is ultimately happy about getting in better shape.

2. Watch what you eat. You don't have to be particular about every single morsel that passes your lips, but you have to make changes. As John Bingham says, 'Rubbish in, rubbish out'. If you don't eat right, your workout programme will be that much more difficult to maintain.

3. Running is a process. It changes every day. You won't really learn to appreciate running until you learn to appreciate that every run is a new adventure. You can't be sure what's going to happen. But go with it. Ride the ups and downs. You'll be glad you did.

---

when you learn to balance effort and recovery. Now I mix lots of easy-run days around my harder workouts.

My body, my self. As soon as I began running regularly, I waited for my body to magically change into that of a runner. I expected my legs to grow longer and leaner, my muscles to become tight and sinewy. This never happened. My body may be leaner now, but it's still basically the same body I had when I started. It just works better.

Size matters, at least when it comes to shoes. I'd worn size 8½ shoes since I was 17 years old. So at the age of 42, when I shopped for my first pair of running shoes, I bought – you guessed it – size 8½. I didn't even try them on. The result? I didn't lose all my toenails before I realized these shoes were too small, but almost. Now I buy shoes that really fit, without considering the size on the manufacturer's label.

Being a runner is a process, not a destination. I was convinced that I could get into shape and stay there. I thought that once I had achieved a certain distance or speed, I'd won. But there's always something new to learn, some new workout to try or some new pace to achieve. Running is a continual process of assessing and evaluating where you've been, where you are and where you want to be.

THE BEST WAY

Q: What's a tried-and-tested way to get faster?

A: Run more. Lose a little weight. Run more. Wait for the fast times to come. As your fitness improves, you'll gradually begin to run faster relative to your first workouts. That doesn't mean you'll ever make it to the Olympics, however. Not everyone who plays the violin is invited to join a professional orchestra. At some point – many experts believe it will take 7 years – you'll get as fast as you ever get. So start training for that milestone.

WEBWISE

John Bingham's popular *Penguin Chronicles* online and in *Runner's World* magazine have made him the pied piper of the second running boom – people running for health, fitness, energy and that 'can do' attitude.
www.waddleon.com

CHAPTER 3

Making Time for Exercise

Why You Can Never Say Never to Running

Of course, you lead a busy life. But no training programme can work if you keep missing the workouts. So here are 30 strategies to help you find the time and stick to the plan. Survey after survey reveals that lack of time – whether actual or perceived – is the primary reason why exercisers don't get in a workout.

Obviously, this is a problem. Particularly when you're a beginner. Every workout that you miss is a workout that's not advancing you towards your goal.

That's why this chapter is about beating the restricted-time barriers that are conspiring to steal away your workout time. There are basically three time-management issues that you need to deal with: making time (questions of when, where and how); saving time (little do's and don'ts that add up to serious savings); and rethinking time (new ways to examine the relationship between your running and the time you need to do it).

We all lead busy lives, but this should never be an excuse to miss a workout – you'll only be cheating yourself.

Here are 30 can't-fail time-management tips from all three of these categories. Now stop making excuses. Get out for your run.

MAKING TIME

Your week actually has plenty of space for regular workouts as long as you've got a plan to make good use of the time.

1. Leave out time in your schedule for all the workouts you want to do in a given week. Do this first thing, at the start of the week before the blank spaces start filling up with errands and other time thieves. Use your PDA, computer calendar, desk diary or whatever other system you have for scheduling your week's activities. Just make sure you give your workouts the highest priority.

2. Get the most for your money. Several times a week, think quality, not quantity. It's the effort you put in that counts. If you've only got 20 minutes, use them. Don't miss your workout. Just do something a little shorter and harder than you might have planned.

3. Receive your bonus for focusing on quality. You don't just get stronger, but leaner too. Alternating faster with slower workouts not only builds running strength and speed, it also burns more fat. What's more, according to a 2001 study in *Medicine and Science in Sports and Exercise*, alternating fast and slow running helps you lose weight faster than a steady-pace effort.

4. Run earlier. Many runners have found that the early morning is the perfect time for a workout. It jump-starts your day with a jolt of energy that lasts for hours and relieves you of having to worry all day about when you're going to get the workout done. Not a problem. It's already done. If you have children, an early-morning run allows you to log your workout before they get up and need your attention.

5. Run even earlier. If rolling out of bed at 5:30 a.m. still doesn't give you enough time, then 'Get up earlier,' advises

'If you've only got 20 minutes, use them. Don't miss your workout. Just do something a little shorter and harder than you might have planned.'

1972 Olympian-turned-coach Jeff Galloway, 'and have a
stronger cup of coffee.'

6. Get a dog. 'There's no way you're not going to get up at
5 a.m. when there's a wet snout in your face saying "now,
now, NOW!"' says Greg Chaimov, whose pooch pulls him
through 4 miles, five mornings a week.

7. Tag-team tot patrol. One morning, afternoon or evening,
your spouse looks after the kids, you run. The next day,
reverse roles.

8. Park the kids. Many gyms now feature in-house nurseries.
In 60 minutes, you can get in your treadmill time, with
additional time left over for a basic strength workout, a core
strength workout on a Swiss exercise ball or an excellent
circuit-training workout that takes you rapidly through a
number of strength stations.

Owning a dog can help you get up, out and running – he always needs walking.

9. Circle the kids. While your kids are playing football (tennis, rugby, whatever), run and/or walk loops around the outside of the field. 'I do this twice a week,' says mother-of-two Judie Simpson. 'Once I'll do a steady run. Another day, I'll do sprints on the long side of the field and slow jogs on the short side.'

10. Give up the commute. Take your togs to work and do your run from the office after work while everyone else is spending a miserable hour in fingernail-gnawing gridlock. By the time you've finished your run – sweating, pleasantly tired, totally detorqued from the day's workplace rigours – the whole smoggy mess will have cleared out and you can cruise home comfortably (while feeling very, very clever).

11. Fast-forward to free time. Many would-be exercisers who whine 'No time to run' find plenty of time to develop blisters on their remote-control thumbs. Well, hidden away inside more than half the TV shows on the box are precious minutes of running time. They're called adverts – and they're your friends. Instead of watching the original broadcasts of your favourite shows, watch them on tape – freeing up enough time for you to fit in a decent little workout.

12. Goal for it. Too many runners think too long range – a 6-month or year-long plan – when laying out their training. 'But that vision can be lost pretty quickly when you're feeling down,' warns Dave Scott, six-time Ironman winner. 'Instead, set a 2-week goal and make it specific: run your goal workouts for the next 2 weeks.' Then set another 2-weeker. And so on.

13. Just bet it! A study found that people who bet money that they could stick to their training programme for 6 months had a 97-per cent success rate. On the other hand, fewer than 20 per cent of those who didn't place a bet stuck it out. Bet a running partner that the first to slack off pays up. Open time slots will suddenly, almost magically, start popping up.

14. Especially good for beginners: run often, not long. If you want to run regularly, aim for frequency, not duration

---

Avoid going home at all costs

Even if your post-work commute is easy, do not go home before doing your workout – even if it means parking several streets away from your house and heading out from there. 'Doing that can be deadly,' says marathoner Matt Henderson about walking through the door straight after work. 'Go home, and the odds are you'll end up not doing your workout.' Instead, you'll encounter TV, your dinner, stuff to put away, kids who want to play, newspapers to flick through, phone calls, beer. Way, way too many distractions.

to make running a regular part of your life. Instead of trying to find time for a 45-minute workout two or three times a week, aim for shorter sessions – 15 to 20 minutes – but make sure you fit them in most days.

15. Rope in your friends. Recruit a regular workout partner and agree on time, place and distance. If someone is expecting you to show up, you're more likely to – and less likely to scratch around for excuses not to. 'When you commit to running with a friend a few times a week, it becomes just another part of your weekly routine,' says Laurie 'Housebound-with-Two-Children' Doane.

16. Evolution, not revolution. OK, the prospect of all of a sudden getting up to run every morning (Yikes!) – or during every lunch hour (What? No tuna sarnie?) – can seem daunting. Because it is. So, here's the deal: commit to running just one morning and/or one lunch hour per week for just a month and stick to your usual schedule the rest of the time. See how it goes. Two small steps rather than a giant leap is always the wise way to go.

SAVING TIME

Timing is everything. Fifteen seconds here, a minute there. They don't seem like much, but watch how fast these precious time periods add up.

17. The night before, lay out your gear. All of it. Even loosen up your laces so your feet slide straight into your shoes. That way, you sit down and dress for battle quickly. No scurrying back-and-forth from dresser to wardrobe to laundry room, back to dresser, hunting out clean shirt, shorts, socks, shoes. No, they're all there. Waiting for you to take them out for some sweaty fun.

18. The 8-second breakfast. After you lay out your togs in the evening, also shove your favourite smoothie ingredients in a blender, and put it in the fridge. After your workout the next morning, hit a switch and 8 seconds later: breakfast. OK, 11 if you count pouring.

' On extra busy days, you can beat the clock by adjusting your workout plan downwards. '

Buddy up: if others are expecting you to turn up for a run, you're more likely to be there.

19. Don't spend time stretching cold muscles. Instead, walk briskly for a few minutes, then jog slowly into your run.

20. Go, then gab. Too often, you turn up, you meet your running partners, you start talking while doing some pathetic trunk twists as a 'warm-up'. This isn't what you turn up for. Time to change this scenario. Just don't do it. Instead, say 'hi' and start jogging slowly into your run. Start gossiping then, once you're under way.

21. The ultimate timesaver. Do all four of the timesaving strategies listed above (numbers 17 to 20) and you will save 7 to 10 minutes – a nice addition to your usual workout! Over the course of a working week, you gain at least 35 extra minutes of workout time. That's enough to pay real benefits.

22. 'I wear running shorts as underwear,' says Olympic marathon runner Galloway, thus rendering himself run-ready the instant his antennae pick up a 10-minute block of free time. 'Accumulate enough short runs,' he tells us, 'and they add up.' Jeff's dialled in here. One study found that 'multiple bouts of moderate-intensity exercise produce significant training effects.' Which leads us to . . .

RETHINKING TIME

Some time barriers to running are external – work, picking up the kids, root canal work. But equally restrictive are internal roadblocks: negative attitudes towards running and/or ourselves. So let's change a few perceptions here.

23. Be realistic. Cut back on your running if you need to now and then. It's OK. Just don't throw in the towel because of what is a fact of life: workplace deadlines, sick kids, holidays etc., can severely cut into free time. Ride these periods out and shoehorn in a workout of some kind – 15 minutes, 10 minutes – every second or third day. Then resume your regular exercise routine ASAP. When your impeccably laid-out schedule implodes, think short-term glitch, not catastrophe and don't fret your way into becoming a sofa sloth. Don't get caught in that 'all-or-nothing' snare.

Divide to conquer

Even on the off chance that Jeff Galloway's solution (number 22) seems too unconventional for you, don't ignore the underlying message: on extra busy days, you can beat the clock by adjusting your workout plan downwards. But don't scrap it altogether. Remember, every mile counts. If you can only do one mile, fine. That's much better than nothing.

24. Be like Sue. 'When I'm really busy, I run for maintenance – 20 minutes or so every other day,' says Susan Jones, 31, a biology teacher. 'When my schedule lightens, I pick up the frequency, distance and intensity.'

25. Think of it like sex or a tax rebate. A little bit is always better than nothing. If all you have is 17 minutes to fit in a run, then run for 17 minutes.

26. Be selfish. No, not really. But don't ignore yourself either. By giving your run a high priority a few days a week, you're boosting your own physical and emotional health and living up to your obligation to your family to be as healthy and happy as you can be.

27. Be flexible. Don't throw up your hands and not run if circumstances suddenly change, as they do. If a surprise meeting cancels the 30-minute lunchtime run, then do your miles after work while the traffic clears. If you forget to set the alarm, take your gear to work and run at lunch.

28. Burn the alternatives. Take a torch to 'I don't feel like it' or 'I should wash the car/water the plants/sort out my loose change.' If you allow too many options to invade your commitment to run, you'll lose the battle.

29. Make your exercise programme just like brushing your teeth. 'If you really want to run, you'll find the time,' says Ron Hill, a former British marathon star. 'It's really no different than finding time to shave, eat or read the paper.' Think about it. Why do you always seem to have time for those activities? Then plan more ways to help you find time for exercise.

30. 'Have fun during every run,' says running coach Bob Williams. It greatly increases the likelihood that you'll want to – and will – find time for the next one. Run a new route; run an old one backwards. If you usually run on roads, hit the trails and run through the trees. Do something silly during your run (like singing the Bee Gees' 'Stayin' Alive' in your head).

' When your impeccably laid-out schedule implodes, think short-term glitch, not catastrophe and don't fret your way into becoming a sofa sloth.'

WEBWISE

For information on a wide range of running shoes, apparel and other running-related equipment including reviews and product tests, *Runner's World* website is the place to go. Click on 'Gear' to find out more.
www.runnersworld.co.uk

THE FINISH LINE

Three things to remember about this chapter:

1. Keep your bags packed. You can waste a lot of time looking around for the socks, shoes, shirts, shorts and jogging bottoms that you need for a workout. Or you can always have a bag packed and ready, with all the gear you need. Have your gear organized at home and at work. Some runners always have an extra bag in their car.

2. Same for your meals. We live in a fast-paced world, but that doesn't mean you have to succumb to unhealthy, fast-food meals. Always keep a stock of healthy drinks, snacks, and other foods in your cupboard and refrigerator. It's easier than you may think, as food manufacturers are continually producing more healthy alternatives for active people.

3. Find a training partner. Or several. You might only run with this person once a week, but it still makes a big difference to have someone who's counting on you (while you're counting on him or her). Even if you only run together once a week, you can keep in close contact through e-mails and phone calls.

PUTTING IT ALL TOGETHER

So here's the game plan: pick any three of the foregoing strategies – one from each section – and road test them for a month. If any (or – dare we hope? – all) work, yippee! Good for you. Stick to them.

If they don't work, pick three more and take them for a spin. Keep repeating the same process until you've gone through the whole list and found those that help you the most. Then make sure you keep repeating them and keep finding time for your workouts.

THE BEST WAY

Q: How much time do I need to do a worthwhile workout?

A: Whatever time you've got. Ideally, 30 minutes is a good starting point. In that amount of time, you can warm up, do a solid 20 to 25 minutes of workout, and briefly cool down. So if possible, put at least 30 minutes into your planner. But if you simply don't have 30 minutes, do whatever you can. This includes stretching at your desk, walking stairways in your building or taking a quick lap or two around the block. Don't fall into the all-or-nothing trap. Instead, tell yourself that every little bit helps.

CHAPTER 4

Strike
a Balance

Not Too Much, Not Too Little, but Just Right

To succeed in running, you need to balance many aspects of your life, from your diet to your family to the intensity of your workouts. Here's how.

Running is a simple and sometimes solitary activity, but it doesn't exist in a vacuum. It affects every other part of your life, and every other part of your life also affects your running. To live and run harmoniously, you need to find the right balance between all the parts.

This sounds easy and obvious, but it's not. It won't happen unless you pay real attention to it. Why not? Because we live in a hectic, fast-moving world. It's a world where you'll encounter 'quick fixes' at every turn. The problem is, these fixes might be quick but they don't last long.

They tend to violate the principle of balance, usually by demanding excess. On a diet, you're allowed to eat only one kind of food. On an exercise programme, you should focus on just one body part, not your whole body (and mind). If you're saving for your child's education, or your retirement, you put your money in just one great opportunity. OK, this is one approach, but there's a better way – the balanced way. By keeping things in perspective and viewing your whole life through a long-view lens, you'll make small improvements that lead to lasting results. This approach works in many areas of life and most certainly provides the best foundation for your beginning running programme.

Here are some of the key balance points you should keep in mind. They'll help you stay healthy and happy in your running and all the other areas of your busy life as well.

STRIKE A BALANCE BETWEEN . . . NEW AND CUSTOMARY

If you always tend to run or run/walk the same route for the same distance, it's time to stir up your routine. When you do the same workout day after day, you are seldom challenged, and your motivation is bound to flag. Think about this: if you eat a tuna sandwich four days in a row, you'll probably notice how delicious a different kind tastes on the fifth day. Same with running. Even a little variation will reinvigorate your experience.

■ **Too boring:** you run or run/walk the same course day after day. You get in a rut and lose interest in your programme.

■ **Too radical:** you follow a different course every day, moving from park to local streets to the centre of town. This takes lots of planning and driving around.

■ **Just right:** you have a favourite, convenient training route, but you're not afraid to change it several times a week. In fact, when you have time, you look for alternative courses that add variety to your training, giving your body and mind a chance to 'recharge'.

STRIKE A BALANCE BETWEEN . . . EATING WELL AND EATING TOO WELL

Soya burgers and salads are super, but if you carry a calculator to keep a running tally of your carbohydrate, protein and fat intake, it's time to relax. Moderation, not obsession, is the key to long-term health and weight control. Be aware of what goes into your body, especially saturated fats, but don't stress out over it.

> '*By keeping things in perspective and viewing your whole life through a long-view lens, you'll make small improvements that lead to lasting results.*'

■ **Too inflexible:** do you do all your shopping at the health food store? Loosen up a little. You can find plenty of healthy products at supermarkets. And do you spend a small fortune on nutritional supplements? You'll be just as healthy and energetic by simply following a balanced diet and taking a multivitamin for insurance.

■ **Too piggish:** do you count French fries as vegetables? Pineapple pizza as fruit? A six-pack of beer as carbohydrate-loading? You'll harm your running, and eventually your health, by letting your cravings call all the shots.

■ **Just right:** a balanced, sensible diet emphasizes whole grains, fruit and vegetables, but allows you an occasional indulgence without feeling guilty. (Give Ben & Jerry a good home, just not every night.)

STRIKE A BALANCE BETWEEN . . .
SLOWER AND FASTER

Varying the pace of your runs is another key to ducking the doldrums and improving your fitness level. Instead of cruising at the same speed every day, alternate between slower and faster efforts. This may mean shifting between 11 versus 9 minutes per mile, or between workouts where you run hard for 1 minute, walk for 2 minutes and repeat six or eight times. It's the contrast that's important. Running fast all the time can lead to injuries, while always going slow can lead to staleness. Occasional hard efforts, on the other hand, will improve your fitness and make your easy runs feel easier.

■ **Too slow:** on every run, you resort to the same sluggish shuffle. You could run faster, but tend to say to yourself, 'I'm not out to break any records' or 'I'm not racing'.

■ **Too fast:** most runs feel difficult. Your breathing is laboured, your legs feel heavy and you struggle to maintain your pace.

■ **Just right:** your runs are at a comfortable, relaxed pace, but once or twice a week you run at least 1 minute per mile faster.

STRIKE A BALANCE BETWEEN . . .
RUNNING AND RESTING

Take a day or two off after any run that leaves you feeling depleted the next day. Take several days off when you have a cold or a stressful week at work or at home. If your

Pigging out will not be good for either your running or your health. Aim for a balanced diet.

muscles are sore as you begin a run, stop running until the pain goes away. Never try to run through the pain of an injury.

■ **Too driven:** if you have a particular workout planned, you go ahead with it even though you're ill, injured, sore or worn out.

■ **Too lazy:** if you have a run planned and feel a little tired, you use that as an excuse to skip it.

■ **Just right:** if you have a workout scheduled, stick to your plan unless you have a legitimate reason to call it off. You'll feel a whole lot better – and more motivated – once you've completed the run.

STRIKE A BALANCE BETWEEN . . . RUNNING AND CROSS-TRAINING

Aerobic activities such as cycling, vigorous hiking, swimming, pool running and using your health club's cardiovascular exercise machines offer an array of benefits. On days when you don't run, a good cross-training workout will burn up calories, reduce stress, work up a sweat, and strengthen your heart, lungs and major muscle groups. At the same time,

'To live and run harmoniously, you need to find the right balance between all the parts.'

If you feel completely worn out after your run, it's time to take a few days off.

cross-training offers you a physical and mental break from running.

■ **Too much:** you spend more time wearing a bike helmet or swimming goggles than running shoes. You want to be a triathlete? Fine. But the training law of specificity dictates that to be a runner, there's nothing like the real thing.

■ **Too little:** you hate the smell of chlorine and don't even own a bike. And the prospect of trying any new sport is intimidating.

■ **Just right:** find an aerobic alternative you enjoy and cross-train once or twice a week, on days you don't run. Even old dogs can learn new tricks. Give it a try.

STRIKE A BALANCE BETWEEN . . . RUNNING AND STRENGTH WORK

Running will develop your lower-body muscles but doesn't do much for your top half. Strengthening neglected upper-body muscles will make you fitter in the fullest sense. Schedule time with a club trainer or a friend who strength trains to learn how to develop your 'core' and upper-body muscles. While you're in the gym, include some lower-body work to strengthen your quadriceps, hamstrings and hip flexors.

■ **Too strong:** your work ethic on the running path takes over in the gym, and you begin to bulk up. Unfortunately, bodybuilders make useless distance runners, because they have to carry all that muscle on the run – and we don't run on our arms.

■ **Too weak:** you won't lift anything heavier than a Lucozade bottle – and it shows. When your kids draw stick people, you're the model.

■ **Just right:** twice a week, spend about 30 to 45 minutes in the gym. Choose weight amounts that you can lift 10 to 12 times before fatiguing, and do a variety of exercises, lifts and stretches for upper- and lower-body muscles.

STRIKE A BALANCE BETWEEN . . . HILLS AND FLATS

One or two hilly runs a week will make your legs stronger and more resistant to injury. (If you have no hills around, a treadmill will work.) Any more than twice a week, however,

Shorten your stride when running uphill and lengthen it when running downhill.

can inflict damage on your muscles and joints. Running descents too fast can cause problems, so beware of exceedingly steep downhills. Walk if you have to.

■ **Too steep:** if a hill is so steep you feel stress on your lower back, hips, knees, shins or Achilles' tendons, you need to pick another hill.

■ **Too gradual:** if a hill is so negligible that it isn't obvious whether you're running up or down, it doesn't count.

■ **Just right:** any ascent between wheelchair-ramp and nursery ski-slope severity will build leg and lung strength without causing damage. Just add hills in measured doses. And be careful on the downside.

STRIKE A BALANCE BETWEEN . . . TAKING ADVICE AND IGNORING IT

Feel overwhelmed by the sometimes contradictory running advice that bombards you from books, magazines, websites and your fellow runners? Then ignore the recommendations targeted at runners with different goals and capabilities from yours. Instead, home in on the advice that's most applicable to your running circumstances.

■ **Too dependent:** you follow every training programme and gimmick. You do every workout your friends do – at their speed. Your running stumbles along with no coherent plan and numerous setbacks. Eventually you want to give up.

■ **Too independent:** you reject all advice and blaze your own trail, believing you'll learn from your mistakes. The learning curve (and injury factor) of this approach, however, proves so steep that eventually you give up.

■ **Just right:** like a discerning customer at a salad bar, choose only the most healthy and appealing items, rather than impulsively piling everything on your plate. Select only the expert advice that conforms to your individual goals.

STRIKE A BALANCE BETWEEN . . . RUNNING AND LIVING

Running deserves a regular spot in your appointment book, but it shouldn't be sacrosanct. With careful and flexible scheduling, you should be able to fit in 95 per cent of your runs while still meeting the rest of your family and

THE BEST WAY

Q: What's the best way to run hills and gradients?

A: First of all, understand that there are no secrets or shortcuts. Hills are difficult for all runners. That's why every runner talks and worries about them so much. When running uphill, simply shorten your stride and run a consistent effort. You can't maintain pace on a hill, but you can maintain effort. Listen to your breathing and keep it steady and regular. On the downhills, relax and lengthen out your stride a little but not too much. Don't overstride and don't start sprinting. Maintain control.

professional obligations. As for the other 5 per cent, don't sweat it. Nobody's perfect.

■ **Too obsessed:** you planned a workout the morning of your cousin's wedding. You finish the workout, but miss the 'I do's'.

■ **Too lax:** Test cricket matches are on all day, so you let the TV listings pre-empt your scheduled run.

■ **Just right:** when meaningful responsibilities conflict with running plans, do the right thing and run another time. But if you have to shampoo the dog, get a haircut, clean the windows or watch a television repeat, postpone those plans until after you run.

STRIKE A BALANCE BETWEEN . . . LOW GOALS AND LOFTY GOALS

If your running goals are too easily attained, it's hard to stay motivated. Set your goals too high, however, and you'll fail to achieve them, which will also dampen your motivation. The best way to preserve your enthusiasm is to set and regularly reset specific time, distance and performance goals that are reasonably challenging, yet achievable. Take a risk, but make it a calculated, achievable risk.

■ **Too timid:** you resolve to finish a 5-K without walking, although you've already been there and done that. After succeeding, you resolve to do the same race again next year. But without an important short-term goal, you don't run a step for months.

■ **Too ambitious:** you resolve to finish a 5-K at a pace of 10 minutes per mile, although you never train faster than 9-minute pace. When you flake out after 2 miles and end up walking, you're so frustrated you don't run another step for months.

■ **Just right:** resolve to run a 5-K at a slightly faster pace than your fastest training runs. Pick out several races in a year, and aim to run each one successively faster.

STRIKE A BALANCE BETWEEN . . . SHORT VIEW AND LONG VIEW

Keep running in its proper perspective: It is just an activity that has a meaningful place in our lives. And well it should, since running is a lifetime endeavour that will deliver all its

OK, take a break from your schedule now and then – but not too long a break.

WEBWISE

The Road Runners Club is a national organization with over 2,000 members worldwide, and Time Outdoors is a good place to find your nearest local running club.
www.roadrunnersclub.org.uk
www.timeoutdoors.com

THE FINISH LINE

Three things to remember about this chapter:

1. Vary your running courses. This will provide novelty and motivation to your workouts. Include friends when you are able to schedule the time together. But don't worry if you have a particular routine that you like repeating on most days of the week. Routine is good and necessary.

2. Strength train several times a week. Running is good for your aerobic health and capacity. Strength training is good for maintaining your muscle mass and posture, particularly as you age. The two together are the perfect complementary workouts.

3. Eat as many different kinds of foods as possible. Variety is often good in training routes, but it's always good at the kitchen table. The greater the variety of foods you eat, the greater the number of vitamins and minerals you'll consume.

---

health and fitness benefits for years to come. Don't let it rule your life. Use it to enhance your life.

■ **Too serious:** the thought of not running during a week-long cruise with your family is driving you mad. So even before you find your cabin, you measure the perimeter of the deck and work out how many laps add up to a mile.

■ **Too indifferent:** when the baby arrives, you decide to take a complete break from running until he or she is old enough to run with you.

■ **Just right:** you shrug it off when you can't run for a week or even a month. Some experienced runners take 1-month sabbaticals from running every year to recharge themselves physically and mentally. That's fine. Remember, you're in this sport for the long run.

'*Keep running in its proper perspective: it is just an activity that has a meaningful place in our lives.*'

CHAPTER 5

Train
Your Brain

Learn the Secrets of Visualising Successful Running

Many people would like to become runners but don't even try because they believe they have the wrong kind of body. Their legs are too short. Their stomach is too big. Their shoulders are too broad. Their total body fat is too high. Their total body weight is too much.

These people are wrong. The body is unimportant. The mind is everything.

They simply need to train their brain more effectively.

Others begin running but then give up after a few days, a few weeks, maybe a few months. They get discouraged. They assume they'll never succeed. They can't run as far as they'd like. They can't run as fast as they'd like. They can't run as easily as they'd like. They see other runners who look thinner, faster, smoother than they are. It's so-o-o-o discouraging.

These people are right. No one can run as far, fast, smoothly or effortlessly as they'd like. Not even the Olympians. But this is no reason to give up. If you feel like this, you simply need to train your mind more effectively.

Running is not a physical sport. It's a mental sport. The people who succeed are not the ones who have the longest legs or the leanest torsos. The champions are the ones who understand how to harness the power of the brain.

EXAMPLE NUMBER ONE:
THE WOMEN'S RUNNING BOOM

Here's an example – not a solitary anecdote, but an entire-population anecdote. As recently as 30 years ago, women

To run better and faster, you need to hone your mental skills.

were told they couldn't run. They were too small and delicate. They weren't strong enough. Their bodies carried too much fat. And so forth.

From one perspective, all these statements are true. Women *are* smaller on average than men. They have less testosterone, so they don't build as much muscle. They naturally and normally carry more subcutaneous fat on their bodies than men – up to 10 per cent more.

So the statements are basically true. And yet millions and millions of women have taken up running in the last 30 years and done absolutely amazing things. Some have even won Olympic gold medals. But, more importantly, women in every walk of life have become fitter and healthier through a regular running programme.

How did this happen? It happened because the statements are true, but the assumption is wrong. It's wrong to believe that you need a certain physical body type to run. All body types can run. It's not about your legs, muscles or cellulite. It's not about the physical side of things.

If you train your brain, your body will follow. It's that simple. The hard part isn't getting your body in shape. The hard part is getting your mind in shape.

THE FEMALE MENTALITY

So let's return to our women's running story. How did so many women succeed in running? It was easy for them. Because many women already possess the essential mental skills.

Determination. Discipline. Organization. Time management. Friendship-making. These skills are what it takes to succeed in running. You have to want it, you have to plan for it, you have to fit it into a busy day, you have to be mentally tough, you have to use others to help you. Women are outstanding at this, and it makes them great runners.

Running is just an example. Women haven't achieved equality with men in some sports like football and basketball because those sports *do* demand a certain physicality – be it height, strength, speed or whatever.

But women are rapidly becoming 50 per cent of the worldwide running population because you don't need to be tall, strong or fast to reap all the benefits of running. You don't

'Keep thinking about the reasons why you want to become a healthy, fit runner, and more reasons will pop into your head.'

need a certain set of physical qualities. You only need a certain set of mental qualities.

The rest of this chapter lists a number of ways any runner, male or female, can train the brain. Or, to put it another way, these are tricks, tips and systems you can use to keep your motivation going.

There's only one important thing to remember: if you train your brain and pave the way to your success, you will succeed. Repeat after me: running is a mental activity. Now let's look at these motivational secrets.

TRAINING LOG

A training log is for runners as a captain's log is for the captain of a ship. It tells where you have gone and what you have encountered – the good and the bad. The purpose of a log is basically twofold. First, a log serves as a simple but compelling get-up-and-go device. Once you have a log, your brain knows it's there and wants you to enter something into it on a regular basis. After all, no one wants to carry around a log full of empty pages. Many studies have shown that a training log is one of the most effective motivational tools for runners: it gets you out of the door.

That's the reason that this book actually contains your first training log. Whether you decide to use the 8-week (see page 274) or 24-week (see page 284) training plan that appears later in the book, you'll find a training log exactly suited to your needs. And, unlike most training logs, which are essentially blank pages meant to be filled in, this one tells you what to do for each workout. Plus, it provides inspirational quotes and training tips for each week of your programme.

Before long, you'll fill up this training log, and it will be time to start another. You can buy a simple, inexpensive training log at many bookshops or running stores, or you can make one of your own from a loose-leaf notebook or any diary or journal. Pick what you like, but be sure to keep using a training log. It'll help you maintain your training programme and also serve as a vital feedback tool.

That's the second purpose of a training log. It lets you see where you've been and learn from your experiences. If you get injured, your training log can help you work out why.

Log it: track your running progress by recording your mileage, PBs and other achievements.

' If you train your brain and pave the way to your success, you will succeed.'

If you become ill, your training log could have the answer. Experienced runners keep a bookshelf full of their training logs and refer back to them often.

MOTIVATIONAL QUOTES

Just about everyone loves a good inspirational quote, and many people use quotes to motivate a particular behaviour that they are trying to adopt. The practice is so common among runners that you can actually find one or two whole

Take on a training partner

A training log is great; a training partner is even better. There's nothing like the human element to get you out and exercising. Picture a dark winter morning in February. The alarm goes off, and it's time for you to get up for your early-morning workout. Only you're tired. It's warm in bed. You tell yourself that a single missed run can't make that much difference. So you don't do it.

Now picture the same morning, only you know that your friend who lives down the street is going to be waiting for you on the pavement. You're not going to disappoint your friend. You don't want to be the one who cancelled the appointment. So you get up and do the workout. In fact, it's easy. Because someone else is out there with you.

We humans are social animals who enjoy social activities. And even though running is the perfect individual, solitary exercise (you don't need to assemble a full team of players before you can do it), it's also an unusually good social activity. You can run side-by-side with your friend or friends. Most workouts are casual and conversational. In other words, you don't run so hard that you're gasping; you run so slowly that it's easy to talk to each other as you move on down the road or trail.

When you plan your workout week, try to do as many runs as possible with friends and professional colleagues. You may have just one steady training partner, or you might have several – different ones on different days of the week and in different places. You can join a running club or workout group for larger, team training. Of course, you can continue to enjoy running alone on those days when it's exactly the tonic you need.

But you'd do well to develop several training partners, particularly several beginning running partners. Rest assured, you know plenty of people who would like to get in shape with a running programme but have never worked up the resolve to get started. You can help them, and then you can both help each other by encouraging, motivating and running together. It's one of the best ways to ensure your success.

books of quotes gathered together specifically for runners. The best of these books is American writer Mark Will-Weber's *The Quotable Runner*.

The best runner's quotes are about courage, struggle, determination and themes like these, as those are the qualities you will need the most to succeed in your training programme. It's helpful to know that many other great individuals have had a tough go of it and haven't always succeeded with consummate ease. Some runners like to read a quote or two before they head out for a workout, some like to memorize a quote they can repeat while running and others like to surround themselves with quotes at all turns, at home and in the office, so they are never far from inspiration.

'WHY I RUN' CARDS

Running is not easy and not always fun. Most of the time, it's just plain hard work. That's why it's so effective. If running were easy, it wouldn't produce so many positive benefits.

Because running is hard, you need to remind yourself why you are doing it. Chapter 1 listed many of the most compelling health and fitness reasons for running, but you should also create a pack of running cards that includes your own personal reasons for running. The first time you sit down to write some 'I am running because . . . ' cards, you might soon exhaust your list of reasons. You might only come up with a couple of very basic reasons.

But keep at it. Keep thinking about the reasons why you want to become a healthy, fit runner, and more reasons will pop into your head. They may come while you are running, or they may come at any time during the day.

Regardless, write down all the new reasons on separate cards and keep the cards together in one place. Then review the cards regularly. Each rereading of your cards should boost your motivation dramatically.

A PIGGY BANK

Motivation comes in many forms. One of them is cash. We're all motivated to some extent by monetary gain, so it makes sense that cash would be a good way to help you stick to your training plan. Unfortunately, neither Richard Branson nor some

---

A fridge fact

Your fridge contains perhaps the most valuable property in your house. This is where you stick photos of your loved ones, favourite recipes, important date reminders and the like. It's also a great place to put a mini training log or similar workout reminders. For example, you could cut a page from a magazine and put it on your fridge to remind you to do a certain strength-building exercise at least twice a week.

To remind you of your running workouts for the week, simply write them on a small index card and attach the index card to your fridge with a magnet. List the days of the week and the workouts you are supposed to do on those days. If something else will inspire or motivate you, include that in the plan. Some people like to 'reward' themselves by putting a star next to every day when they do the planned workout.

When using your fridge in this way, it's crucial to actually slow down and look at your card every time you open the fridge. Force your eyes to read the card whenever you go to the fridge. It won't be long before your workouts have lodged in your brain, and then it won't be long until you do them.

other rich person is going to give you a big cheque every time you finish your 30-minute workout.

In fact, the only person who's likely to pay you is you. So do it. Many runners have used the piggy-bank trick to keep themselves motivated. It sounds silly, and it is, but so what? Here's how you do it: first, buy yourself a garish little piggy bank. Second, after every completed workout, put some money into your piggy bank.

Before long, your piggy bank will shake, rattle and roll every time you pick it up. The sound of the coins in the bank will provide visceral proof of all the successful training you've done. It's almost guaranteed that a smile will come to your face whenever you pick up the piggy and shake it. Your friends will also be impressed as the piggy gets heavier.

If you make the piggy-bank deposit part of your training ritual, you'll quickly begin looking forward to it. You can play music if you like. Or pronounce a favourite quote or statement from your 'I Run Because' cards.

Keep it light, and make it fun. And when your piggy bank is full, empty it out and go and buy yourself something you've been wanting. You deserve it!

MUSICAL MOTIVATION

Many runners like to use music to motivate themselves, and several race series with musical themes (like the Rock 'n' Roll Marathons) have become huge successes, in the US especially. No one has clearly defined exactly why running and music make such perfect partners, but it might be as simple as this: music is rhythmic, and so is running. When you jog down the street, your feet make a regular, metronome-like beat on the road. Adding another musical rhythm to your workout seems to reinforce the running.

Different people like to listen to different music when they run. There doesn't seem to be one style or rhythm that is the best. Some runners like classical music, some like the big-band sound and of course others like listening to one of the many varieties of rock music. Simply make a selection of your favourites, and go with it.

A word of caution: many running groups discourage the use of headphones while you're running outdoors. These

THE BEST WAY

Q: How can I increase my discipline?

A: One successful running coach used to tell his athletes to 'live like a clock'. In other words, you should do the same things at the same time every day. Go to bed at the same time, wake up at the same time, eat your meals at the same time, and do your workout – you guessed it – at the same time. This isn't always practical, but just by trying you'll make it easier to fit in your planned workouts. Second: develop external networks – that is, people and resources that will motivate you to do what you want to do.

The humble piggy bank – the source of funds for those new running shoes you want to buy.

groups worry that you'll fail to hear a vehicle, an attacker or some other sound that you should be hearing. It's true, the groups are right to issue their cautions. When you run, the single most important thing you must do is to take care of your own safety, and that requires the use of all your senses, certainly including your sense of hearing.

Nonetheless, there are places where you can run safely with headphones: treadmills and well-lit, non-vehicular paths, trails and roads where you are surrounded by other people (perhaps runners and walkers). Many popular parks and riverside pathways fit this description. Deep forest trails do not, however, nor do any night-time running areas. Use common sense when deciding whether or not it's OK to run with headphones. If you feel relatively alone or threatened in any way, don't do it.

Here's a good alternative to headphones: listen to the music before you run. Use music to psych up for your workout. Sit or lie down quietly, and listen to 3 to 5 minutes of a favourite tune. Let your body relax and gather strength, while your mind is soaking up the energy of the music. Then head out for your run, without headphones.

THE DIGITAL WORLD

The latest and one of the best ways to practise brain-training is through the varied resources of the digital world. These include e-mail training partners and Internet forums (or 'message boards'), but other forms of social networking are also gaining speed on the Web.

On a forum, you can find and learn from like-minded individuals. At *Runner's World Online,* for example, you'll discover a Beginners Forum dedicated to supporting new runners like yourself. You can participate as a quiet observer at first, until you are comfortable with the format. Then join in: ask questions, discuss injuries and listen to other forum participants share secrets that have worked well for them.

You might also develop a special connection with one or two forum participants, who could then become direct e-mail training partners. This friendship can develop into a more personal and sharing one than you would normally post on a forum. You can telephone your new friend(s), in addition to

Listening to music before running is a safe and effective way to psych yourself up.

> *' When the brain says 'Go', the rest of the body follows.'*

THE FINISH LINE

Three things to remember about this chapter:

1. Your brain is your most important muscle. A runner needs a healthy heart, and strong legs, and a well-developed 'core', but the brain is more important than all the other parts combined. Without it, you won't succeed in your training programme. When the brain says 'Go', the rest of the body follows. When the brain says 'No', nothing happens. So every minute you spend developing links between your brain and your running routine will pay multiple dividends. (Note: the brain isn't actually a muscle, but you get the point.)

2. Keep a training log. It can be as simple as an index card or as special as a deluxe personal journal that you buy at a bookshop. Your entries into the log can be as short as a couple of ticks or as involved as a long and intensely personal diary essay. Go with the approach that seems most normal and natural to you. But keep some kind of training log. It will soon become a close friend, it will motivate you to do your workouts (so you can fill up the blank spaces and pages in the log) and it will become an important history of your fitness progress.

3. Reward yourself. Running is hard work, and anyone who sticks to a regular training programme deserves regular rewards. Since you can't depend on anyone else to reward you for your good training behaviour, you're going to have to do it yourself. The list of possible reward behaviours is infinite; pick simple, mostly inexpensive rewards, and lavish them on yourself. Buy a new running book; go to a favourite restaurant for a delicious meal; take a long, relaxing bath with your favourite bath oils. The better you treat yourself, the more likely you are to stick to your workouts (which are also a form of treating yourself and your body well).

e-mailing and you may eventually plan to travel to the same event together for a face-to-face meeting. When a larger group of forum participants does this, it's called a forum encounter. In the running world, a forum encounter is often a trip to a famous race, mixed with the spirit of a barbecue at a family reunion. It's feel-good running.

Even though you won't be meeting your digital training partners at the local park every week, these people can have a powerful effect on your success. A quick e-mail, or several, is so easy. E-mails quickly take on a natural, uninhibited feel, and each one can carry a 'thread' of messages or exchanges with it, so that it seems much like an extended conversation. You'll enjoy this social side of things, and you'll be sure to do your next workout because you'll want to share all the details with your digital friends.

WEBWISE

Check here for full-text articles on a wide range of topics of interest to runners, especially injury prevention and nutrition. The information comes from a widely respected and authoritative US sports medicine magazine, *The Physician and Sportsmedicine*.
www.physsportsmed.com

2
GETTING
STARTED

CHAPTER 6

First
Steps

Getting Off on the Right Foot

Every runner remembers his or her first days of running. And they're not necessarily pretty. But when you keep at it, you find unexpected surprises and payoffs.

As runners, we all remember our first runs . . . or attempts at running. We remember the awkward, lumbering steps. The heavy breathing. And especially the way our muscles ached for the next few days.

Yet we persisted. Soon things got better. Often, things got much better. And we looked forward to our next run.

All runners discover their own best reasons for running, and there are as many reasons as there are runners. To each his own. The surprise is this: after a few miles, weeks or years, you'll discover reasons you never imagined when you began. The path includes magic and mysteries that are only revealed as you travel down it.

O f course, some of you might not have begun yet. To you, a simple word of advice: today is a great day to start. You'll never find a better one. No one can honestly tell you that running will be easy. That would be a lie. But this much can be guaranteed with absolute certainty: the rewards will be worth the effort.

As proof, here's testimony from 11 runners who tell why and how they got started – and what kept them going.

'1 Could Not Have Found a Better Stress Reliever'
I started running while I was at nursing college, raising two young boys and dealing with the end of a very bad marriage.

After a few miles, weeks or years, you'll discover more reasons to run than you could ever imagine.

They were difficult times. I decided that in order for the boys and me to survive, I needed to get strong, both mentally and physically. I had done aerobics and strength training before, but I most admired the people in my gym who ran for miles on a treadmill. I started with 1 mile and worked my way up. I could not have found a better stress reliever if I had been given a lifetime supply of Prozac.

S. M., registered nurse

'I Was 35 Kg (5½ st) Overweight'

At the time of my 40th birthday, I was 35 kg (5½ st) overweight, with high blood pressure and high cholesterol. My doctor told me to change my lifestyle, or I was looking at type 2 diabetes. I had just lost an uncle because of his unhealthy habits, so I joined Weight Watchers and bought a treadmill. I eased myself in slowly. I started walking 3 days a week, then did some gentle jogging. Eventually, I worked up the nerve to enter my first race, a 15-K. And believe it or not, I finished third in my age group, which gave me the motivation to continue. That and the fact that I lost those 35 kg (5½ st).

B. L., machine operator

'Running Is More Fun than Smoking'

When I moved to London to start a new job a few years ago, I discovered my office was on the course of the London Marathon. I'm ashamed to admit it now, but back then I didn't even know how long a marathon was. And I made fun of the people who were training for it. But after watching the marathon from my office window, I made a pact to run a marathon some day.

A week later, I registered for the next year's marathon. I began running a few consecutive nights, but I was a smoker and I couldn't go any further than a half-mile. Still, I kept at it and found that the more I ran, the better I felt and the less I wanted to smoke. One evening late in my training, I walked to a nearby newsagent and bought a packet of cigarettes. Back home, I threw the packet away. I did my marathon and I'm already planning another. In the end, running is more fun than smoking.

D. R., accountant

> **"** *All runners discover their own best reasons for running, and there are as many reasons as there are runners.* **"**

'It Was Like We Were Girls Again'

My sister and I ran cross-country at school, but life soon got too busy: college, work, marriage. When my sister came to visit me once, we went running together, and it was like we were girls again. I enjoyed the time spent with her and started adding more miles to my workouts. Then I found a woman in my aerobics class who ran at weekends. We became training partners. It has been a year of accomplishment, pride and self-awareness.

K. K., publishing manager

'I Started Running to Beat the Lights'

When I started my new job, I was always in a rush. I never ran, but walked fast to and from work each day. One day, to save time, I started running to beat the lights. If I hit the lights right, I'd sometimes run across a few streets at a time. This gradually shortened my commute, so I could make earlier trains. One morning, I hit all the green lights and suddenly realized I was a runner.

L. G., advertising executive

> **"** *I love telling people I ran 8 miles before coming to work this morning. I love the way I feel when I'm running.* **"**

Finding a training partner can make your running more consistent, fun and rewarding.

'My Batteries Died'

It sounds strange, but I started running because the batteries in my Walkman died. I was a walker and worked out on an indoor track. Seventeen laps to a mile. Yuck! When the batteries died, I decided that if I jogged, I would finish my workout faster. Soon after, I noticed a poster for a 5-K race. That was 10 years ago, and just recently I completed my first marathon. Good thing my batteries weren't Energizers, or I'd still be a walker.

L. Z., executive assistant

'I Couldn't Play Squash without Feeling Out of Breath'

One Sunday night when I was at my health club, a woman turned up to play squash. Nothing bizarre about that, but she explained that she had just completed a marathon that morning! I couldn't even play a long rally at squash without getting out of breath, so I started running. Since then, I have mowed my lawn after a marathon, but I have never played a squash match following one.

K. F., engineer

'I Thought about a Girl Undergoing Chemotherapy'

I knew some day I might want to do a marathon. I'm not sure why. But the real spark came a few years back, when I received a letter about raising money for people with leukaemia. I thought about our babysitter's daughter, who was undergoing chemotherapy. I ran three half-marathons before I did my first full marathon. Now I have completed five and am looking forward to two more this year.

D. F., lawyer

'I Succumbed to Peer Pressure'

As a tennis player at college, I was forced to run every day after practice. Following graduation, I swore I would never run again. Then, at 30, I got a new job where a number of colleagues ran during the lunch hour. They lured me out. I did several 5-Ks with them, then a half-marathon. Against my will, I found myself enjoying the experience. I ran two marathons last year and have more planned for the future.

A. F., project manager

THE BEST WAY

Q: What's the best way to guarantee I'm successful at running?

A: Sports psychologists often advise their athletes to 'visualize' success. This doesn't mean that you avoid all obstacles – after all, obstacles are a real part of life for everyone. But you can still visualize yourself succeeding. Visualize how you're going to look at your next school reunion. Or how you're going to feel when you run a mile non-stop for the first time. Or what it will be like to do workouts with your partner and/or children. Make mental pictures of your success, and you'll soon have it.

WEBWISE

Longtime *Runner's World* senior writer Hal Higdon maintains one of the most complete sites with training advice and training schedules for runners. A great place to go when you're ready to race. **www.halhigdon.com**

THE FINISH LINE

Three things to remember about this chapter:

1. You need to take care of yourself. It's not anyone else's responsibility – it's yours alone. You need to make the time for exercise and be sure you stick to your training schedule. Excuses are everywhere, but don't listen to them. Get in shape so you can live a fuller life for yourself and all the others around you.

2. The weight will come off. But it might not come off exactly when, where and how you expect it. Every body reacts differently to exercise, depending on your unique genetic makeup. But the body can't change one basic rule of biochemistry: if you burn more calories than you consume, you'll lose weight. The weight might not fall off as fast as you like, but stick with it, and it will definitely start to drop away.

3. Running will surprise you. The reasons you continue to run will be different from your reasons for starting. When you begin to exercise, you start down the path to an adventure with twists and curves and scenic views that you can't imagine at first. But you'll find them, and you'll be glad you kept moving down the road.

'I Was Curious about My Father's Running'

When I was young, my father ran marathons. I was curious about all the time he spent on the local running track, so one day I decided to join him. I was 11. I remember feeling so proud of being able to boast to my mother that I actually had run a mile. I waited 14 years after that first mile before I ran 26 at one time, but it was worth the wait. I will complete my 12th marathon in April, and I owe it all to my father.

A. M., library assistant

'I Love the Way My Backside Looks'

At secondary school, I was the only girl in the track team, and the coach trips to races with the boys were fantastic. But after university, I only ran sporadically. Last spring I thought about running a local 8-K but decided to skip it, because the distance was too far. Then, 20 weeks before my local marathon, I signed up. I don't know why. I'd never even watched a marathon before. I just pulled out my credit card and registered. I'm still amazed that I did it. I love those yelling supporters. I love telling friends I ran a marathon. I love telling people I ran 8 miles before coming to work this morning. I love the way I feel when I'm running. And I love the way my backside looks!

J. K., lawyer

Make time for exercise. It's not anyone else's responsibility – it's yours alone.

CHAPTER 7

Running
Fundamentals

Take the Experts' Advice to Help You Run Better

When an experienced runner and running-book author leads a running course for beginners, he learns as much as he teaches. And in this chapter, he passes the lessons along to you.

In recent years, Joe Henderson has been teaching a running course for beginners, drawing on his many years as a competitive and recreational runner, his years as editor of Runner's World *magazine, and the more than a dozen running books he has written. But most of all, Henderson has made use of what his running students have taught him. Their experiences will also help you.*

Henderson's classes meet twice a week for 50 minutes at a time. For homework, he suggests that class members do an additional workout or two each week.

From his own running and the feedback of his students, Henderson has put together what he terms the most important 'mini lessons' for beginners. These are the points he asks them to concentrate on during the 10 weeks of their class meetings. Henderson thinks of these lessons as a sort of *Pass Notes for Running*. Master them, he says, and your beginning-running efforts are certain to be rewarded with an 'A' grade.

1. Welcome to the starting line. This might be your first try at running, or a return visit, or an attempt to improve on what you already do. The less running you've done recently, the more you can expect to improve your distances and speeds in the next 10 weeks. On the other hand, the less you've run lately, the more likely you are to hurt yourself by doing too much running too soon. That's why it's so important to set two related goals as you start or restart your running programme: maximize improvements and minimize injuries. You win by improving. You lose by getting hurt. Learn and remember this principle.

2. Buy the right shoes. They are the biggest equipment expense for runners, so it's important to get it right – first time. You can't afford to damage your feet. Spend wisely by buying well-made shoes from a major brand. Look for a model that fits you properly and is designed for the surface you'll run on most often – roads, tracks or trails. If you're not sure which shoe will work best for you, shop at a specialist running store staffed by experienced runners and shoe experts. After you buy your shoes, remember that even the best have a limited life span. Plan to replace them after about 400 to 500 miles of wear.

3. Make a plan. The two basic raw materials of a running routine are time and space. And the two main reasons given by those who don't run? 'I don't have time for it' and 'I don't have anywhere to do it'. Let's dissect those excuses. You can run well and get in great shape with as little as a 30-minute session every other day. Think of it as the time you won't waste by watching a sitcom repeat.

'Anywhere that's safe for walking is also fine for running.'

THE BEST WAY

Q: What's the best running form?

A: First, relax. Run naturally. Don't force your body into any unnatural positions. Next, run 'tall'. Pretend you are a marionette and there is a string coming out of the middle of your head that extends straight up to your puppeteer-master. Feel the slight pressure of that string helping you to run tall, with your ears, neck, hips and feet all in the same line. Don't lean forwards. Don't run with a long, bouncy stride. Instead, try to glide over the ground, moving smoothly as you go.

As for finding places to run: anywhere that's safe for walking is also fine for running. Off-road routes (parks, bike paths, school running tracks) are better than busy streets, and soft surfaces (grass, earth) are better than paved ones, but any choice is better than staying at home. Major suggestion: map out the best courses in your immediate area. That saves time, solves the 'place' issue and makes it much more likely that you'll actually do your planned runs.

4. Take the mile trial. Friends who hear that you've begun running will soon ask, 'What's your best mile time?' so you might as well get used to it. Before long, you'll be calculating your pace per mile on longer runs, but you should begin with a simple 1-mile test run (four laps on a standard track) to determine your starting point. Run at a pace a little beyond easy but less than a struggle, and count on improving your mile time in later tests as your fitness improves.

Where you run is up to you – parks, cycle paths and school running tracks make ideal locations.

5. Get F-I-T. Dr Kenneth Cooper, a giant in the fitness field, long ago devised a simple formula for improving as a runner: run 2 to 3 miles, 3 to 5 days a week at a comfortable pace. It's easier to remember as the F-I-T formula: frequency (at least every other day); intensity (comfortable pace); and time (about 30 minutes). Even with walking breaks, you can cover 2 miles in 30 minutes, and you might soon be running 3 miles in that time. It's important to run these efforts at an easy, comfortable pace. Think of yourself as the tortoise, not the hare. Make haste slowly.

6. Find your pace. OK, so you understand that you need to keep it comfortable. Sounds simple enough, doesn't it? The problem is that most beginning runners don't know what a comfortable pace feels like, so they push too hard. Result: they get overly fatigued and discouraged, or even injured. And then they quit. Here are some more guidelines to help you. A comfortable pace is 1 to 2 minutes per mile slower than your mile trial time. Or you can use a heart-rate monitor and run at 65 to 75 per cent of your maximum heart rate. (Note: Max heart rate is 205 minus half your age.) Or, my favourite because it's so simple: listen to your breathing. If you aren't gasping for air and you can talk while you're running, your pace is just right.

7. Remember to warm up and cool down. Don't confuse a little stretching with a good warm-up. Stretching exercises generally don't make you sweat or raise your heart rate, which is what you really want from a warm-up. A proper warm-up begins with walking or running very slowly to ease your body into the session.

My recommendation is to walk briskly for 5 minutes (about 400 metres), then break into your comfortable running pace. (Don't count the warm-up as part of your workout time or distance.) When you finish your run, resist the urge to stop suddenly. Instead, walk for another 5 minutes to cool down more gradually. Then comes the best time for stretching – after your run when your muscles are warm and ready to be stretched a little. This reduces the chances of pulling muscles.

Run roads right

Think about where you run. On the road, the biggest threat you'll face as a runner, by far, is the car. Traffic zooms past you only centimetres away. A moment's attention lapse from either you or the driver can bring disaster, and you'll be the one to suffer, not the well-protected driver.

8. Don't hesitate to walk. Walk is not a four-letter word for runners. Pausing to walk during a run is not a form of cheating, but a common practice among experienced runners. It is a form of interval training that breaks a big piece of work into smaller pieces, making it more doable. Mix running and walking in these ways: when you're starting to run for the first time; to regain fitness after a long layoff, injury or illness; to make your fast running faster, which is the classic use of interval training; to make long runs longer; and to make easy runs easier. You'll find that walk breaks work best when you walk for at least 1 minute but no longer than 5 minutes.

9. Run safely at all times. Choosing where you run is one of the most important decisions you will make. Running on roads is a popular choice, but it can be a dangerous business. The best way to lower this risk is to avoid running on roads completely. But for many of us, this is a near impossibility. Or it's an approach that adds time and complexity to our routine (if we have to drive to a park, for example). So most of us just learn to be extremely cautious when we run on the roads. We try to find wide, low-traffic roads; we run on the right side of the road, facing traffic; we obey road signs and traffic signals; and we follow every road rule our parents taught us by the time we were seven. Every runner should run as if every car is a lethal weapon. Because it is.

10. Use pain as your guide. Runners get hurt. Of course, we rarely hurt ourselves as seriously as skiers and rugby players, but injuries do happen. Most are musculoskeletal, meaning that we recover rapidly when we take days off or other appropriate action (like ice treatment). And most are self-inflicted. We bring them on by running too far, too fast, too soon or too often. Prevention is often as simple as a change of routine. Use pain as your guide. If you can't run steadily without pain, mix running and walking. If you can't run/walk, simply walk. If you can't walk, cycle. If you can't cycle, swim. As you recover, climb back up this fitness ladder.

11. Pay attention to your form. Running form is as individual as a fingerprint and is too inborn to change very

Cycling is a great way to recover from muscle soreness caused by running.

much. But with practice, you can make minor modifications to become a more efficient runner. Run 'tall' and upright, not with a pronounced forwards lean. Look towards the horizon, not at your feet. Run faster by increasing your stride turnover, not by overreaching with each stride. On uphills, shorten your stride and drive more with the arms. Try to maintain even effort, not pace. When running downhill, let gravity work for you by leaning slightly forwards.

12. Eat and drink the right foods. Sports nutrition is too big a topic to cover thoroughly here. But in general, the rules for good nutrition and fluid consumption are the same for runners as everyone else. Three areas of special interest to runners:
■ Control your weight, as extra bulk will slow you down.
■ Eat lightly an hour before training and 2 hours before racing.
■ Avoid dehydration – drink 230 to 460 ml (eight to 16 fl oz) of water or sports drink an hour before running.

13. Add a little stretching and strengthening. Running is a specialized activity, working mainly the legs. If you're seeking more complete, total-body fitness, you need to supplement your running workouts with other exercises. These should aim to strengthen the muscles that running neglects and stretch those that running tightens, which means strengthening the upper body and stretching the legs. Add a few minutes of strengthening and stretching after your running workouts, because that's when these exercises tend to do the most good.

14. Follow the hard-day/easy-day training system. Most runs need to be easy. This is true whether you're a beginning runner or an élite athlete. (Of course, the definition of 'easy' varies hugely for these groups; an easy mile for an élite runner would probably be impossible for many beginners or even veteran runners.) As a new runner, make sure you limit yourself to one big day a week. Run longer and slower than normal, or shorter and faster than normal, or go to the starting line in a race where you'll try to maintain your best appropriate pace for the entire race distance.

' Add a few minutes of strengthening and stretching after your running workouts, because that's when these exercises tend to do the most good.'

WEBWISE

When you're starting out, you'll need all the information you can get on the basics of running. The *Runner's World* website will help and will also carry you through to more advanced training.
www.runnersworld.co.uk

THE FINISH LINE

Three things to remember about this chapter:

1. Run safely. Many runners do their regular workouts in the areas where they live, simply because this is so convenient. You open the front door, walk down the pavement, and you're ready to run. But you're also sharing the road with cars and vans. So face traffic as you run, and always run defensively.

2. Warm up and cool down. This age-old advice is one of the best ways to increase the relaxation of your runs and to help avoid injuries. Even experienced runners like to walk a little before and after a workout. Whatever your particular plan, allow time for a relaxed warm-up and cooldown.

3. Listen to your body. This is one of the most frequently repeated and important running mantras. In other words, if you have pain anywhere, take several days off or go very, very easy. You've got to expect a little muscle soreness from time to time. But pain is another matter altogether. Don't even think about going there.

15. Congratulate yourself: you're a winner. One of the great beauties of running is that it gives everyone a chance to win. Winning isn't automatic; you still have to work for success and risk failure. But in running, unlike in other sports, there's no need to beat an opponent or an arbitrary standard (such as 'par' in golf). Runners measure themselves against their own standards. When you improve a time, or increase a distance or set a personal best in a race, you win – no matter what anyone else has done on the same day.

You can win even more simply by keeping at it for the long haul, for years and decades. You don't have to run very far or fast to outrun people who have dropped out. It's the tortoise-and-hare story all over again. Slow and steady always wins the race.

‘*One of the great beauties of running is that it gives everyone a chance to win.*’

CHAPTER 8

Moving Down the Road

What Other Runners Wish They'd Known at the Start

To learn more about beginning running, you can't do better than to visit others who have been there and to listen to them. They've been in your shoes. They know how hard the early days and weeks can be. They know what works and what doesn't.

Best of all, like all runners, they're eager to share. Any time you have a question, don't hesitate to ask friends, colleagues and others who have more running experience than you. Chances are they'll quickly and happily offer to help.

B ut back to those beginners, some of whom are actually editors of *Runner's World* magazine. After all, everyone was a beginner at some point. In the pages that follow, these one-time beginners tell you the most important things they learned in their early running days. They'll answer some things you've been curious about, raise some issues you haven't even considered and, most importantly, give you the confidence that you won't be a beginning runner for long. In the near future, you'll be a happy, healthy veteran runner.

Let's get started. Let's find out 'what I know now that I wish I knew then'.

Do it for you. 'I wish I had been less self-conscious when I started, but I listened to a group of women runners who thought they were on display when

Sharing your fears, hopes and expectations with others who are beginning running will set you off on the right path.

they ran. Eventually I saw beyond that. Now I run for me, and I don't care what others think about it.'

Mary, 45. Years running: 5

Embrace recovery. 'I wish I'd known 15 years ago that recovery was more important than continuing to train hard. Now I pay attention to my body and more clearly understand what I can and can't do.'   *Paul, 33. Years running: 22*

Race by feel. 'Don't worry about your mile splits when training or racing. You'll enjoy it a lot more if you just give it your best effort. Personal best times are nice, but the feeling of doing your best can be achieved in any race, regardless of your age.'   *Amir, 39. Years running: 25*

Think it, then do it. 'I ran my first 5-K last April and my first marathon 8 months later. In that time, I learned that running

Got something on your mind? Part of the pleasure of running can be sharing and solving problems with your companions.

long distances is 90 per cent mental and 10 per cent physical. Be prepared to change both inside and out. If you think you can, you will. If you think you can't, you won't. It's that simple.'

Chris, 29. Years running: 1

Enjoy the ride. 'You need to enjoy the running experience if you want to continue and succeed at it. But this can take time. You need to be patient. Running doesn't always jump out at you as the greatest thing since sliced bread. Eventually, though, you realize it is.'   *Jack, 45. Years running: 25*

Support your pals. 'I've learned how powerful it is to support my fellow club members. For me, the real fun of running is being with others and helping them out.'

Kelly, 21. Years running: 5

Listen to pain. 'Localized pain can be an early warning that something isn't right. It may mean it's time to back off from running and evaluate the causes of your discomfort. Listen and react to the pain, and you may lose a few days of running. Ignore it, and you can do serious damage.'

Michael, 45. Years running: 18

Protect your knees. 'The knees are prone to injury, so it's important to build up your quadriceps muscles to protect them, especially before you try long runs or speedwork. Doing half-squats or using a leg press works well for this.'

Marc, 30. Years running: 10

Go for quantity time. 'If you're preparing for a long race and your goal is simply to finish, emphasize mileage quantity, not quality. Quality mileage only comes into play if you're aiming for a specific time.'   *Ben, 24. Years running: 3*

Do a form makeover. 'I wish I'd known about proper form. I started running for fitness, but my bad form made it such a struggle. Now, after correcting my form and stride rate, I've increased my weekly mileage, run marathons and run much more easily.'   *Kenneth, 29. Years running: 15*

THE BEST WAY

Q : What's the best way to make sure I succeed as a runner?

A : Smell the roses. Appreciate the small things – the small improvements in your running ability. Don't expect miracles. Your goals should be realistic first, and then challenging, second. The big payoff is down the road: years and years of increased energy and better health.

Look for the softer stuff. 'For me, a track, treadmills and trails are the only acceptable surfaces to run on. They help you run. Streets and pavements can really beat you up. If these are your only choices, do a fast walk instead, then run when you reach the trail.'   *Harry, 44. Years running: 15*

Ease into it. 'Starting out nice and easy in a race will help you, no matter what the distance. How do I know this? My four marathons, a half-marathon, two 30-Ks, a 25-K, five 15-Ks and countless shorter races have offered me proof enough!'
Melissa, 32. Years running: 7

Drink fluids. 'I used to wonder why I'd have bad runs on some days and good runs on others. After one long run, I finally realized I wasn't drinking enough. Now on all my long runs I carry a water bottle or plan my route through areas where I can find water. My running is much more consistent now.'   *Andrew, 19. Years running: 5*

Race long. 'I had an incredible feeling of peace, well-being and joy when I finished my first long race – a half-marathon. It made the effort worthwhile. There's nothing quite like the first time.'   *Jim, 52. Years running: 27*

Create a performance pantry. 'Pay close attention to your diet, and determine which foods work best for you before a run or race. It's partly mental I'm sure, but I've found some pretty strange foods that help me. They're my secret weapons.'
Aimee, 34. Years running: 10

Stay inside if you want. 'When I started running in my mid-twenties, I thought running on a treadmill was cheating, so I'd push myself to go outside on the worst days. Now I realize that I can sometimes get a better-quality workout on the treadmill.'   *David, 41. Years running: 16*

Do a morning assessment. 'If I wake up in the morning and my legs are still aching, then I know I overdid it the previous day. I take it easy and get extra rest and sleep before training hard again.'   *William, 68. Years running: 13*

Run trails: they're kind on your knees, and your surroundings can be breathtaking, too.

Hit the speed limit. 'If you want to become faster, you have to train for it, and that means doing speedwork. It sounds obvious, but I always thought I could improve just by going a little faster on my daily training runs. I improved, but only marginally. It took me 12 years to learn that speedwork was the way to go.'

Dave, 46. Years running: 15

Wear shades. 'I have just finished my 24th marathon, but only learned recently how important it is to protect my eyes with sunglasses. My optician told me I should wear them even on wintry, cloudy days.'

Franceska, 57. Years running: 21

'*Starting out nice and easy in a race will help you, no matter what the distance.*'

You should always wear sunglasses to protect your eyes, even during the winter months and on cloudy days.

Buy the right stuff. 'Shamefully, I used to run in tennis shoes. Then a friend suggested I try running shoes, and the difference was amazing! Now I've become a running-shoe evangelist to all my new running friends.'

Molly, 30. Years running: 12

Stretch often. 'I'd much rather run than stretch, but now I have chronic Achilles tendinitis, a recurring muscle tear in my left calf and a dodgy IT band, so I have to stretch. If I'd stretched more in the past, I probably wouldn't have these problems. Don't do as I did. Your legs will thank you.'

Doug, 40. Years running: 26

Stay the course. 'Early on, every run can seem difficult. And they are for some people. But if you're steady, train sensibly and take your time, eventually the pain goes away, and running becomes natural, powerful and enjoyable.'

Don, 42. Years running: 26

STRAIGHT FROM *RUNNER'S WORLD*

The following advice comes straight from *Runner's World* editors. This doesn't make them any cleverer or more knowledgeable than any other runner, but working at *Runner's World* does help them see the 'big picture' and understand the concerns of beginners.

Stay healthy. 'Taking care of myself and staying uninjured is more important than any training run or race. If I'd worked that out last winter when I twisted my ankle badly, I would have taken the time to get better, even though it would have meant missing a marathon. Instead, I tried to train through it and made the injury worse. So I missed the marathon – and months of training besides. I've made a solemn vow to never do that again. You must be patient and sensible about injury recovery.'

Daniel, 26. Years running: 14

Run with a partner. 'I'd taken years off from running when I had children, so when I started up again, I felt so slow that I was too embarrassed to run with anyone else. That was a mistake. Finally when I started training for a half-marathon,

Treadmill versus the road

What's the difference between running on a treadmill and running outdoors? Firstly, a treadmill 'pulls' the ground underneath your feet, and secondly, you don't face any wind resistance when you're on a treadmill – so running is made somewhat easier. Many treadmills are padded, making them a good option if you're carrying a few extra pounds or are injury prone and want to decrease impact. To better simulate the effort of outdoor running, you can always set your treadmill at a 1-per cent incline.

I joined a group for long runs at weekends. Being in a group motivated me tremendously and made 10 miles seem like two.'

Claire, 42. Years running: 15

Don't overdress. 'In the past, whenever it was a touch chilly, I would pile on the clothes. In the early part of the run, I'd feel nice and cosy. But then I'd get too hot. This made the remainder of the run feel as if I were running in a sauna. Now I wear just enough to keep me from freezing, knowing that within a mile I'll heat up.'

Ken, 45. Years running: 6

Keep a training log. 'I wish I'd kept running logs when I started running, and that I'd done a better job on them once I did start recording my workouts. I have decent logs going back to the late 1980s, and a few times a year I'll flip through them. This is a great motivational tool; it helps me recall good races and special training runs. More practically, it helps me see what worked and what didn't.'

Martin, 49. Years running: 35

Use the lube tube. 'I had spent most of my life running shorter distances, so I was clueless about chafing. Then I set my sights on the marathon. My first long run was a 13-miler, and I thought I was equipped with all the essentials: water, gels, money for a taxi, etc. I had a great run and felt fine when I finished. Then I stepped into the shower and felt the painful sting of hot water on chafed skin. I realized that my sports bra had rubbed parts of my chest raw. That was the last time I ran without using an anti-chafing lotion.'

Melanie, 27. Years running: 13

Know that there's time. 'When I started running, I thought I had to do everything "right now" or the opportunity would be gone for ever. I thought that if I missed a day of training due to injury, I had to run harder or for longer the next day to make up for it. If I ran a bad workout, I had to run a good one the next day. If I missed a race, I had to find another one. Now I know that I have all the time I need. I no longer measure running by what it can do for me today. Instead,

Keeping a training log will help you see what works for you and what doesn't.

> *You must be patient and sensible about injury recovery.*

I love running for the promise and rewards it brings me year after year.'　　　　　　　　　　　　*Bob, 54. Years running: 38*

ESSENTIAL QUESTIONS

At some point, almost every beginner asks most of the questions that follow. With these answers, you'll save time and avoid mistakes.

Q: How do I get started?

A: Very gradually. Start walking for a length of time that feels comfortable – anywhere from 10 to 30 minutes. Once you can walk for 30 minutes easily, sprinkle 1- to 2-minute running sessions into your walking. As time goes on, make the running parts longer, until you're running for 30 minutes straight.

Q: Is it normal to feel pain during running?

A: No. Some discomfort is normal as you add distance and intensity to your training. But real pain isn't normal. If some part of your body feels so bad that you have to run with a limp or otherwise alter your stride, you have a problem. Stop running immediately, and take a few days off. If you're not sure about the pain, try walking for a minute or two to see if the discomfort disappears.

Q: Can I wear tennis shoes instead of running shoes?

A: The short answer is 'no'. Running doesn't require much investment in gear and accessories, but you have to have a good pair of running shoes. Unlike tennis shoes or plimsolls, running shoes are designed to help your foot strike the ground properly, reducing the amount of shock that travels up your leg. They're also made to fit your foot snugly, which reduces the slipping and sliding that can lead to blisters. Visit a specialist running shop to find the right shoe for you.

Q: Where should I run?

A: You can run anywhere that's safe and enjoyable. The best running routes are scenic, well lit, free of traffic and well populated. Think of running as a way to explore new territory. Use your watch to gauge your distance, and set out on a new adventure on each run. Find the best local routes.

Start slowly: imagine your running future as a moderate marathon, not an outright sprint.

WEBWISE

As well as a huge volume of training advice, the *Runner's World* website is the best place to find and enter races around the UK.
www.runnersworld.co.uk

THE FINISH LINE

Three things to remember about this chapter:

1. Some days it's more important to rest than to run. Often you'll know first thing in the morning. If you feel sluggish and tired getting out of bed, it might be time to take a rest day. No running. You can start again tomorrow, when you'll probably feel much better.

2. Dress for running, not for walking or standing still. Many runners overdress because they don't appreciate how much heat the body produces after it has been moving vigorously for 4 to 5 minutes. Yes, you might be chilly for the first few minutes. But then you will warm up dramatically. Dress in several light layers – that way, you can peel off one layer at a time and wrap your clothes around your waist as necessary.

3. Train your whole person. Running isn't a one-dimensional activity; it's many-dimensional. You need to train regularly, but you also need to eat well, sleep enough, do some stretching and strengthening work, and maintain a modest level of stress. Don't focus on just one area of your fitness life. Plan to improve them all. A little goes a long way.

Q: I always feel out of breath when I run. Is something wrong?

A: Yes. You're probably trying to run too fast. Relax. Slow down. One of the biggest mistakes beginners make is to run too fast. Concentrate on breathing from deep down in your belly, and, if you have to, take walking breaks.

Q: I often suffer from a side cramp when I run. Will these ever go away?

A: Yes. Side stitches are common among beginners because your abdomen is not used to the jostling that running causes. Most runners find that stitches go away as fitness increases. When you get a stitch, breathe deeply, concentrating on pushing all of the air out of your abdomen. This will stretch out your diaphragm muscle (just below your lungs), which is usually where a cramp occurs.

Q: Should I breathe through my nose or my mouth?

A: Both. It's normal and natural to breathe through your nose and mouth at the same time. Keep your mouth slightly open, and relax your jaw muscles.

'*You need to be patient. Running doesn't always jump out at you as the greatest thing since sliced bread.*'

CHAPTER 9

Shoes, Clothing and More

Essential Advice for the Beginner

Every beginner has to know, well, how to begin his or her training programme. With these 33 tried-and-tested running tips, you can't go wrong.

To succeed at any sport, you've got to follow the basic principles. Golf: keep your head down. Tennis: remember to follow through. Running: train, don't strain.

Wander too far from the basics, and your performance suffers. It's as inevitable as a stock-market fall when interest rates rise. And no runner is immune, particularly not the beginner. Accept that you're bound to make some mistakes. You haven't learnt the ropes yet. You'll need guidance nearly every step of the way and answers to dozens of commonplace questions: What should I eat? What should I wear? How fast should I go?

Don't be afraid to ask: beginning runners have plenty of questions that need answering.

Here are the answers, all in one place. The information is conveniently divided into six key running topics: training, shoes, clothing, running surfaces, nutrition and injury prevention. Read this chapter carefully and refer back to it often. It will form a firm foundation for your future efforts.

TRAINING: NOT ROCKET SCIENCE, BUT TRICKIER THAN YOU THINK

1. Mix running and walking. Few people can run a full mile the first time out of the door. Don't even think about trying it. You'll only get discouraged and give up. This method of slowly building up your endurance without overtaxing your muscles and cardiovascular system has been proven by thousands of successful beginners. And that's why I recommend that you follow it, too.

Parts 9 and 10 of this book will provide specific programmes geared to your current fitness. You can choose an 8-week training plan or a 24-week training plan. But the specifics aren't important now. What's important is that you understand that you're not going to open the front door and go out for a 20- or 30-minute run.

You're going to walk a little and run a little. Then you're going to walk a little more and run a little more. And most important of all, you're going to succeed.

2. Take the 'talk test'. Always run at a pace that's relaxed and comfortable for you. This isn't the Olympics; it's a lifelong fitness quest. To check your effort level, you need to take the 'talk test'. Start a conversation with your training partner. You should be able to speak without gasping or feeling out of breath. If you can't, slow down.

3. Go further, not harder. Once you reach the magic 24-minute mark, build up to 30 minutes (and then 40, 50 and 60). Don't make the mistake of trying to get faster. Don't try to run your 24-minute course in 22 minutes. Increasing endurance is your first priority.

4. Be a tortoise, not a hare. There's no need to retell the old children's story here. Running works just like the tortoise-and-hare race. It rewards the patient (with weight loss, steady progress, less stress, more energy and a whole host of health benefits) and penalizes the over eager (with injuries, burnout and so on). This isn't a sport for sprinters. Be slow, not sorry. You'll thank yourself for it.

5. Don't compare yourself with anyone else. The world is full of runners, so you'll probably see one every time you go round the block or your favourite park. Some will be thinner than you, some smoother-striding, some faster. But don't let this get you down. There's only one runner who really counts: you. Running is *your* activity. Make it work for *you*, and don't worry about anyone else.

THE BEST WAY

Q : I'm so slow, and I don't look very good when I'm running. I'm worried about embarrassing myself. How can I avoid this?

A : Well, there *are* ways. You can run at home on your treadmill, where no one else can see you. Or you can run in a safe place under cover of darkness, when very few will see you. But a better way is to be slow but proud. Walk and be proud. Run slowly, even awkwardly, but be proud. We live in an age of decreasing fitness and increasing obesity, and anyone who resolves to fight these twin scourges should be proud. Remember: even if you don't look like an Olympian, you're doing something very few others have the courage to do. So be proud. You deserve it.

SHOES: THE MOST IMPORTANT PURCHASE YOU'LL MAKE

6. Go to a specialist running store. When you're looking to buy running shoes, don't just head for the first sports shop you see. Go instead to a shop that specializes in running footwear – one that you know is recommended by other runners, if possible. At a specialist running store, you'll find a wide selection of shoe models and sizes, as well as trained salespeople who are runners and understand the particular needs of beginners. (To find a running store, go to *www.runnersworld.co.uk* or *www.ausrun.com.au* and check out the Shoes section.)

7. When shopping for shoes, do these four things to ensure you buy the right pair.

■ Go late in the day, when your feet are their largest (feet swell during the day and during running).

■ Take along the socks you'll wear while running – this way you'll get an exact fit.

■ Have both feet measured by a salesperson, even if you think you know your shoe size. (One foot is often larger than the other, and you'll need to be fitted for the larger foot.)

■ Try on both shoes.

8. Be fastidious about fit. The running shoes you buy must fit properly to work properly. A well-fitting running shoe will feel snug but not tight. There should be room at the front of the shoe to allow your feet to spread during running. Press your thumb into the shoe beyond the big toe. Your thumb should fit between the end of your toe and the end of the shoe. At the rear, your heel should also fit snugly so the shoe will hold your foot securely.

9. Take the shoes for a test run. Most running stores will allow you to jog around in the shoes you're considering buying. Take advantage of this. As you run, pay attention to how your toes feel: Are they sliding forwards? Do they feel pinched together? Also, notice how your heels feel: Are they sliding out of your shoe slightly? In general, are the shoes comfortable? If not, try another pair.

Some shoe sense

You need a pair of shoes to run in? Some advice: buy the real thing. Get a quality pair of running shoes. Not basketball, tennis, aerobic or cross-training shoes, but shoes made specifically for running. It's worth spending extra to get a really good pair from a major manufacturer.

CLOTHING: NOT JUST A FASHION STATEMENT

10. Layer it on thinly. Sweat moves more easily through two thin layers than it does through one thick layer. A well-designed layering system keeps you warm and dry during the colder months, yet still allows freedom of movement.

11. Make it breathable. A sweat-soaked cotton T-shirt will stick to your body, and its coarse, rough fibres may chafe your skin. Breathable, synthetic fabrics, such as Coolmax, wick perspiration away from your skin and out to the next layer of clothing or to the outer surface, where that moisture can evaporate quickly. Result: you'll stay cooler in hot weather and warmer in cold weather.

12. Consider the weather conditions you'll be running in. If you rarely run in rain, sleet or snow, you don't need a waterproof jacket. If winter temperatures in your area rarely drop very low, you may only need one layer, so buy a good one. And unless you live in a really cold climate, you probably won't need more than two or three layers on your upper body and one or two layers on your legs.

13. Don't overdo it. Many runners make the mistake of overdressing when it's cold outside. A good rule of thumb: you should feel slightly cold during the first mile or so of your run. If you feel cosy straight after heading out of the door, you're probably going to get too hot later on.

14. In sunshine, protect your skin with a dark shirt. Dark-coloured clothing absorbs UV light, protecting your skin better than light-coloured clothing, which lets light through. You may feel a little warmer wearing a darker shirt when the temperature soars, but sun protection is more important.

RUNNING SURFACES: THEY MAKE A HUGE DIFFERENCE

15. Sidestep the pavement. Many pavements are made of crushed rock, and over time, they'll crush your legs. A little running on pavements (say, 5 minutes) is OK, but never do

Think before you run: take a look outside before you run and dress for the weather ahead of you.

The ground rules

Run on the dirt. Smooth dirt tracks are easy on the legs and great for the mind. And there's less chance of running into hazards on dirt than on grass. Nothing's better than running on a great track through woods or along a scenic river or lakeside. The pounding's minimal, the mind wanders, the miles flow.

the bulk of a daily run on pavements. Apart from the pounding your legs will take, pavements are crowded with people and obstacles, uneven and cracked, so you can easily trip on them. Avoid them as much as possible.

16. Beware the one-track mind. Tracks are definitely easier on your legs than pavements, but they're tougher on your psyche. Many beginners go to a track for their initial runs and, not surprisingly, find circling a 400-metre track to be mind-numbing. Tracks are for speed sessions or races, not fitness runs.

17. Look for the open road. Asphalt is the surface on which runners generally log the most miles. Asphalt isn't the softest and most forgiving surface, but it's a lot softer than concrete. Don't run on the side of steeply cambered roads, because it can lead to injuries. If possible, run on the most level part of the road. Asphalt cycle paths are a good option, as they usually have the smoothest surface and no cars.

18. Go for the green. Parks are excellent places to run. Usually there are plenty of grass fields to run around.

'Nothing's better than running on a great track through woods or along a scenic river or lakeside.'

A green and grassy park will help you run more miles with fewer aches and pains.

Beginners who made it

At a recent marathon, the editors of Runner's World *asked a handful of runners, 'What was the most important thing you learned when you started running?' Here are their answers.*

'You have to start slowly and take a conservative approach. I used to push too hard and get injured often. Eventually I got a heart-rate monitor to force myself to go slower.'

G. L., 29

'You have to eat well to fuel your running. I've never been a big eater, and I found that I didn't have enough energy when I started building up my mileage. I'd get muscle cramps, too. I had to concentrate on eating and drinking more.'

C. T., 18

'I found it was easier to train on a circuit course. I marked every mile, and I was never far away from where I started. If I felt good, it was easy to go further. If I didn't feel good, I could stop at the end of the circuit.'

M. W., 49

'It's not just about running. It's a whole lifestyle thing. When I started, I weighed 110 kg (17 st). Now I've lost 32 kg (5 st) and finished several marathons. When I took up running, I started skipping the daily sweets and ice cream. Now I usually park further away from the shops, and I take the stairs instead of the lift. Everything adds up.'

M. G., 32

'Having a support group is so important. I got pulled into running by my friends. It's great fun. Make sure you enjoy it as you're going along.'

C. Y., 50

You can do loops around the entire park or laps around the football pitches. You'll find that most parks have amenities like toilets, water fountains and telephones, and are safe for solo running. Grass is the softest surface to run on, but it can be uneven. So be alert to hard-to-see bumps, holes and sprinklers, which can trip you up.

NUTRITION: FUELLING THE FIRE

19. Never run on an empty stomach. Many beginners skip breakfast and eat a salad for lunch in an attempt to lose weight. This is a mistake. Your body needs fuel to run. If you don't take in steady calories during the day (this is called grazing), you'll be sluggish and your legs won't want to move. And you'll hate running. Also, make sure you eat 200 to 300 calories about an hour before your run so you'll have fuel in the tank, advises sports nutritionist Dr Nancy Clark.

For the health of it

Running does wonders for your body. It boosts 'good' HDL cholesterol, conditions your heart and lowers your risk of certain types of cancer. But maybe you've heard all that. Here are some more surprising benefits.

• You'll stay warm in winter. A US Naval Medical Center study of fit women found that they conserve heat better than overweight, unfit women.

• You'll get cleverer. Your daily run may be all you need to beat your peers at Scrabble, chess or any other game that requires brain power, according to a recent study from the Journal of Aging and Physical Activity. *In the study, men who were more physically fit performed better mentally than their less-fit peers.*

• You'll prevent age-related disabilities. Researchers from Stanford University in the US found that people who exercised, maintained a healthy weight and didn't smoke were half as likely to become disabled by the age of 75 as those who didn't have those habits.

• You'll improve your hearing. Regular runs can even help your ears survive a loud rock concert. Researchers from the University of Northern Iowa in the US found that physically fit people recover their normal hearing faster after being exposed to loud noise than less physically fit people.

• You'll live longer. Finnish research shows that walking or jogging for 30 minutes or more six times a month can reduce your risk of premature death by more than 40 per cent.

20. But don't pig out. Some new runners take the opposite approach by eating too much before their workouts, especially too much sugar. If you feel as if you're running with a brick in your stomach and you often end up doubled over with a side stitch, rethink your fuelling scheme. A banana or a slice of toast is a great snack before a workout. A doughnut is not.

21. Avoid taking pit stops. Many beginners (and even some experienced runners) worry that drinking fluids before a race or workout will translate into annoying pit stops. Not so. It takes your body roughly 45 to 90 minutes to process the fluids you drink. 'If you load up on fluids an hour and a half before your workout, you'll give yourself enough time to get rid of the excess before you start running,' says Clark.

22. Drink and eat on the run. Keeping adequately hydrated is critical to your running. This means drinking the equivalent of eight large glasses of water every day, and probably twice that in warm weather. And it means taking in around 230 ml (8 oz) of fluid every 15 to 20 minutes of running. For runs lasting an hour or more, you also need to replenish spent energy stores with carbohydrate. Optimal intake: 50 to 100 calories of carbohydrate per 30 minutes of running.

Don't run on empty: keeping adequately hydrated is critical to your running.

23. Eat a balanced diet. Don't be fooled by all the fad diets out there. The healthiest way to eat is also the best fuelling plan for your running. Try to stick to the food guide pyramid Most of the food you eat should be whole grains, fruit and vegetables. Strive for six to 11 servings of grains (one serving equals a slice of bread, 30 g (1 oz) of cereal, or a cup of pasta), five to nine servings of fruit and vegetables, and two to three servings of meat and dairy products a day. Keep sugary, fatty foods to a minimum.

INJURY PREVENTION: FIVE DO'S AND FIVE DON'TS

24. Do warm up by walking. Even if you're fit and not overweight, make sure that you start each run with 2 to 3 minutes of brisk walking. It's the ideal warm-up for any runner, regardless of ability.

25. Do take it easy. Either do a run/walk programme or run at a pace at which you can chat with a friend without being out of breath. Running harder increases your risk of injury, not to mention early burnout.

26. Do run by time, not distance. Measure your run by the amount of time spent running, not by how far you have covered. That is, try to run for 30 minutes rather than for 3 miles. Doing this will help prevent you from trying to go faster and faster over the same route.

27. Do progress slowly. You should only increase the actual time spent running by 1 or 2 minutes a day (or less). Another good rule to follow: never increase your mileage by more than 10 per cent a week. Instead of running longer, you may want to add an additional shorter run during the week. The leading cause of injuries to beginners is running too far before they're ready.

28. Do stretch and strengthen. Learn how to stretch properly – and devote 10 minutes to it after each run. Pay particular attention to the hamstrings, calves and quadriceps. Also, consider light strength-training exercises for the same muscle groups.

29. Don't run with the Joneses. Running with a partner, best friend or anyone else who is faster and fitter than you can be very frustrating for a beginner. And it can cause tension between you. Instead, seek out someone who is also a beginner.

30. Don't run with pain. If something hurts, stop. Don't try to 'run through it' (infamous runner's term), even if you've heard that's what good runners do. It isn't. It's what stupid runners do – runners who get hurt again and again.

31. Don't leave the flatlands. Once you gain experience, hills are a great way to boost fitness and strength. But not now. Running up and down steep hills can increase the risk of pain and injury from jarring.

> *'Always run at a relaxed and comfortable pace. This isn't the Olympics; it's a lifelong fitness quest.'*

All in the timing: measure your run by time spent running, not by distance covered.

THE FINISH LINE

Three things to remember about this chapter:

1. Buy good shoes. They don't have to be expensive shoes, but they should be proper running shoes, made by one of the major running-shoe companies (there are about a dozen of them). Other kinds of athletic shoes – like tennis shoes and cross-trainers – are made for other activities, not running. Runners need *running shoes*.

2. Eat a varied, healthy diet. Yes, runners need certain foods like carbohydrates for energy. But runners don't need special or exotic diets. They just need to stay properly hydrated and to eat a variety of foods from all the healthy food groups.

3. Stick to it. Running doesn't produce miracles. It produces slow, gradual progress. You won't lose much weight in the first week, and you won't be able to run a marathon the first month. But if you stick to a regular training programme, your body will slowly get in shape and shed the weight.

32. Don't race. And don't even think about running a marathon. Not yet. You're learning how to run, and you're conditioning your body. Racing is for runners who already know how to run and are ready to test their bodies. If you must run a race, look for a low-key 5-K and consider walking part of it.

33. Don't apply ice or take painkillers before you run. If you're hurting, take a day off. Which isn't a bad thing to do now and again, whether you're feeling pain or not. Building planned rest days into your programme can both motivate you and help keep you injury-free.

WEBWISE

Buying shoes online is best left until you know what you want, but once you're more familiar with your requirements Bourne Sports has a great range of running gear with clear descriptions and good prices.
www.bournesports.com

CHAPTER 10

The Run/Walk
Plan

Why You Need to Learn to Walk before You Can Run

A simple training technique can increase your endurance and calorie burning, decrease injuries and guarantee you success as a runner.

Until recent times, beginners didn't have it as good as you do. To progress as runners, they had to endure pain and suffering. Often they got injured or frustrated before reaching their goal. Result: they gave up. They never became lifelong recreational runners or gained the health and emotional benefits that come with the fit way of living.

Why did they fail? Because most beginners were told to get out there and run. Of course, as with starting any new physical activity, they were told to go slowly and make gradual progress. But they were only informed about running. No one told them how walking – and a mix of walking and running – could help them become successful runners.

Now we know better. Walking, and a mix of walking and running, is not only crucial for beginning runners, it's used by many other runners as well. Even advanced runners. Consider the following.

■ When world-class runners peak for the Olympics, this is

the time that they concentrate on 'interval' training – the still-unsurpassed method for achieving maximum results. They run hard for 1 to 5 minutes, then walk or jog very slowly until they're ready to run hard again.

■ When ultradistance runners participate in those seemingly crazy races of 100 miles or 6 days (or more), they inevitably alternate between running and walking. Which only makes sense. It's hard to imagine any other way to cover the mega-mile distances that they endure.

■ Early man also used a mix of running and walking to hunt down game in the Palaeolithic period. These people knew nothing about marathon running – unlike us, they weren't lucky enough to have been born in the marathon era – but studies have shown that they covered close to 10 miles a day. *Every* day. It was an integral part of their lives. And they managed 10 miles a day by combining walking and running.

When you do a workout, any workout, the goal isn't to avoid walking. This point bears repeating: the goal of a workout is *not* to avoid walking. The goals are to feel better, get in better shape, reduce tension, lose weight, train for a forthcoming race and so on. Take your pick. They're all positive steps. They're all worthwhile goals.

And here's the important thing: you can achieve these goals more easily if you combine some walking into your running. It really is that simple.

Enough talk. Let's pause for a moment to take a look at many of the similarities between walking and running. Some are small, others more significant.

TWO OF A KIND

Running and walking do have much in common. Running is basically fast walking, with this difference: Runners 'jump' from foot to foot; walkers don't. When you run, the knee flexes more than in walking, the quadriceps muscles contract, and you 'toe off' in more or less the same way as the long jumper who explodes off the jump board.

Because you toe off and jump, you come down forcefully on the other foot. This is the infamous 'impact shock' of running – said to be two to three times your body weight – that can lead to overuse injuries of the foot, knees, tendons

---

THE BEST WAY

Q: I like the run/walk idea. But how much should I do of each?

A: Keep it flexible. Let your mood and energy level decide. Of course, when you're just beginning, you'll do much more walking than running, maybe 4 minutes of walking and 1 minute of running. As you get in better shape, this ratio will move in the direction of more running. Ultimately, there's no limit to the varieties of run/walk training. You can walk and run slowly for hours to build your endurance. Or you can walk and run, with short, fast run periods, to build your speed.

'*Listen to your body and don't run further or faster than what feels right.*'

and so on. Walkers don't jump, so they are less likely to get injured. There's less risk involved because they don't absorb as much pressure.

But because you jump, you can cover ground much faster than a walker and burn many more calories per minute (because moving faster requires you to consume more oxygen). In other words, you get a superior workout in less time, which is one of the major benefits of running.

Unfortunately, many potential runners never get into the rhythm of running, because it can be hard work. They set out to run around the block a few times but find themselves breathless and bedraggled at the first corner. Not a pretty sight. So they repair to the sofa and never leave it again.

Or maybe they do try another time, but on this next effort they decide to skip the running. They walk. It's hard to fail at walking. But a leisurely stroll, while better than nothing at all, probably doesn't produce as many health and fitness benefits.

These leisurely walkers are the ones who need to learn about run/walk training. They're already motivated to exercise; they just have to step up the pace a little. Which is what a programme of running and walking does. You won't get exhausted and frustrated (thanks to the walking breaks), and you'll get all the benefits that vigorous exercise brings (thanks to the running). Not a bad deal.

THE GALLOWAY MARATHON

Some runners have even found that the run/walk approach is the best way to tackle the marathon distance. Olympic marathon runner and inspirational trainer Jeff Galloway has pioneered the idea of walking breaks during marathons. He advocates this programme not only for many first-time marathon runners, but also for those who have previously 'hit the wall' and experienced the crushing fatigue and depression of those last few miles. By walking early and often, Galloway has found, most runners survive the final miles in much better shape. They feel better, and they often run faster.

You can run/walk a marathon any way you want, but the simplest is to run the first mile, then walk 60 seconds. Run the second mile, then walk 60 seconds (and enjoy a gulp of sports drink). Repeat 24 more times, then hold your head

'A run/walk workout is an offshoot of the classic interval workout, so it's easy to make it a real gut-buster.'

Build steadily using the run/walk programme and you'll reach your first mile much more quickly.

high and sprint like a cheetah – sorry people, but there has to be a little hard graft in all this.

The Galloway run/walk marathon has now been used successfully by thousands of marathon runners. Jeff says it's possible to run under 3:30 this way, and we know several runners who have done so in major marathons like Chicago, London and Boston. But fast times aren't the point. The point is that you can finish the marathon, you can feel good, you can run strongly to the end and you can admire that gleaming finisher's medal for the rest of your life.

OTHER APPROACHES

There are many other varieties of run/walk training. And just as many benefits. Some are physical, some are mental, all are guaranteed to get you into better shape. Here are just a few of the benefits.

1. Running further, easier. All runners, from beginners to veteran marathon runners, would like to run for longer and more easily. The run/walk system gives you a new tool to achieve this. Does it come at a cost? Of course. Your overall workout is slower, so you get slightly less training effect. But usually you run for longer to build overall endurance and increase your body's ability to burn fat and calories in general. A long run/walk workout does this just as well. (For pacing information, see 'How Fast Are You Going?' on page 91.)

2. Increased variety. Far too many runners do the same workout at the same pace every time they run. It's boring, and it's not a wise way to train. A run/walk workout naturally has many small segments, which encourages you to experiment. You can, for example, do an hour of 4/1 run/walking, with each 4-minute run being totally different. You can do everything from 4 minutes very slowly to 4 minutes at a varied pace to 4 minutes at a hard, steady pace. Experiment a little to find your favourite plan.

The run/walk programme is suitable for everyone, from the beginner to the marathon runner.

3. Better speedwork. Same as point 2, but with harder effort. A run/walk workout is an offshoot of the classic interval workout, so it's easy to make it a real gut-buster. Here's a particularly successful workout, again built on the 4/1 pattern. During each 4-minute running segment, jog for 1 minute, run hard for 2 minutes, and jog for 1 minute. Then do the 1-minute walk. Repeat this eight times, and you've come reasonably close to the 8 × 400-metre interval torture training that many top runners use.

4. Fewer injuries. Walking doesn't cause as many injuries as running, and run/walk training shouldn't cause as many either. No, this can't be proved, but it makes intuitive sense. Since walking uses the leg muscles and connective tissues in a slightly different manner than running, it should reduce overuse injuries. During run/walk workouts, you can walk with a deliberately slow, elongated stride – quite different from a normally short, choppy running stride. When you do this, you'll feel other muscles coming into play.

5. More sightseeing. What's the point of running in some gorgeous, natural environment if all you see are the rocks and gnarled roots on the trail right in front of you? Yet that's all many trail runners see, because they're concentrating so hard on avoiding falls and twisted ankles. Take your new run/walk philosophy to the trails, however, and you can drink in those scenic views during your walking breaks.

6. More effective recovery days. This one's easy and obvious. Some days you need to run slowly. Maybe you just don't feel like exerting yourself. Maybe you ran long or fast the previous day. Maybe you've been having a tough time at work or at home. You want to run, but you're not exactly bursting with mental or physical energy. Try a run/walk workout. You won't regret it.

7. Faster comebacks. You've had a sore knee, a bad Achilles or a nasty, week-long cold. You're ready to get back into your training routine but want to make sure you don't overdo it

---

Slow things down

Further proof that the run/walk plan works: exercise physiologist Dr Jack Daniels recently had two groups of women run three times a week, either continuously or with walking breaks. After 12 weeks, the run/walk group was more fit. Why? 'In effect, the walking breaks turned the workouts into one big interval session,' says Dr Daniels. 'It allowed the women to go faster overall.'

and suffer a setback. A series of progressive run/walk workouts may do the trick. Try a couple of 2/1 workouts, then a couple of 3/1 runs and keep building. Listen to your body and don't run further or faster than what feels right.

8. More quality time. Maybe you and your wife run, but your teenage kids don't. They do all the other stuff kids do – play football, use their computers, take part in tae kwon do – but probably wouldn't make it through a steady 30-minute run. They will, however, do a run/walk workout with you. Just pick something easy, keep it relatively short, chat a lot and enjoy the time together.

FINAL THOUGHTS

The part of run/walk training that's most appealing to some people – the mental breaks provided by the brief walking periods – won't prove equally compelling to everyone. Many will staunchly resist. 'I didn't start running to become a walker,' they'll snort. We runners succeeded as runners because we're an extremely determined, motivated breed, and we don't take easily to anything that smacks of laziness.

OK. Fair enough. Run/walk training isn't for everyone. Or for every workout. You might choose to do it just a couple of

'The goal of a workout is not to avoid walking. The goals are to feel better, get in better shape, reduce tension, lose weight, train for a forthcoming race and so on.'

How Fast Are You Going?

Most runners want to keep track of their pace. It's how we measure many workouts. So what happens to your overall pace when you combine running and walking? You slow down, obviously. But not as much as you might think.

The following table shows per-mile paces for someone who runs a mile at his or her normal pace, then walks for 60 seconds before running the next mile. These estimates assume that you walk at a steady (but not fast) pace between running efforts.

If you run at the pace in this column and then walk for 60 seconds after each mile . . .	Your overall pace will be . . .
8:00	8:34
9:00	9:31
10:00	10:29
11:00	11:26
12:00	12:23

THE FINISH LINE

Three things to remember about this chapter:

1. Don't get discouraged. When you begin running, you won't be able to dash out of the door and spin around the block for 30 minutes. Tens of thousands of runners have begun with no more than 20 or 30 seconds of running, followed by walking breaks. Don't imagine yourself winning the Olympics. That's a one-in-a-million shot. But always remember the parable of the tortoise and the hare. You're in a race where slow-but-steady always wins.

2. Don't do all workouts at the same pace. After the first couple of weeks of a training programme, you should be able to do some walk or run sections at a slightly faster pace. Do this. Not to go for the gold. But to add some variety and different muscular challenges to your workouts.

3. Go further, not faster. Notwithstanding the above, remember that it's always better, in the big picture and the long run, to go further rather than faster. So don't try to beat your times on certain courses that you repeat often. Instead, try to extend the number of minutes of your workout.

times a week. Maybe when you run alone. Maybe on your long-run efforts.

But – and this is the most surprising thing – this variety of approaches may motivate you to do more speedwork and tempo training. That's because run/walk training is so close to classic interval training that it seems to nudge you in that direction. In fact, you could simply say that run/walk training is classic interval training that's been liberated from the track and allowed to roam wherever you want to take it. Free at last. Enjoy yourself. And get fit the easy, injury-free way.

WEBWISE

When you're looking for current, indepth research on many topics relating to your personal performance, the Peak Performance website is crammed with info-packed training, nutrition and injury-prevention articles.
www.pponline.co.uk

CHAPTER 11

Try a Treadmill

Make the Treadmill Work for You

In the past, treadmills were clackety pieces of almost-useless indoor machinery. Now they're smooth, sleek and great to run on, in summer and in winter, in daylight and (especially) in darkness.

There are as many reasons to run on a treadmill as there are workouts you can run on one. Jamey Canipe, for example, recently had a skin-cancer scare and doesn't want another one. She'd rather do her running indoors.

And Karen Williams has a 14-year-old autistic son and needs to be at home with him. These runners are just a couple of converts in what is quickly becoming a national obsession. According to recent figures, the number of people exercising on treadmills has grown an amazing 772 per cent in the past few years.

From anecdotes and surveys, it's clear that runners are using treadmills in innovative ways to improve their motivation, health, training and racing performances. The following real-life examples reveal what treadmill running can do for you, too.

TALES OF TREADMILL SUCCESS

Stay-at-home mums . . . frequent business travellers . . . world-class athletes . . . they all have a story to tell about how the treadmill has become a feature of running in their lives.

■ **Lose weight and get in super shape.** When Kevin Dear began running in June 2002, he went straight to the treadmill at his local gym. He figured it was the safest place for a

More runners than ever before are incorporating the treadmill into their running regimes.

beginner to start, particularly since he was worried about injuries. Dear desperately wanted to lose weight, but he knew his running and weight-loss programme could succeed only if he managed to stay healthy. He increased his mileage gradually, progressed nicely, and decided to enter a marathon. By then, he'd lost weight and felt more confident about his running. Dear ran 3:31 and improved his time to 3:17:31 just 4 months later in his next marathon. 'I do about 80 to 90 per cent of my training on the treadmill,' says Dear. 'Where I live, the winters are cold and the trails few and far between. The treadmill lets me run in good conditions and provides the cushioning I need to prevent injuries.'

■ **Stay in shape while you're travelling.** Frequent business travellers may be called road warriors, but it's not because they're training hard on the roads. For the most part, they're racing from airport to hotel to meetings to airport to hotel, and so on. It's exhausting stuff. But many of these road warriors are in fact runners who believe their miles logged in their hotel gym make them more energetic and productive while travelling. 'Treadmills help me run when I'm travelling and can't do runs in familiar territory,' says Dave Malloy. 'A treadmill offers low-impact running, controlled weather conditions and ready availability. I can maintain a training programme that would otherwise be difficult with the time pressures of getting to early-morning meetings.'

■ **Beat the weather.** This one's so obvious that it hardly deserves a mention. It gets one, however, because it's so powerful. When treadmills began improving and attracting more runners a decade or so ago, most were bought for winter running. Now that the treadmills are widely available, many runners turn to them in summer as well. 'I run on treadmills whenever there's too much heat and humidity, or when there is too much snow and ice, and when the flies and wasps are about,' says Robert Cohn.

■ **Get over your fear of embarrassment.** Many people like the idea of beginning a running programme, but hate the thought of doing it in public. They know they'll be slow and perhaps awkward. Why put yourself on display? With a home treadmill, you don't have to. It's the perfect solution. 'I'd tried running a few times but was too embarrassed to run slowly

Trust the treadmill to help your knees

Many runners train on treadmills because their decks are softer than asphalt roads. Some treadmills go too far – last year Runner's World *tested one brand that felt more like a trampoline than a treadmill – but most strike a reasonable balance between cushioning and stability. And it's a balance your body will appreciate. 'The treadmill is a good alternative when I feel my legs are taking too much of a beating on the roads,' says Sharon Wilson. 'Every couple of weeks I do one of my long runs on a treadmill to give my knees a break.' Some sound advice.*

enough for my fitness level, so I wore myself out quickly and then gave up on the sport,' says Jeffrey Windsor. 'On the other hand, the treadmill in my cellar lets me run at a slower speed that's more appropriate for me. When I started using it, I couldn't go very far at first, but after a month I could run 3 miles. In 6 months, I ran a 2:05 half-marathon.'

■ **Fix your form.** When you run on a treadmill, especially one that's positioned in front of a mirror, you have little choice but to check where your feet are landing and how you're holding your arms. What else you going to do? 'When I'm running on a treadmill without any worries about traffic or other road obstacles, I use the time to concentrate on my form,' says Ken Pliska, a top US marathon runner. 'I used to have more of a heel-strike, but the treadmill has helped me correct this and develop a better push-off from my toes.'

■ **Stay home with the kids.** Tess Aguirre has five daughters under the age of 10 and still manages to fit in her workouts. More than that, she trained for and finished a recent marathon (in 5:17) and a half-marathon (2:22). 'There is no way I could maintain my training schedule if I had to run outside,' says Aguirre. 'That would require a babysitter, which isn't always a possibility. I have my treadmill in the garage, with an assortment of toys, bikes and our favourite CDs. The girls seem to enjoy our "playtime" together, and my treadmill training allows me to stay active and healthy.'

■ **Stop sneezing.** Seasonal allergies come and go, causing problems for runners who are sensitive to certain pollens. You can't run a great workout when you're sniffing and sneezing, so indoor training offers a welcome alternative. Canada's Courtney Babcock set a national record for 5,000 metres at the 2003 Paris World Championships shortly after a great training workout on a treadmill. 'I have allergies and don't train that well outdoors in the spring and summer, so my coach and I decided to try a hard indoor workout just before I left for Europe,' she says. 'I wasn't sure how feasible it was, but I pushed really hard and finished it.'

■ **Get off the sofa.** OK, we all have days when we just can't get it together for the workout we'd planned. You wouldn't think Laurie Kearney is one of those runners, not when you consider that she's completed 92 marathons, but she swears

> '*A treadmill offers low-impact running, controlled weather conditions and ready availability.*'

THE BEST WAY

Q : What's the main thing to look for when buying a treadmill?

A : Buying a treadmill is like buying a pair of shoes (only it's just a little more expensive!). That is, just as every runner has a best and favourite pair of shoes, you will also have a best and favourite treadmill. Look for these key attributes: stability (the treadmill shouldn't shake, rattle and roll), a smooth ride (the belt shouldn't feel jerky), and a control panel and control buttons that are easy for you to use.

she is. She also believes the treadmill is the secret to her many successes. 'I'm very lazy,' she claims, 'and the treadmill forces me to run at a required pace. I get injured when I run the turns on a track, but on my treadmill I have a favourite workout of 8 miles starting at 8 miles per hour, increasing by 0.1 miles per hour after each mile mark. This is one excellent marathon workout.'

■ **Find your rhythm.** Although elite US marathon runner Kevin Collins lives in an area that has very bitter winters, he makes it work for him by spending most of his time on a treadmill. 'The treadmill training teaches me an incredible rhythm,' says Collins. 'I do all my steady runs on the treadmill and some of my tempo runs. The treadmill keeps me under control. I'm amazed at how many 5-minute miles I can string together.'

■ **Get in shape while watching TV.** Every indoor runner knows TV-watching helps pass the time, but Carl Rundell has worked out how to make good use of adverts. He turns his workout into an interval session, filling commercial breaks with fast repeats. 'I like to go to the gym when a good sitcom is on, and I find a treadmill close to the big-screen TV,' says Rundell, a top marathon runner. 'I run at an easy pace during the actual sitcom but really push it during the adverts, either by increasing my pace or the incline of the treadmill.'

■ **Practise running faster.** Training on a treadmill can help you improve your performance for almost any distance. The reason for this is that the treadmill allows you to select the precise pace you need to get faster. Last March, Heather Housley ran a 2:06 half-marathon. Soon afterwards she began doing a weekly speed workout on a treadmill. Five months later, she improved her half-marathon time to 1:46. 'I like the way the treadmill helps you run exactly as fast as you want,' says Housley. 'You don't have to measure anything or constantly check your watch. You just set your pace and keep up with the belt.'

■ **Run for ever.** Top US marathon runner Kim Jones has run on a treadmill for more than 15 years. She began because she was frustrated by the harsh weather where she lived. To fight back, Jones bought a treadmill and then began doing many of her weekly miles on it. Things even got personal; she gave

Finish with a kick

On an undulating road or trail course, it's virtually impossible to have complete control over your pace every mile. On a treadmill, it's easy. This makes a treadmill the perfect place for running negative-split workouts (start slow, finish fast), arguably the simplest and most effective 'hard day' workout for any runner to do. 'I normally run a 6- to 8-mile workout with a 1-mile warm-up and then try to increase my pace by 15 to 30 seconds each mile,' says Phyllis Drake. 'These negative-split workouts have helped me tremendously in races. I'm able to hold or increase my pace, while others are slowing down.'

THE FINISH LINE

Three things to remember about this chapter:

1. The treadmill is a great all-weather training device. On a treadmill, you never have to worry about the heat and humidity or the biting wind chill. You never have to dress in layers of bulky clothing. You can simply enjoy running the way it was meant to be – free and light. This will help you stay motivated.

2. The treadmill gives you total control. You can run as fast or as slow as you want, and you will know your pace exactly from the treadmill controls. This makes the treadmill an excellent device for slowly, gradually increasing your running workouts.

3. The treadmill is kind to your body. In general, treadmills are softer than the roads, tracks and concrete you might otherwise have to run on. This shock-absorbing quality of a treadmill helps keep you running healthy and injury-free.

her treadmill a name! 'I find the treadmill very stress-free, since I don't have to worry about the weather or cars or anything like that,' says Jones. 'The key for me is listening to music or watching the news on TV to avoid boredom.'

WEBWISE

If you decide to invest in a treadmill, Powerhouse Fitness is a great place to start your search. The site has a huge range of treadmills (and other home gym equipment) and gives more than enough details to help you make your decision. **www.powerhouse-fitness.co.uk**

3
NUTRITION AND
RUNNING

CHAPTER 12

The Best Foods for Runners

Fuelling the Fire to Keep You Running Longer

Don't limit your diet. Eat as many healthy foods as possible, starting with the ones listed in this chapter.

You might think a list of best foods for runners would include only a handful of items. Perhaps just the foods you could find in a health food store. Or maybe the kinds of foods you would see on the finish-line tables after a local race: bananas, sports drinks and standard high-carbohydrate fare.

Well, those do work well. But runners don't have to limit their foods to just a few. Many others also provide the energy you want for running along with the vitamins, minerals and micronutrients you need for optimal health. Some of these foods are surprising ones, too. Like chocolate. And steak. And red peppers. Yes, you need plenty of carbohydrate to fuel your workouts. But as a runner, you also need higher amounts of certain vitamins and minerals – especially antioxidants – than your sedentary peers. You need more protein, too. And you can find these important nutrients in some of the most surprising places.

The following foods will give you all the nutrients you need to run faster, recover more quickly and feel more energized all day long. Most are low fat, so they're good for your waistline, too. What's more, it's a certainty that there'll be at least several kinds of food you love. Whether it's almonds you adore, salmon you salivate over or pasta you pine for, the best foods for runners are also some of the tastiest.

Good sources of carbohydrate, such as pasta, are an intrinsic part of the successful runner's diet.

The Optimal Energy Foods

Many studies show that these tasty treats will reduce your risk of heart disease and cancer. Since they're easy to prepare, you'll have plenty of time for your workouts as well as healthy meals.

SEMI-SKIMMED MILK

Serving: 230 ml (8 fl oz)

Carbohydrate: 10.8 g **Protein:** 8 g

Fat: 3.9 g **Calories:** 106

Benefits: Drinking semi-skimmed milk or skimmed milk is the easiest way to get high amounts of calcium into your body. Calcium is one of the more important nutrients for runners, because it's involved in crucial bodily functions such as bone-mineral formation, muscle contraction and nerve conduction, says number-one calcium fan Dr Ellen Coleman, author of *Eating for Endurance*. Consuming adequate calcium helps prevent stress fractures, shinsplints and possibly muscle cramps. Lastly, milk is a great post-run recovery food because it provides both carbohydrate and protein. (Avoid milk just before running, however, because it can cause side stitches.)

Serving suggestions: Drink it straight from the fridge, whizz up a fruit milk shake, pour it over your favourite high-fibre cereal or enjoy it in hot chocolate as a pre-bedtime drink.

RAPESEED OIL

Serving: 1 tbsp

Carbohydrate: 0 g **Protein:** 0 g

Fat: 11 g **Calories:** 99

Benefits: For optimal performance, runners need to obtain about 30 per cent of their calories from fat. And of all the different sources of fat out there, rapeseed oil is the best, says *Runner's World* magazine nutrition columnist Dr Liz Applegate. Compared to other oils, rapeseed has the lowest level of artery-clogging saturated fat and one of the highest levels of monounsaturated fat, which lowers your risk of heart disease. Rapeseed is also rich in omega-3 fatty acids, which are found in fish and are known to fight heart disease.

Serving suggestion: Use rapeseed oil instead of other fats, such as butter and margarine, when cooking or baking.

BAGELS

Serving: 1 plain bagel

Carbohydrate: 40.5 g **Protein:** 7 g

Fat: 1.5 g **Calories:** 191

Benefit: This easy-to-eat snack comes packed with muscle-fuelling carbohydrate. Truly one of the old standbys before or after a run.

Serving suggestion: If you have a bagel before running, eat it either plain or with jam to avoid adding fat such as cream cheese, which slows digestion.

BANANAS

Serving: 1 medium banana

Carbohydrate: 23 g **Protein:** 1.2 g

Fat: 0.5 g **Calories:** 95

Benefits: Chock-full of carbohydrate and easy to digest, bananas are another classic. They come with a nice dose of potassium, an important mineral that helps keep blood pressure low. Bananas also supply plenty of vitamin B_6, which helps fuel your running.

Serving suggestions: Eat alone or combine with peanut butter.

Eat bananas for energy and to fend off those sugar cravings.

SALMON

Serving: 90 g (3 oz)

Carbohydrate: 0 g	**Protein:** 17 g
Fat: 9 g	**Calories:** 150

Benefits: Salmon and other types of fatty fish come packed with omega-3 fatty acids, important oils that keep your immune system strong. Scientists say that these types of fish can prevent strokes, heart attacks, asthma, dementia, prostate cancer and premature births. They also may boost blood flow, which could improve your running.

Serving suggestion: Grill salmon and top it with a fruit salsa of sliced kiwi, papaya, coriander and a chilli pepper. The salsa provides important antioxidants as well as fibre, says Applegate.

FIG BARS

Serving: One 40 g fig bar

Carbohydrate: 23 g	**Protein:** 3 g
Fat: 6 g	**Calories:** 160

Benefits: These mini 'energy bars' are great high-carbohydrate snacks that satisfy your sweet tooth without packing fat into your arteries.

Serving suggestion: Eat 'em right out of the pack.

ALMONDS

Serving: 25 g (¾ oz) (about 12 almonds)

Carbohydrate: 2 g	**Protein:** 5.5 g
Fat: 14 g	**Calories:** 153

Benefits: Because almonds are loaded with the antioxidant vitamin E, they may help reduce muscle damage as well as fend off age-related diseases. Almonds also come with a healthy dose of important minerals such as magnesium, iron, calcium and potassium. Almonds do contain a hefty amount of fat, but it's mostly the heart-healthy monounsaturated type.

Serving suggestions: Make a trail mix of almonds, cereals, and assorted dried fruits and seeds. Or lightly toast almonds in a non-stick pan and eat them plain.

Fill up on heart-healthy almonds when a snack attack hits you.

BREAKFAST CEREAL (eg branflakes, fruit and fibre)

Serving: 30 g (1 oz)

Carbohydrate: 21 g*	**Protein:** 3 g*
Fat: 1 g*	**Calories:** 100*

*Amounts vary by type of cereal

Benefits: Packed with carbohydrate and fortified with vitamins and minerals, a bowl of cereal is a lot like a multivitamin, but with much more fibre. Best of all, cereal takes less than a minute to prepare and only a little longer to clean up.

Serving suggestions: Eat with semi-skimmed milk or mix with low-fat yogurt and fruit.

ROOT GINGER

Serving: 1 tsp

Carbohydrate: 0.5 g	**Protein:** 0.1 g
Fat: 0 g	**Calories:** 2

Benefits: Besides settling your stomach, this spice may act as a natural anti-inflammatory, reducing joint and muscle pain. It also may prevent heart attacks by thinning your blood.

Serving suggestion: Look for dense roots. Grate the root for stir-fry dishes, cold salads and smoothies.

The Optimal Energy Foods (continued)

KIWI FRUIT
Serving: 1 medium kiwi
Carbohydrate: 7.5 g   **Protein:** 0.7 g
Fat: 0.3 g   **Calories:** 35
Benefits: This tart and tasty fruit is an excellent source of vitamin C. It's also high in potassium, which can help keep blood pressure low. A juicy kiwi makes a perfect post-run snack on a hot day.
Serving suggestions: Simply peel a kiwi after your run and eat it plain. Or mix it into fruit salads or your favourite smoothies.

CHOCOLATE
Serving: 30 g (1 oz)
Carbohydrate: 18 g   **Protein:** 1.5 g
Fat: 8 g   **Calories:** 143
Benefits: You have to splurge every once in a while to keep your diet from getting boring, says Applegate, a certified chocoholic. Chocolate tastes great, and unlike many other sweet treats, it contains the same phyto-chemicals found in red wine, known to fight heart disease. In fact, when researchers recently studied the antioxidant capacity of various foods, chocolate beat other powerhouses like strawberries and tea.
Serving suggestion: Stick with dark chocolate, since it contains more phytochemicals than milk chocolate. (White chocolate doesn't contain any.)

Fight cancer with the phytochemicals found in chocolate.

BROWN RICE
Serving: 180 g (6 oz) cooked weight
Carbohydrate: 57 g   **Protein:** 5 g
Fat: 2 g   **Calories:** 253
Benefits: All types of rice pack a powerful carbohydrate punch, but brown rice does more, because it provides a wealth of antioxidants. These will help in the battle against heart disease and even muscle soreness.
Serving suggestions: One problem with brown rice is that it takes 45 minutes or more to prepare. So cook up lots and freeze it. That way, you only need to add 2 tablespoons of liquid per serving and cook it in the microwave. Or buy instant, though this has slightly less fibre and nutrients than ordinary brown rice.

PORRIDGE OATS
Serving: 40 g (1½ oz) dry weight
Carbohydrate: 26.5 g   **Protein:** 4.5 g
Fat: 3.5 g   **Calories:** 150
Benefits: Porridge is one of the best breakfast foods for those watching their weight because, as the saying goes, it sticks to your ribs. The high amount of water-soluble fibre in porridge does more than keep you full: it also lowers your blood cholesterol. High in muscle-fuelling carbohydrate, porridge is also a good source of iron.
Serving suggestions: Porridge is perfect before a long run, as it provides slow-release carbohydrates to your bloodstream. Make it more nutritious by adding dried or fresh fruit.

BROCCOLI
Serving: 90 g (3 oz)
Carbohydrate: 1 g   **Protein:** 3 g
Fat: 0.5 g   **Calories:** 22
Benefits: Broccoli has it all. It's a great source of vitamin C, which may reduce exercise-induced muscle damage. It's also a good source of folic acid and the bone-builders calcium and vitamin K. Broccoli also comes packed with cancer-fighting phytochemicals.
Serving suggestions: Steam broccoli and squeeze some lemon over it. Or chop it up and add it to your favourite pasta dish.

SEAFOOD COCKTAIL (prawns, mussels, squid, crabsticks and cockles)

Serving: 100 g (3½ oz)

Carbohydrate: 3 g   **Protein:** 16 g

Fat: 2 g   **Calories:** 87

Benefits: An excellent low-fat protein source, each 100 g serving contains 5.6 mg of iron (around 40 per cent of RNI). Seafood also supplies a healthy amount of zinc, an immunity-boosting mineral that's notoriously low in many runners' diets. Zinc is needed for wound healing, healthy skin and fertility. Be sure you're consuming the 7 mg (for women) or 9 mg (for men) of zinc you need each day.

Serving suggestion: Add seafood cocktail to tomato sauce, suggests clam connoisseur Dr Scott Fisher, a sports nutritionist and physiologist.

RED PEPPERS

Serving: 75 g (2½ oz), chopped

Carbohydrate: 5 g   **Protein:** 0.8 g

Fat: 0.3 g   **Calories:** 24

Benefits: These crunchy, colourful vegetables supply more immunity-boosting vitamin C than oranges. They're also loaded with carotenes, a family of plant pigments known to fight heart disease and cancer.

Serving suggestions: Use them as a colourful addition to any pasta dish or salad. Or cut them up and take them to work.

ORANGES

Serving: 1 orange

Carbohydrate: 16 g   **Protein:** 1.5 g

Fat: 0 g   **Calories:** 64

Benefits: An excellent source of carbohydrate, oranges are packed with vitamin C. This powerful antioxidant may help your muscles recover faster after exercise and will keep your immune system running strong, says Coleman. Oranges are also a great source of folic acid, which helps maintain optimal levels of red blood cells and may protect against heart disease. The white pith on oranges is loaded with flavonoids that keep LDL cholesterol from turning into plaque.

Red peppers provide more vitamin C than oranges.

Serving suggestion: Get in the habit of gulping down a large glass of orange juice after a run. You'll be:
(1) Replenishing your muscles with carbohydrate.
(2) Boosting your immune system with vitamin C.
(3) Rehydrating your body with fluid.

FLAXSEED (LINSEEDS)

Serving: 1 tbsp

Carbohydrate: 4.1 g   **Protein:** 2.3 g

Fat: 4 g   **Calories:** 59

Benefits: Sold as seeds, oil or a ground meal, flaxseed contains high amounts of alpha-linolenic acid, a type of fat that can boost immunity, blood flow and possibly even endurance. Flaxseed also keeps your platelets (flat cells in your blood) from clumping together and forming dangerous clots.

Serving suggestions: Use ground flaxseeds when cooking muffins, buy breakfast cereals that contain flaxseed (check the label) or mix linseed oil into your salad dressings. Store flaxseeds in your fridge to keep them from turning rancid.

The Optimal Energy Foods (continued)

BEANS

Serving: 150 g (5½ oz) cooked weight

Carbohydrate: 29 g   **Protein:** 13 g

Fat: 1 g   **Calories:** 180

Benefits: If you're a vegetarian, black beans, lentils, chickpeas and other beans are your best source of protein, iron and soluble fibre. High in carbohydrate, beans are also loaded with folic acid, which may prevent birth defects during pregnancy and fight heart disease.

Serving suggestions: Buy tinned black beans, chickpeas, kidney beans or any other beans. Throw them in a blender with some spices to make tasty sandwich spreads or add them to soups and salads.

RAISINS

Serving: 90 g (3 oz)

Carbohydrate: 62 g   **Protein:** 2.4 g

Fat: 0.4 g   **Calories:** 245

Benefits: High in carbohydrate and low in fat, this convenient snack supplies plenty of potassium as well as some iron. Like grapes, raisins contain an abundance of heart-healthy phytochemicals.

Serving suggestions: Sprinkle them on your cereal, add them to yogurt or simply snack on them throughout the day.

Raisins are cholesterol-free, fat-free and low in sodium.

Pasta with marinara sauce makes the perfect pre-race meal.

PASTA

Serving: 60 g (2 oz) dry weight

Carbohydrate: 44 g   **Protein:** 7 g

Fat: 1.1 g   **Calories:** 205

Benefits: Famous as the quintessential carbo-loader, pasta is low in fat and is a great source of folic acid, which decreases your risk of heart disease. Pasta also serves as a great vehicle for other good-for-you foods like tomato sauce, tofu and seafood.

Serving suggestions: Enjoy pasta with a low-fat marinara sauce for the perfect pre-race meal that's loaded with both carbohydrates and antioxidants (from the tomatoes in the marinara sauce). Avoid creamy pasta sauces that are loaded with artery-clogging, hard-to-digest fats and cheeses.

PRETZELS

Serving: 30 g (1 oz)

Carbohydrate: 22.5 g   **Protein:** 2.6 g

Fat: 1 g   **Calories:** 108

Benefits: Both hard and soft pretzels are high in carbohydrate and low in fat. Even salted pretzels are fine for those who don't have high blood pressure, as the sodium helps you retain the fluid you drink before and after running.

Serving suggestions: Keep a bag of pretzels at work and on the kitchen counter at home. And make sure you drink plenty of water or fruit juice with them.

SWEET POTATOES

Serving: 1 baked sweet potato

Carbohydrate: 30 g   **Protein:** 2 g

Fat: 0.5 g   **Calories:** 126

Benefits: Sweet potatoes are packed with carbohydrate, fibre and carotenes – a family of antioxidants that helps in the fight to prevent cancer.

Serving suggestion: Microwave the sweet potato until it's soft to the touch (about 4 minutes), split it open, and add a pinch of brown sugar and cinnamon plus a touch of butter or low-fat yogurt.

TOFU

Serving: 120 g (2½ oz) cooked weight

Carbohydrate: 1 g   **Protein:** 10 g

Fat: 5 g   **Calories:** 88

Benefits: Most vegetarians know that tofu is one of the best non-meat protein sources. It also supplies a decent dose of bone-building calcium and B vitamins. According to research, the soya protein found in tofu may help prevent cancer, heart disease and osteoporosis, and it may decrease menopausal symptoms.

Serving suggestions: Try tofu in pasta sauces and stir-fry dishes. You'll normally find it in the refrigerated section of your supermarket.

SPINACH

Serving: 90 g (3 oz)

Carbohydrate: 0.7 g   **Protein:** 2 g

Fat: 0.7 g   **Calories:** 17

Benefits: High in carotenes, calcium and iron, spinach is a true 'power food'. The carotenes help ward off age-related diseases as well as protect your muscles from damage. The calcium keeps your bones strong. The iron keeps your energy high. Research also suggests that spinach may hold a cure for some forms of blindness.

Serving suggestions: Use spinach instead of iceberg lettuce to boost the nutritional value of your salads. Also, sneak cooked spinach into lasagne and other casseroles. Make sure you eat something acidic or high in vitamin C, such as tomatoes or oranges, along with your spinach to increase iron absorption.

STEAK (rump)

Serving: 100 g (3½ oz) raw weight

Carbohydrate: 0 g   **Protein:** 21 g

Fat: 10 g   **Calories:** 174

Benefit: Lean red meat is your best source of absorbable iron. Skimping on red meat in an effort to cut calories and fat can lead to iron deficiency, low energy levels and poor running performance.

Serving suggestion: Make fajitas by marinating sirloin or rump steak, which tend to be lower in fat than other cuts. Chop the steak up with some tomatoes, onions and peppers and toss them on the grill. Once cooled, wrap it all in a tortilla.

Steaks are high: eat lean red meat for a great source of iron.

The Optimal Energy Foods (continued)

Many varieties of wholegrain bread contain B vitamins and iron.

WHOLEGRAIN BREAD

Serving: 1 slice

Carbohydrate: 15 g   **Protein:** 3 g

Fat: 1.1 g   **Calories:** 75

Benefits: High in carbohydrate, wholegrain bread contains many of the same healthy phytochemicals as fruits and vegetables. Most whole grains also contain B vitamins, and some come with iron added.

Serving suggestions: Use wholegrain bread for your sandwiches.

STRAWBERRIES

Serving: 145 g (5 oz)

Carbohydrate: 9 g   **Protein:** 1 g

Fat: 0.2 g   **Calories:** 40

Benefits: Strawberries – and many other berries – are low in fat and high in vitamins, especially vitamin A, vitamin C and folic acid. They also provide lots of fluid, making them good snacks after a workout, especially on hot days. Strawberries are loaded with ellagic acid, a powerful antioxidant that can inhibit tumour growth.

Serving suggestions: Mix strawberries and other berries into a fruit salad or blend them with milk or yogurt for a nutritious post-run shake. Or slice up several juicy strawberries to put on top of your pancakes or French toast instead of maple syrup.

NATURAL YOGURT

Serving: 150 g (5½ oz)

Carbohydrate: 11 g   **Protein:** 8 g

Fat: 1 g   **Calories:** 84

Benefits: Yogurt is a terrific source of muscle-fuelling carbohydrate, protein and calcium. Look for yogurts that list 'live and active cultures' on the label, as they may boost immunity.

Serving suggestions: Great for a quick breakfast. Or add your own fresh fruit and muesli to plain, low-fat yogurt to create a snack loaded with vitamin C, fibre and other nutrients.

Sprinkle strawberries over cereal or enjoy them on their own.

THE FINISH LINE

Three things to remember about this chapter:

1. Eat many foods, not few. Some runners and health food nuts go on 'special' diets where they emphasize one or several foods over all others. However, a healthy diet contains many different kinds of foods, not few. You'll eat best, feel best and perform best when you eat from a wide range of foods.

2. Eat carbs before and after running. When you eat carbohydrate foods in the hours before a workout, you stock your body with its most efficient energy source. Carbs 'burn cleaner' in the body than fats and proteins. You also need to restock on carbs as soon as possible after a workout. The rest of the time, you don't have to obsess about carbohydrates.

3. Eat lots of fruits and vegetables. Not only do these foods have the vitamins, minerals and micronutrients you need, but they're also good sources of the daily water that runners must consume. This way you can eat and hydrate at the same time.

EAT MORE, WEIGH LESS

Many runners worry too much about the foods they eat, often dividing them into 'good' and 'bad' foods. Nutritionists, surprisingly, don't take the same approach. Yes, they agree, there are many healthy foods (such as the ones listed in this chapter). But other foods aren't sinful. They simply shouldn't be consumed in large quantities.

Another surprise: surveys show that the thinnest people often eat more than their obese counterparts. How can this be? It happens because most overweight people do too much sitting. Most thin people are on the go constantly, at work, at home and while exercising. That's what makes them thin.

THE BEST WAY

Q : Isn't it important for runners to eat lots of carbohydrates?

A : It's crucial for runners to eat enough carbohydrates to fuel their workouts, as your muscles burn carbs more efficiently than they burn fats or protein. But that doesn't mean you need to eat all carbs all the time. In fact, the best diet for runners is a highly varied one that includes plenty of proteins, healthy fats, and especially fruits and vegetables. The most important time to eat carbs is before running and immediately after running.

WEBWISE

For great food-nutrition information, the British Nutrition Foundation has a very useful website. Learn more about how to achieve a balanced diet throughout life. **www.nutrition.org.uk**

CHAPTER 13

The Right Food at the
Right Time

From Breakfast to Bedtime, Choose the Best Foods for Running

Good nutrition is important all day long, but different foods are healthiest and most important at different times of day. Here are the best foods for a number of situations that runners often encounter.

Runners need to train right and eat right. To do one without the other is like sleeping just 4 hours a night. You're only doing half the job.

On the other hand, when you train and eat as you should, the results are greater than the sum of the two parts. This doesn't guarantee that you'll feel great every minute of every day. No one gets that guarantee. But you'll feel a lot better than you would if you didn't train and eat correctly.

As you move through your daily, weekly and monthly training programmes, there are times when certain nutritional practices are particularly important. That's what this chapter is about: the right foods at the right times.

You might remember how, in the early Popeye comics, our hero would often find himself in a jam, usually when he was about to be pummelled by Bluto. On these occasions, Popeye would quickly inhale a tin of spinach, and the green stuff would give him bulging muscles. Result: he'd pop Bluto right in the kisser and send him flying through the

Different foods will reward you best at different times of the day.

air. Spinach was the original 'quick fix'. It's the iron it contains that makes it a 'power food'.

Runners get in jams too, and this chapter gives you 20 quick nutritional fixes to provide the strength and energy you need. You'll find plenty of opportunities to put these fixes to good use and then to run and feel your best.

Before a Longer-than-Normal Workout
■ **The food:** Peanut butter
■ **The benefit:** Peanut butter is super-high in vitamin E, the most potent antioxidant vitamin in foods. For pre-workout energy, spread 2 tablespoons of peanut butter on half a bagel and eat it 2 hours before you begin to exercise. The good fats (monounsaturated) in peanut butter will 'stick to your ribs' and help you feel full. Plus, you'll be energized with slow-release carbohydrates. Bonus: recent data from the US Nurses' Health Study indicates that peanut butter and nuts can help reduce the risk of type-2 diabetes in women.

When You Have a Joint Injury
■ **The food:** Glucosamine and gelatine
■ **The benefit:** According to several studies, supplemental glucosamine – about 1,500 mg daily – helps soothe joint pain, possibly by stimulating cartilage growth. Taking glucosamine may also speed healing in ligaments and tendons. Most recently, a study from Harvard University has shown osteoarthritis improvements with gelatine-based products.

Before a Short Run or Race
■ **The food:** Coffee
■ **The benefit:** A study published in the *British Journal of Sports Medicine* reported that runners who drank 1½ cups of coffee (containing a total of about 3 g of caffeine) prior to running 1,500 metres ran faster and had higher max VO_2 levels than those who didn't drink any coffee. In addition, related studies have suggested that the antioxidants in coffee can help cut the risk of developing both Alzheimer's and Parkinson's diseases. Just keep in mind that coffee's energising effect is that of a stimulant; it doesn't provide true energy calories – so try to eat a little something that does.

Drinking a cup of coffee before you run can bring you some positive results, including faster times.

'For pre-workout energy, spread 2 tablespoons of peanut butter on half a bagel and eat it 2 hours before you begin to exercise.'

A Week When You're Tapering for a Big Effort

■ **The food:** Oranges

■ **The benefit:** Stay healthy during the week by eating an orange a day – each one packs 75 mg of vitamin C. Recent studies suggest that vitamin C can help beat arthritis. For even better reinforcement, eat organic oranges, which according to research may contain as much as 30 per cent more vitamin C than conventionally grown oranges.

After a Harder-than-Normal Workout or Race

■ **The food:** Cottage cheese

■ **The benefit:** Cottage cheese is full of protein for muscle repair, and it's a good calcium source as well, making it the perfect post-run treat. It also contains linoleic acid, which boosts memory and protects against cancer, heart disease and diabetes. Bonus: Adding a large handful of fresh blueberries will give you about 20 g (¾ oz) of carbohydrate for recovery fuel. Or, to help with rehydration, mix in cantaloupe or honeydew melon, both of which are 90 per cent water.

The Night before a Long Workout

■ **The food:** Pasta plus a side salad

■ **The benefit:** Stick with one serving of traditional pasta to carbo-load your muscles, but have it with bolognese sauce and include a high-protein salad as well. Mix greens with vegetables, chickpeas, cheese or diced ham for a healthy, protein-rich side dish that will keep you satiated through the night so you're not ravenous during your long workout the next morning.

After a Strength-Training Session

■ **The food:** Tuna

■ **The benefit:** Research has shown that runners need about 50 to 70 per cent more protein than the average couch potato does, which means you should eat 75 to 100 g (2½ to 3½ oz) a day, depending on your body size and the type of mileage you're putting in. This is especially important if you're strength training, as lifting weights increases your protein needs even more. Eating just 90 g (3 oz) of tuna will supply you with about 20 g (¾ oz) of protein.

Add oranges to cooked or cold dishes, eat them as snacks or squeeze them for their delicious juice.

During a Long Workout
■ **The food:** Honey

■ **The benefit:** An excellent source of carbohydrate, honey has been shown to effectively keep blood glucose levels high for optimal endurance. Three studies done at the University of Memphis Exercise and Sport Nutrition Lab in the US report that honey is just as good as energy gels when eaten before and during a workout. One of the studies showed that cyclists who ate 15 g (½ oz) of honey before a 40-mile race and every 10 miles during the race increased their power and speed.

The First Meal after a Long Run
■ **The food:** Mixed seafood on wholewheat pasta

■ **The benefit:** A 100-g (3½-oz) serving of mixed seafood contains 5.6 mg of iron and 2.5 mg of zinc, while 150 g (5½ oz) of cooked wholewheat macaroni packs 30 g (1 oz) of carbohydrates. Since your immune system is weakened after a long run, the zinc in seafood can help boost your immunity, which will lower your risk of getting a cold or flu. The zinc will also repair muscle tissue damage that occurs during a long workout, and the pasta will restock your carbohydrate stores.

The Week after a Particularly Hard Effort
■ **The food:** Stir-fry with meat

■ **The benefit:** To refortify your depleted immune system the week after a big effort, you need vitamin C. And you'll get this by eating plenty of vegetables such as green and red peppers, cauliflower and broccoli. For an added bonus, eat green, leafy vegetables to boost folic acid levels, which will help decrease cancer risk. Adding meat rebuilds muscle tissue.

TEN SUPERFOODS FOR EVERYDAY LIFE
You're not always planning for your next workout or eating to recover from it. But eating well *is* important all the time. So here are 10 more research-proven foods to make you happier and healthier.

1. The Sleep Enhancer
■ **The food:** Turkey

■ **The benefit:** You sleep better after eating turkey because it

Eating a stir-fry with meat after periods of heavy running will rebuild precious muscle tissue.

' An excellent source of carbohydrate, honey has been shown to effectively keep blood glucose levels high for optimal endurance. '

contains tryptophan, an amino acid that is the building block for serotonin, a neurotransmitter that promotes a sense of calmness and drowsiness. So the next time you have trouble sleeping, try a turkey sandwich.

2. The Memory Booster
- **The food:** Blueberries
- **The benefit:** Preliminary studies on blueberries suggest that they may help prevent mental decline as we age. Researchers recently found that blueberries reduced age-related brain damage in rats. These findings, along with preliminary results from a human study, suggest that 150 g (5½ oz) of blueberries a day may be the secret to preventing Alzheimer's.

3. The Pregnancy Helper
- **The food:** Enriched cereals (folic acid)
- **The benefit:** Folic acid may help guard against pre-eclampsia, cervical cancer and the risk of neural-tube defects

' The carbs and fats in chocolate flood the brain with feel-good endorphins and hormones. '

As well as fighting cancer, eggs contain vitamin B$_6$, which is vital to the formation and health of red blood cells and blood vessels.

in foetuses. It's important for women to get the proper amount of folic acid (the RNI for adults is 200 micrograms, and women are advised to consume an additional 400 micrograms before and during pregnancy). Folic acid has been added to some foods, such as cereals and some breads, but can also be found in supplement form.

4. The Sex-Drive Booster (men)
■ **The food:** Oysters
■ **The benefit:** Oysters are said to be an aphrodisiac, and it might just be true. This mollusc is one of the most concentrated food sources of zinc – a nutrient that is key in the production of testosterone. In fact, six raw oysters contain 72 mg of zinc. Eat them on pasta or in the shell.

5. The Mood Lifter
■ **The food:** Chocolate
■ **The benefit:** According to a recent issue of the *American Journal of Psychiatry*, chocolate can be an antidepressant. The carbs and fats in chocolate flood the brain with feel-good endorphins and hormones. They also release peptides in the brain that have an antidepressant effect. Plus, another compound in chocolate called phenylethylamine (PEA) has been shown to boost mood in depressed people.

6. The Breast-Cancer Fighter
■ **The food:** Eggs
■ **The benefit:** A preliminary study published in *Breast Cancer Research* reported that teenage girls who ate at least one egg a day reduced the risk of eventually getting breast cancer by 18 per cent. Other nutrients associated with a reduction in breast-cancer risk were fibre and vegetable fats.

7. The Heart Protector
■ **The food:** Cranberry juice
■ **The benefit:** A recent study reported that drinking three glasses of antioxidant-rich cranberry juice a day significantly raises levels of 'good cholesterol' (HDL) and may help reduce certain risk factors of heart disease. Factor in the cystitis-fighting properties of cranberry juice, and it's a natural wonder drink.

THE BEST WAY

Q: What's the best pre-workout food to eat to give me extra energy?

A: There are many ways to answer this question that all runners try to answer for themselves. The first, and most important, is to eat foods that work for you – foods that make you feel good and don't upset your stomach. Here's one good approach: Have half a cup of coffee an hour before your workout with a light carbohydrate snack like a banana or an oatmeal biscuit, and then drink 115 to 230 ml (4 to 8 fl oz) of a sports drink about 30 minutes before your workout. You'll get a little pick-me-up, some carbs and the fluids you need.

WEBWISE

The British Dietetic Association is dedicated to providing information on optimal nutrition and well-being. If you live in the UK you can search the website for a registered dietitian near you. It's also a good source of the latest food news. **www.bda.uk.com**

THE FINISH LINE

Three things to remember about this chapter:

1. Eat well after a hard workout. It's not only important to eat well before a workout, but also after, and the meals are remarkably similar. After running, you need fluids and carbs, the sooner the better. Some endurance athletes actually eat a small meal – or at least an energy bar – before taking a shower.

2. Eat low-fat protein foods: runners put so much emphasis on carbohydrates that they sometimes ignore protein. That's a mistake, as runners actually need more protein than non-exercisers.

The best proteins: low-fat or fat-free dairy foods, healthy fish like tuna and salmon, and seeds and nuts (which do contain a lot of fatty acids, but most of them are very heart-healthy).

3. Eat plenty of citrus fruits: all the vitamin C-containing fruits – oranges, grapefruits, kiwis and more – make excellent foods for runners. The juices are great, and the whole fruits even better, as they contain more micronutrients and fibre. Vitamin C is an antioxidant that keeps your body and all your tissues healthy in many different ways.

8. The Prostate-Cancer Fighter (Part 1)

■ **The food:** Tomatoes

■ **The benefit:** Tomatoes are loaded with lycopene, an antioxidant that helps fight prostate cancer as well as heart disease. Aim for seven to 10 servings of tomato-based products each week. One tomato serving is equal to about 4 tablespoons of pasta sauce, one medium tomato or one slice of pizza with tomato sauce.

9. The Prostate-Cancer Fighter (Part 2)

■ **The food:** Watermelon

■ **The benefit:** A recent article published in the *Journal of Nutrition* reported that watermelon has even more lycopene than tomatoes. Bonus: watermelon is also 92 per cent water – making it a great choice for when you need to rehydrate after a run. Use it in fruit salsas or salads.

10. The Cholesterol Reducer

■ **The food:** Porridge oats

■ **The benefit:** This breakfast favourite can help reduce the risk of heart disease. One particular study published in the *American Journal of Clinical Nutrition* found that a daily serving of oat bran significantly reduced total cholesterol and LDL cholesterol in healthy men and women.

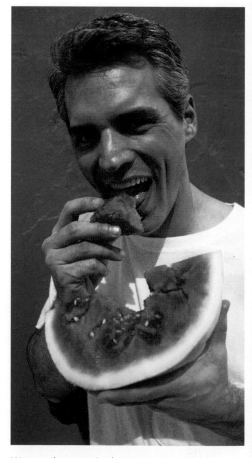

Watermelon contains lycopene, an antioxidant that studies show can help fight infertility in men.

CHAPTER 14

Eat Snacks for
High Energy

Why Grazing Is So Good for Runners

Runners love snacks and need them – they're one of the best ways to get the energy you need. As long as you pick snacks such as the ones presented in this chapter.

We're sure you can still hear that voice of admonishment: 'No more snacks; you'll ruin your appetite for dinner!' Could have been your mum, or maybe it was your dad. For some of us, it was both.

But it's time to silence that guilt-inducing voice in your head once and for all, because snacking is in. Actually, it's not even called snacking any more – it's called grazing. And nutrition experts now believe that grazing on five smaller meals throughout the day is better than eating three big ones.

How come? Because a steady food intake keeps your energy levels consistently higher. Also, when you graze, you never become overly hungry, so you don't get the urge to overeat. You don't binge, and this, of course, makes it easier to maintain your weight exactly where you want it. Added bonus: if you don't let yourself get too hungry, you're more likely to choose higher-quality foods at mealtimes.

Still, you've got to make the right choices and pick the snacks that are best for you. To help you find them, five top sports nutritionists (they're all grazers too) give their recommendations here. So look at the following suggestions and start snacking – I mean, grazing. You'll feel and perform better all day long.

The advice you've always wanted to hear: have a snack.

The Greatest Grazing Foods You Can Eat

The science behind grazing is something called energy balance. It's based on the idea that you want to have a constant high level of energy throughout the day. This doesn't happen when you skip breakfast (after 8 hours of no eating) and then consume a gluttonous lunch. In fact, breakfast is the most important meal of the day, as it re-establishes your energy balance. After breakfast, eat small, nutritious meals every 3 to 4 hours.

STRING CHEESE

Why it's good: Many runners fail to meet their calcium requirement, especially those who don't eat many dairy products. String cheese is a tasty, convenient way to take in calcium and protein as well as some fat.

When it's good: Have a stick or two with some high-carbohydrate foods after a long run or race. Research shows that eating a little protein along with carbohydrates can speed your recovery.

Calories: 69 per 20-g (³/₄-oz) stick.

CARROTS

Why they're good: Carrots are low calorie but filling, so they're excellent if you're watching your weight. They contain beta-carotene and vitamin A, which promote eye health and strong immune function.

When they're good: Eat them at night when you want something to munch but don't want extra calories. Or eat them before dinner if you're famished. This way, you won't over-indulge once you sit down for your meal.

Calories: 30 per medium-size carrot.

It's no myth: carrots promote good vision, especially night vision.

ENGLISH MUFFIN PIZZAS

Why they're good: These pizzas include three food groups – grain, dairy and vegetable – and supply protein, calcium and beta-carotene. All are important for strong bones.

When they're good: Eat any time after running or as an afternoon snack to keep you energized for your evening run.

Calories: 300 per 2 muffin halves, including 2 tablespoons of tomato pasta sauce and 60 g (2 oz) of low-fat mozzarella cheese.

BREAKFAST CEREAL WITH EITHER SEMI-SKIMMED OR SKIMMED MILK

Why it's good: A large bowl of cereal in the morning will set you up for the rest of the day. Most cereals are vitamin and mineral fortified, and they're great with fresh fruit sliced on top. Cereal is a quick-to-prepare, easily digestible and healthy way to satisfy your sweet tooth. (Even sweetened cereals such as Alpen, Crunchy Nut Cornflakes and Frosties are a better low-fat alternative to biscuits.) Choose cereals that have 3 g of fibre or more per serving.

When it's good: Fine as a pre-run snack, a post-run pick-me-up or even as a trail mix during a long, easy run.

Calories: Between 200 and 300 per 45 g (1¹/₂ oz) of cereal plus 230 ml (8 fl oz) of semi-skimmed milk.

MUESLI AND CEREAL BARS

Why they're good: A low-calorie muesli or cereal bar will satisfy your sweet cravings without the fat calories of a chocolate bar. And unlike chocolate bars, they come with B vitamins and iron. They also provide you with energy.

When they're good: Any time you feel like satisfying your sweet tooth – without feeling guilty.

Calories: about 110 per 30-g (1-oz) bar.

HUMMUS ON WHEAT CRACKERS

Why it's good: This filling snack packs plenty of protein, fibre, vitamin B₆ and folic acid. The latter is especially important for a healthy pregnancy and has recently been shown to prevent anaemia and breast cancer.

When it's good: Hummus works well as a substantial mid-morning or afternoon snack. It's also a more healthy evening alternative to peanuts or other fried party snacks.

Calories: 340 per 2 tablespoons of hummus and 5 wheat crackers.

COTTAGE CHEESE

Why it's good: It's packed with protein, which runners need more of than sedentary people for muscle rebuilding and repair. Cottage cheese serves as a good calcium source as well.

When it's good: Any time except just before running. Great with fruit after an intense workout or race.

Calories: 110 per 125-g (2½-oz) serving.

ENERGY BARS

Why they're good: You can choose from high-carb, 40-30-30 or protein-plus bars designed especially for runners. They're tasty and come in all flavours.

When they're good: Pre-race, mid-marathon or post-race – so any time!

Calories: 150 to 230 per 50- or 70-g bar.

PRUNES

Why they're good: Prunes contain no fat and are packed with carbohydrates. They're also a good source of fibre and potassium. Eating potassium-rich foods like prunes helps lower high blood pressure.

When they're good: Prunes make a healthy snack at almost any time. But don't eat them just before your

Apricots in your diet are a delicious way to increase fibre intake.

run, as they can act as a laxative.

Calories: 60 per 5 prunes.

DRIED APRICOTS

Why they're good: These chewy little morsels are low fat and high carbohydrate and provide a decent amount of vitamin A, fibre and potassium.

When they're good: Any time. Toss chopped apricots over your cereal at breakfast or eat whole ones plain before your afternoon workout or as a sweet treat after dinner.

Calories: 100 per 8 dried apricot halves.

FIG BARS

Why they're good: Chewy fig bars are a tasty, convenient source of carbohydrates and fibre. They are carbs that are quickly digestible, making them great 'on the run' snacks.

When they're good: Any time, even during the middle of a workout when you need to refuel in a hurry. Of course, if you're fibre sensitive, save them until after the race.

Calories: 160 per 40-g (1½-oz) bar.

Create your own favourite smoothie for a healthy and tasty drink.

SMOOTHIES

Try blending frozen fruit, semi-skimmed milk or soya milk, orange juice and ice.

Why they're good: If you use fruit and soya milk, smoothies are an easy way to consume a healthy dose of fibre and soya. Smoothies also supply plenty of vitamins C and A, plus potassium, fibre and calcium.

When they're good: A cooling summer treat, a smoothie works well for breakfast, before a run or as a refreshing, re-energising post-run treat.

Calories: Around 150 per 250 ml (8½ fl oz).

RICE CAKES WITH PEANUT BUTTER

Why they're good: Rice cakes are low in calories, most of which come from energising carbohydrates. Peanut butter is an excellent source of protein and heart-healthy polyunsaturated and monounsaturated fat. It also contains vitamin E, which helps with muscle recovery.

When they're good: A perfect 'stick to your ribs' snack for mid-morning or mid-afternoon.

Calories: 220 per 2 rice cakes, thinly spread with peanut butter.

FRUIT JUICE ICE LOLLY

Why they're good: This refreshing low-calorie treat is loaded with vitamin C, which fortifies your immune system and helps boost iron absorption.

When they're good: They're great any time, but they're best immediately after a tough, hot run.

Calories: 75 per lolly.

BANANAS

Why they're good: Bananas are chock-full of carbohydrates. They are a good source of vitamin B_6 and are vital for managing protein metabolism. (Runners need more protein during and after workouts.)

When they're good: Before, during or after exercise. They're great blended into a fruit smoothie. Or simply whip frozen banana chunks with milk in a blender for an excellent recovery shake.

Calories: 95 per medium-size banana.

GREEN SOYABEANS

Why they're good: Soyabeans in any form are a high-quality source of protein, iron, B vitamins and heart-healthy isoflavones (which boost bone health). Soya protein has been shown to lower risk of heart disease and cancer. (Try ethnic supermarkets for green soyabeans.)

When they're good: Eat them after your workout or as a low-calorie but filling afternoon snack.

Calories: 125 per 3 tablespoons, boiled.

CHOCOLATE MILK

Why it's good: Chocolate milk is mostly water and helps keep you hydrated. It also provides plenty of protein, carbohydrates and B vitamins. The calcium in milk will help keep your bones strong.

When it's good: An ice-cold slug of chocolate milk is the perfect reward after a hot summer run.

Calories: 170 calories per 250 ml (8 fl oz) of low-fat chocolate milk.

The live bacteria in yogurt can bolster your immune system.

LOW-FAT FRUIT YOGURT

Why it's good: Yogurt is a great source of calcium, protein and potassium, plus it's low in fat and fairly high in carbohydrates. The live and active cultures in yogurt will also boost your immune system.

When it's good: Any time. Many runners enjoy it as a pre-race snack, despite its protein content.

Calories: 120 per 150-g pot.

TUNA

Why it's good: Tuna comes with protein and heart-healthy omega-3 fats. Research shows that men who eat at least 90 to 115 g (3 to 4 oz) of fish per week are less likely to die of a heart attack, and that women who eat at least 2 servings of fish per week reduce their risk of rheumatoid arthritis. Eating tuna also helps to maintain healthy brain function.

When it's good: Perfect for lunch or an afternoon snack. Consider a tuna salad with low-fat mayo and sliced tomatoes. Or cook up a tuna steak for dinner – however you eat it, tuna offers great health benefits.

Calories: 99 per small (100 g) can, in water.

TORTILLA FILLED WITH REFRIED BEANS, SALSA AND CHEESE

Why it's good: Bean tortillas are high in protein and folic acid and also provide calcium, phosphorus, iron and zinc. To make this snack even lower in fat, you can substitute a wholewheat tortilla, low-fat refried beans and low-fat cheese.

When it's good: As a post-run snack or light meal.

Calories: 300 per flour tortilla, 2 tablespoons salsa, 30 g (1 oz) low-fat mozzarella cheese and 2 tablespoons refried beans.

PORRIDGE OATS

Why it's good: Studies show that porridge helps lower cholesterol. Porridge will also fill you with plenty of carbohydrates to boost energy and alertness.

When it's good: Excellent pre-race or any time you wake up feeling hungry and ready for a hearty breakfast.

Calories: 150 per 150-g (5½-oz) serving, cooked.

THE FINISH LINE

Three things to remember about this chapter:

1. Have something to eat every 3 to 4 hours. Studies have shown that your blood sugar plummets when you go several hours without eating, and this is what gives you that tired, run-down feeling. To achieve the opposite – all-day energy – don't let yourself get hungry. Have a healthy snack at the ready – in your car or desk drawer or fridge – at all times.

2. Dairy products make excellent snacks. Low-fat yogurt, chocolate milk and cottage cheese are good examples. You can eat them at different times throughout the day, and they can often be mixed with other healthy foods to give you more health benefits – fruit, nuts and seeds.

3. Eat snacks that are fibre and protein rich. And avoid snacks that are just sugary confections. The former will keep you satisfied and energized for hours. The latter will give you a brief surge of energy, followed by a sugar crash that may tempt you to eat more of the wrong kinds of food.

NO APPETITE?

Some runners (OK, not many) find it difficult to eat a healthy snack every 3 or 4 hours, particularly during spells of hot weather. If this happens to you, simply drink a tall glass of orange juice or grape juice, naturally high in calories and nutrients.

THE BEST WAY

Q : What's the best way to maintain my energy all day long?

A : To keep your energy up all day, you need to eat meals and snacks on a regular basis. First, don't skip meals. That's a guaranteed way to lose energy. Second, don't hesitate to eat healthy snacks – such as the ones described in this chapter – between meals. Between-meal snacks aren't bad; in fact, they're good for you, provided you make the right choices.

WEBWISE

If you're worried about the amount of sugar in your diet and how your sugar intake is affecting your insulin response, this website instantly finds the glycemic index of virtually any food.
www.glycemicindex.com

CHAPTER 15

Drink to Your Health

Learn How to Stay Refreshed – But Not Overhydrated

Runners need more water and fluids than just about any other group of people. But recent studies have shown that too much water consumption can lead to a serious health condition. Here's how to drink just what you need, and not any more.

We live in a water-obsessed culture. Every young footballer has a water bottle. Parents keep water bottles in their cars. And every business exec clutches a bottle of 'designer water' while dashing through airports with a laptop and overnight bag. Why? At least in part because every fitness article in every newspaper and magazine insists that you absolutely, positively must drink eight big glasses of water a day.

But where's the proof? Amazingly, there isn't any. Even in marathons, the available evidence indicates that over-hydrating is a bigger health threat than underhydrating. Too much water consumption, called hyponatraemia (low salt levels in the blood), can cause convulsions and even death in serious cases. Too little water – dehydration – makes you slow down on the run or perhaps even stop.

However, it remains true that runners need to drink generously. In fact, runners sweat more than just about any other athletes and therefore need to drink more to replace lost body fluids. But we need to drink with a fuller understanding of the facts, the medical science and the potential risks. Here's what you need to know about hydration and your health and performance.

HYDRATION AND YOUR HEALTH

Water plays a crucial role in overall body health, but tales of near-universal dehydration seem to be exaggerated.

■ **Water, water everywhere:** Water is the largest constituent of the human body, making up about 60 per cent of your total body weight. This large pool of water performs many crucial functions. Among them: it nourishes the cells; carries food throughout the body; eliminates waste; regulates body temperature; cushions and lubricates the joints; and maintains blood volume and blood pressure. Inadequate levels of fluid consumption have been associated with kidney stones and higher rates of urinary tract infections, bladder and colorectal cancers, and even heart disease in one or two studies.

■ **Universal agreement:** Given the above, all experts agree that an adequate water supply is crucial to the body's optimal

The caffeine conundrum

A survey of 2,818 adults in 2000 by the International Bottled Water Association (IBWA) revealed that we are drinking 17.6 230-ml (8-fl oz) cups of liquid a day. The IBWA argues that 6 cups of this amount are alcohol and caffeine drinks (both considered diuretics, meaning they increase urine production), and should therefore be subtracted from the total.

But whom should we really believe in the quest to find out the truth about caffeine? Research conducted in the last two years has reversed the age-old wisdom that caffeinated beverages are diuretics. Actually, to be more precise, the research confirmed that caffeinated beverages are diuretics – to the same degree as plain water. You drink a lot of water, you need to visit the lavatory. Same with caffeinated beverages, no more, no less.

'The research indicates that caffeine stimulates a mild diuresis similar to water,' says heat and hydration expert Dr Larry Armstrong, author of Exertional Heat Illnesses. *Armstrong reached this conclusion after analysing 10 medical articles on caffeinated beverages, and published his report in 2002 in the* International Journal of Sport Nutrition and Exercise Metabolism.

functioning. The only question is how much water and other fluids do you need to drink per day?

■ **The 8 × 8 myth:** Many adults believe that they should drink eight 230-ml (8-fl oz) glasses of water a day. Why do they believe this? Because they have heard it countless times in the media. But there's little or no evidence supporting the idea of 8 × 8.

■ **The good professor:** In the summer of 2002, Heinz Valtin, a professor emeritus of physiology at the Dartmouth Medical School in the US, published a lucid and compelling article in the *Journal of the American Physiological Society*. Basically, Valtin committed himself to searching out medical-scientific verification for the 8 × 8 rule. He couldn't locate any.

'I have found no scientific proof that we must drink at least eight glasses of water a day,' concluded Valtin. 'The published data strongly suggest that we probably are drinking enough, and possibly even more than enough.'

Of course, Valtin was researching the hydration habits of average, non-exercising people. Runners sweat heavily and need to drink more than non-exercisers. And the heavier and more muscular you are, the hotter the temperature and the faster you run, the more you will sweat.

■ **This just in:** While most people seem to be consuming plenty of fluids, many still haven't got the message, including some regular exercisers. A study presented at the 2003 annual meeting of the US IDEA Health and Fitness Association showed that nearly half of all exercisers at several locations were dehydrated before their workouts.

■ **Mars and Venus:** When it comes to sweat rates and fluid-replacement needs, men and women come from different planets. Because men are on average significantly heavier than women and have more muscle mass, they tend to sweat more than women do and so need to drink more. Or to turn things around: Women don't sweat as much as men and don't need to drink as much.

■ **An overlooked truth with real-life consequences:** For the reasons just stated, a woman's hydration need can be up to 30 per cent less than a man's. This essential fact has been largely overlooked in most articles on hydration needs, and it's particularly important for women runners, because most

Differences in biological make-up between the sexes mean that women perspire less than men.

of the marathoners who suffer from hyponatraemia (excessive fluid consumption), including a number who have died from marathon-related hyponatraemia, have been women. More on that later.

HYDRATION, PERFORMANCE AND RISK

Dehydration diminishes performance because it thickens the blood, decreases the heart's efficiency, increases heart rate and raises body temperature. But a modest dehydration is a normal and temporary condition for many marathoners and doesn't lead to any serious medical conditions. Excessive fluid consumption, on the other hand, can prove deadly.

■ **A full tank:** A substantial body of research has shown that anything more than 2 per cent dehydration will worsen performance, and everyone agrees that it makes sense to limit dehydration as you run. Some runners can even train themselves to drink more. Studies have also shown that the more fluid you have in your stomach, the more will reach your blood, where you want it. Hence, the good advice to run with a comfortably full stomach and to 'top up your tank' frequently.

■ **Hyponatraemia deaths:** As marathon running has boomed in recent years, and particularly as it has attracted more women and recreational runners, an entirely new health risk has intruded on our sport. It's called hyponatraemia. Hyponatraemia means low blood sodium, but it's caused by excessive fluid consumption, which lowers the concentration of sodium in the blood. In extreme cases, hyponatraemia can lead to brain seizures and death.

In 2002, both the Boston Marathon and the US Marine Corps Marathon had their first-ever fatalities attributed to this condition. Hyponatraemia is also beginning to appear in other endurance athletes, including ultramarathoners, Ironman triathletes, long-distance hikers and army recruits. While no one knows for sure how many runners typically become hyponatremic, the 2002 Boston Marathon produced a 13-per cent incidence rate. And the condition can be very serious.

■ **Hyponatraemia risk groups:** Women, women and women. This is not a sexist slam; it's a warning. Men can also drink excessively and suffer from hyponatraemia, as has

Regular breaks to 'top up your tank' will keep you hydrated and help you stay at your running best.

happened in the US army. Nonetheless, a high percentage of exercisers suffering from hyponatraemia have been women, including the Boston and Marine Corps deaths in 2002.

Why women? As already noted, they're smaller and less muscular than men, so they don't sweat as much. They also have a smaller blood plasma 'tank' than men, which is easier to overfill. Many women are new to marathon running and are happy to finish in 5 hours or more. They have heard that marathon runners must drink as much as possible, so that's what they do. They reach the 20-mile mark exhausted (who doesn't?) and think, 'If I can force myself to drink more, I'll feel better.' It's a recipe for disaster.

NEW VIEWS ON FLUID CONSUMPTION

The hyponatraemia issue has forced sports and medical groups to take a new look at their hydration guidelines, and several have already adjusted their recommendations.

■ **Marathon medicine:** In late 2002, the International Marathon Medical Directors Association (IMMDA) issued the first fluid-consumption guidelines from a medical organization completely focused on runners. IMMDA, which represents some 150 major marathons on all seven continents, suggests that runners should consume 385 to 800 ml (13 to 27 fl oz) of fluid per hour, with an absolute maximum of 800 ml (27 fl oz). For more, visit *www.aims-association.org/immda.htm*.

That's just over half the fluid requirement proposed since 1996 by the widely quoted 'Exercise and Fluid Replacement' position statement of the American College of Sports Medicine, which calls for 590 to 1,180 ml (20 to 40 fl oz) per hour. For more, visit *www.acsm-msse.org* and click on 'Position Stands'.

■ **Boston Marathon and USA Track and Field (USATF):** For the first time in its 107-year history, the Boston Marathon in the spring of 2003 provided all 20,000 runners with a fold-out pamphlet from the American Running Association and the American Medical Athletic Association. It advised runners to stay hydrated but not to overdrink, to maintain a salty diet, to favour sports drinks and to recognize warning signs. Also at Boston, USATF released its first-ever guidelines, 'Proper Hydration for Distance Running', which recommended that runners weigh themselves before and after long, hard training

> ' *Runners need to pay more attention to their daily fluid consumption than most people, but we don't need to be obsessive.* '

Hydration education

A note from our friends at Gatorade: The Gatorade Sports Science Institute (www.gssiweb.com) has recently published one of the most comprehensive advisory documents on hyponatraemia, 'Hyponatraemia in Athletes'. Here you'll find everything from the possible effects of a recessive cystic fibrosis gene to a section on metabolic water production. Experts at Gatorade want you to know that proper hydration is important, and that you're an experiment of one. That is, each of us sweats at a different rate, produces varying amounts of sodium in our sweat and reacts differently to heat stress. So drink up, but drink carefully.

runs to determine their own unique sweat rate. For more info, visit *usatf.org/groups/coaches/library.*

RECOMMENDATIONS

It's a good time to review your hydration practices. Runners need to pay more attention to their daily fluid consumption than most people, but we don't need to be obsessive. Given half a chance, the body will self-regulate to a normal, healthy state of fluid balance. Follow these recommendations.

Drink generously but appropriately. Know yourself and your needs and make adjustments for the weather. A runner training through the summer months for an autumn marathon may need to drink more during and after a slow 16-miler in August than during and after an all-out marathon effort on a cool October morning.

Use sports drinks. Before, during and after workouts and races, drink specially formulated sports drinks. These drinks contain the water you need, appropriate amounts of carbohydrates and small amounts of sodium. It's the combination of all three that really helps you in the long run.

Pay particular attention to post-exercise rehydration. You're likely to become temporarily dehydrated during a long, hard run, so make sure you drink enough afterwards. The same goes for food. Have your fluids, have your carbohydrates, have a little sodium, have a little protein – and you'll be fine.

Weigh yourself daily during periods of intense training. If you're losing weight, make sure it's from fat loss, not chronic dehydration. You can also check your urine colour. It should be clear or light yellow (unless you have recently taken some B vitamins, which can turn the urine bright yellow).

When running long and slow – 4 or 5 hours or more – monitor your fluid consumption. Make sure you're not drinking more than you need. Also, consider running with a salty snack that you consume at the 20-mile mark. Women need to pay particular attention to this advice.

THE BEST WAY

Q: What's the best fluid for runners to drink?

A: A sports drink that contains added sodium (salt) and glucose (sugar). Many of the most common and popular sports drinks have been formulated to contain just the right amount of salt and sugar to: (1) empty quickly from your stomach and intestines to your blood stream; and (2) provide the electrolytes and energy you need. In general, you should stay away from drinks containing extra vitamins, herbs and stimulants. Your drink needs to contain water, salt and sugar. Those are the key ingredients in an effective drink for runners.

THE FINISH LINE

Three things to remember about this chapter:

1. Drink when you're thirsty. Over millions of years, the body has evolved a wonderful mechanism to tell you when you need to take in more fluids – you get thirsty. If you maintain access to drinks and follow your thirst, you'll naturally consume what you need.

2. Drink more when you're running or racing long and hard. While the body has a great thirst mechanism, runners often don't pay attention to it when they're running hard. The physical effort tends to overwhelm your thirst system. During hard runs, especially in hot and humid weather, you should drink about 230 ml (8 fl oz) every 20 minutes or so.

3. Don't drink too much while running, especially if you're a female. Women need only about two-thirds as much water as men and sometimes drink too much when they are running long, slow distances. This can lead to a dangerous condition called hyponatraemia. Drink about one glass of water for every 2 miles you run. Don't drink two glasses every mile – that's too much.

Drink when you're thirsty. While it's true that your thirst doesn't kick in until you're 1- to 2-per cent dehydrated, there's nothing terribly wrong with that. Remember: your body has an exquisitely tuned water-balance mechanism. Use it.

A PLACE FOR EVERY BEVERAGE

Here's a simple three-point plan to help you decide the best time to drink your favourite drinks.

1. When you're trying to limit calories during the day, stick to water or other calorie-free beverages such as diet drinks or herbal tea.

2. For best performance, choose a sports drink before and during a hard workout or race. The same drink will work effectively afterwards as well.

3. When you want extra carbohydrates, vitamins and antioxidants to improve recovery after a workout or race, drink your favourite fruit or vegetable juice.

WEBWISE

For the best information on the Web about hydration, nutrition and exercising in the heat, the Gatorade Sports Science Institute can't be beaten. A thorough and useful resource.
www.gssiweb.org

'If you're losing weight, make sure it's from fat loss, not chronic dehydration.'

4

BASIC

TRAINING

CHAPTER 16

Simple Training =
Big Success

Keeping Things Nice and Easy Will Make You a Better Runner

The surest way to succeed at running is by following the simplest path. The tips in this chapter will help you cut through the obstacles and focus on the goal.

Running is simple: put one foot in front of the other; quickly repeat; keep going. That formula is burned into our brains – for our ancestors, running meant the difference between eating or being eaten – so the skills are there from day one.

We don't need pads, helmets, bats or rackets. As runners, we don't pump up tyres, keep score with stubby pencils or memorize arcane rules and regulations. We just slip on our shoes and go. It's easy, isn't it?

Well, not always. Sometimes your running can become as cluttered as the rest of your busy life. How do you fit it in? How far do you go? How fast? How often? Where? When? What do you eat? What do you wear?

When things get like this, that's when you need to simplify. The following tips, contributed by *Runner's World* magazine editors and running experts and coaches, will help.

You won't need all this advice, but many of these suggestions will save you time and aggravation. They'll leave you free to enjoy the simple pleasures of running. And they might even make you a better, faster runner.

Get in sync. If your schedule allows it, run at the same time each day. If you have to work out when to fit your run in every day, you waste valuable time and energy.

Back to basics: learn the elementary aspects of running – like stretching – and you'll soon progress.

Bag 'em up. Toss your dirty running clothes into a separate mesh laundry bag, then simply knot it and throw it in with the rest of the wash. No more picking through the whole load to weed out your running gear, and you won't have to worry about melting your favourite synthetic running vest in the dryer.

Cross it off. Do you want a simple way to help you stick to your workouts? Mark an *X* on your calendar on days you exercise. In a recent study, exercisers who did this fared better than those who didn't keep track at all.

Don't worry about your breathing. Lots of runners believe there's a right way and a wrong way to breathe, but that's a lot of hot air. Just do what comes naturally to you. Your mouth, nose and lungs will make sure you're doing things correctly.

Set your alarm. Whenever possible, run first thing in the morning. Not only will you avoid having to shower twice a day, you'll also be less likely to skip your run. (You know how it works: the longer the day drags on, the more time you have to find an excuse not to run.)

Stay with a running shoe that works. It's hard to enter a running store and not be tempted by all the flashy new shoes screaming for attention. But the simplest rule for buying shoes is to stay with the kind you're already wearing – assuming they work for you, of course. Take them with you to the shop, and buy a pair of the same model. If your model has been discontinued, ask the salesperson which new style is most like the old one.

Streamline your stretching. Find yourself busy and don't have time for a 20-minute stretching routine? Compromise and focus on your calves and hamstrings – the most important muscle groups for runners. Here's a stretch that works them both: place the balls of your feet on a low kerb or a piece of four-by-two, with your heels resting on the ground. Slowly bend at the waist as if you're trying to touch your toes. Hold for 30 seconds.

The more marks you make on your calendar, the more likely you are to stick to your workouts.

Stock up. If you normally run from work, double up on toiletries when you shop so you can keep soap, shampoo and other supplies at your office or in your gym bag.

One day a week, go vegetarian. Forsaking meat just one day a week will introduce you to new, healthy foods, and over time you may even develop a hankering for vegetarian fare (which tends to be high in fibre and low in fat). Visit the frozen food sections of health food stores if you lack the time or inclination to cook. Or make a hearty bean soup, a pot of vegetarian chilli or a vegetable curry with tofu.

Listen to your body. How much recovery time should you give yourself between repeats in a speed session? It isn't easy to say because we're all different and all have different needs. Ask three coaches, and they'll give you three unique answers.

> *'If you run in the morning, lay out your running clothes the night before.'*

Running first thing in the morning is a great habit to get into because you're less likely to skip a session.

A better alternative is to follow this ultra-simple advice: rest until you feel ready to run again.

Ditch the watch. Sports watches are invaluable during a race or speed session. But on easy runs, they can become just another stressful distraction. Leave yours at home on your next easy run. And the one after that, and the one after that . . .

Have a running wardrobe. Or, if you're short on space, a drawer or shelf. Use it strictly for your running stuff. Organize it however you like. The point is, every run or trip to the gym won't turn into a housewide scavenger hunt as you search for shorts, top, sunglasses etc. If the drawer starts to overflow, sort through it for any clothes you haven't worn in the past year. Give them away.

Lay out your stuff. If you run in the morning, lay out your running clothes the night before. Put them in plain view of your bed, so at the sound of your alarm, you can easily roll out of bed and into them.

Buy a brand-new bag – with partitions and pockets. If you're like most runners, you probably spend 2 minutes every day rummaging for small items at the bottom of your gym bag. By the end of a year, this means you've wasted . . . a lot of minutes. Instead, use a bag with several compartments, so you'll always know where to find what you need.

Get a grip. Negative thoughts or minor aches and pains can turn a good run bad in a hurry – but only if you let them. 'When I'm on a run and feeling down, I remind myself how miserably out of shape I was 5 years ago. This usually pulls me out of it,' says one keen runner.

Make drinking a habit. You know by now that you should drink ample amounts of water throughout the day, and even more if you're training extra hard or running in particularly hot and humid conditions. Make it simple for

---

THE BEST WAY

Q : What's the best way to be sure I'm getting all the daily food nutrients I need?

A : Eat a wide variety of foods. At each meal, set aside one-half of your plate for fruits and vegetables. That will guarantee you healthy portions of the foods that contain the most vitamins, minerals and micronutrients. The rest of your plate should be one-quarter grains and one-quarter low-fat protein foods.

Bag it up: buy yourself something sturdy and good-looking to hold all your running gear.

yourself: Keep a litre water bottle on your desk, and drain it twice by the end of your work day. (Then request an office closer to the toilets.)

Turn things round. You may have heard that tempo training is one of the best ways to improve your performance, but you've also read so many tempo training workouts that you're not sure how to begin. Don't get stressed. It's easy: run slowly in one direction for 30 minutes, then turn round and run a 'comfortably hard' pace on the return. Experienced runners call this their tempo pace, and it's a pace that provides many training benefits. When that's done, jog back to your starting point. Then use tempo training the next time you run.

Pack in fives. Here's a tip that's guaranteed to save you time: rather than scrambling to pack your gym bag every morning, fill it with a week's worth of clothing every Sunday night. Then you won't have to think about it again until the following Sunday. (Yes, you'll need a big bag – and make sure it has pockets!)

Put it in writing. Creating a 4-month training plan may not sound simple, but it only takes an hour or two, and once it's done, you won't have to worry about it for another 4 months. Work backwards from your goal, and plot out each week's workouts one by one, including long runs, speed sessions, hills and rest days. Nothing is simpler than glancing at a schedule, then heading out of the door to do what it says.

Rethink your wardrobe. Admit it: before a run, you waste time fussing over your outfit. Does this top go with these shorts? Does this floral print go with anything at all? To keep these fashion dilemmas to a minimum, buy running clothes in basic, solid colours that mix and match well.

Don't be embarrassed by your running. You might think you look slow and awkward. Slower than

Come up with a training plan together – the regime that you devise will keep you running for months.

whom? The two-thirds of adults who don't exercise at all? The 95 per cent who couldn't run a mile without stopping? As a slow runner, you're still the cream of the crop.

Do more with less. Coaches often notice that many runners will train more or faster than necessary to achieve their goals. Rather than pile on the miles mindlessly, examine your goals and set your mileage accordingly. Then you can better savour the miles you do run.

Mark up your shoes. A good pair of running shoes should last 400 to 500 miles, but who can work out when that will come? Here's a simpler way: as soon as you buy your shoes, write an 'expiry date' on them somewhere. Work out the date by dividing 400 or 500 by your average weekly mileage.

> *'As a slow runner, you're still the cream of the crop.'*

Learn how to divide up your plate and you'll discover how much protein and carbohydrate you should be eating.

Pop a multivit. Unless you have special medical needs, replace your motley collection of vitamin and mineral tablets with a daily multivitamin that covers all of your nutritional bases. If you're already eating a balanced diet, this should give you extra insurance.

Turn off your brain. Set aside a day a week as Simple Run Day. Get up whenever you get up, drink a cup of coffee and head out. On this run, don't worry about time, pace or distance. Just run.

Find a coach. Training for a race can be complicated: What should be my weekly mileage? How often should I race? When should I taper? Who has time or energy to think all this out properly? A coach does, that's who. A coach can do all the homework for you, so you can just run. To find a coach, ask at your local running store or visit these websites: *www.momentumsports.co.uk, www.ukathletics.net* or *www.atfca.com.au* (for Australia).

Divide up your plate. You'll go bananas trying to calculate whether your dinner breaks down into the ideal ratio of carbohydrate/protein/fat. Instead, use this easy rule: about one-quarter of your plate should be covered with a protein food (lean red meat, chicken, fish) and the rest should be filled with vegetables and complex carbohydrates (such as wholegrain bread, rice or potatoes).

Run further. You'd like to, of course. Every runner does. You'd like to burn more calories and maybe plant the seeds for a possible marathon someday. But you feel too tired after just 30 to 40 minutes. What to do? Take a 1-minute walking break after every 9 minutes of running. If that's still too hard, take a 1-minute walking break after every 4 minutes of running. You should be able to double your run/walk time almost instantly. You'll feel great, and the marathon seeds will take root and grow.

Listen to your heart. Worried that you're overtraining? Find out in 60 seconds by checking your resting heart rate before

Don't feel listless

Make a list, check it twice. Even if you're not normally a list maker, having a pre-race checklist is a tangible, foolproof way to reassure yourself before the big event. Write up the list a week or so in advance, before the serious jitters kick in. (Consider it a note from your calm self to your nervous self.) List every item you need to take to the race, things you need to do the night before and morning of the event, and so forth. Then check off each one before you leave for your race.

THE FINISH LINE

Three things to remember about this chapter:

1. **Buy shoes that work for you.** The goal of shopping for running shoes isn't to walk out of the shop with the newest, fanciest, highest-tech pair of shoes. The goal is to select shoes that will work for you. Often, this is the same model you purchased previously or a very similar style. If it ain't broke, don't fix it.

2. **Manage your gear.** It's surprising how the smallest things can have a big effect on your workouts. If you have your shoes and clothing well organized and ready to go, the workout gets easier. If you can't find anything, well, guess what happens?

3. **Make a commitment, and write it down.** Write it in your private journal, on the fridge at home or on the notice board at work. It depends on how brave you are. But when you put your goal down in writing in a place where you will confront it often, you increase your chances of reaching the goal.

you step out of bed. (Monitor it first for a couple of weeks to establish what's 'normal' for you.) An increase in waking heart rate is a definite sign of fatigue. If it's eight beats or more above normal, take it easy that day.

Ignore all this advice. Or any advice that doesn't deliver the goods. Remember: if it doesn't work for you, it doesn't work.

WEBWISE

With input from all types of runners from all over the UK, *Runner's World* gives you access to great training advice. It's a good way to make use of the experience of experts and fellow amateurs.
www.runnersworld.co.uk

CHAPTER 17

The 8 Habits of Highly Successful Runners

Here's a System That's Guaranteed to Deliver Great Results

The most successful runners have developed training habits that keep them going week after week and year after year. We're all different, of course, but these habits will work for you, too.

The best way to improve your running is to build simple, sustainable training habits. After all, you need to train consistently, week in and week out, year in and year out, if you want to enjoy a lifetime of high-fitness health. The hard part is knowing which habits work best. In this chapter you'll find 8 proven and researched habits that will keep you on the right path.

In 1989, leadership guru Stephen R. Covey wrote his famous book The 7 Habits of Highly Effective People, *in which he identified traits shared by successful individuals from all walks of life. Great concept. The book sold millions. And the same approach will work for running. It's just a matter of applying principles.*

In this case, the highly successful people are a mix of Olympians, pros, coaches, exercise physiologists and ordinary people with 2 or 3 decades of running experience.

An important caveat here: 'successful' doesn't necessarily mean fast, though following these habits will certainly help you get faster. The successful runners in this chapter are those who are happy and motivated for the long haul. If and when these runners race, they race well and get the most from their efforts. They are rarely injured and enjoy total-body strength and fitness. Above all, successful runners are healthy, energized, optimistic individuals. And they got

You want to keep running month after month, year after year, while staying injury-free.

this way because of their running habits, which you can easily integrate into your own running lifestyle. At which point they become second nature.

In the end, successful running isn't always a matter of luck or genes or even personality. It's about doing the right things. Eight of them, to be exact. Here they are.

1. Seek out soft surfaces to rest your legs. Physiotherapist and ultradistance runner David Balsley has been taking broken runners and putting them back together again for 30 years. His advice: get on the treadmill, find a trail, go on the grass – whatever it takes to decrease your time on the pavement. 'The surface is just too hard,' says Balsley. At the very least, he says, 'Avoid concrete roads; tarmac is softer. Better still, try to stay on the verge.'

Surface tension? Then try avoiding the roads and heading out on paths, trails or running on grass instead.

This doesn't mean you should stay off the roads altogether, as they're still the most available surface for most of us. But there are many other more forgiving surfaces.

■ **Make it stick:** Make 1 day a week your 'off-road day'. This week, try running on a treadmill. Next week, seek out a local trail or footpath and run there. On the third week, find an even, grassy surface in a park.

2. Get stronger at the same time as you get fitter. Dr Alan Jung, an exercise physiologist at the University of North Carolina at Charlotte, reviewed the existing scientific literature on the effects of strength training on runners. His conclusion: 'Distance runners of all levels can benefit from a resistance-training programme.' Why? Because it helps prevent injuries; it improves your running economy (the amount of oxygen you use when you run) and thus race performance; and it can offset the loss of muscle that occurs as you age. And because it strengthens the tendons, ligaments and bones that enable you to run smoothly and effectively.

■ **Make it stick:** A programme using free weights or resistance machines is the best way to build strength, and you only need to lift twice a week (after running or on a rest day) to see serious strength gains. But you can begin at home with three basic strength-building exercises. If done properly, these exercises – which require only your body weight as resistance – will boost your total-body fitness in just 3 weeks.

Push-ups: Keep your back straight and your palms flat, slightly wider than shoulder width. Descend slowly, until your chest is almost to the floor. Push up faster than you came down, pause at the top and repeat.

Crunches: Lie on your back with your legs bent at a 90-degree angle and feet flat on the floor. Cross your hands over your chest, then raise your shoulders, keeping your lower back on the floor. Feel the tension in the stomach muscles, then lower your shoulders slowly and repeat.

Squats: Keeping your back straight, your head up and your hands out in front for balance, slowly descend into a seated position, with legs bent at a 90-degree angle (thighs parallel to the ground). Then push up from your heels to a straight-standing position, keeping your feet on the floor.

'*The best way to improve your running is to build simple, sustainable training habits.*'

Depending on your current strength, try doing two sets of 10 to 20 repetitions of each exercise, and work up from there.

3. Listen to advice from a physiotherapist. You won't be a runner for long – certainly not a happy one – if you're constantly injured or feeling burned out. To help keep you energized and raring to go, try this checklist for preventive maintenance of the runner's body. Follow it and you'll stay fit and focused.

Spend on shoes: Change them every 400 to 500 miles.

S-t-r-e-t-c-h: Make sure you do it after every run.

Have hands-on therapy: Have a weekly massage, with emphasis on the legs.

Bed down: Get sufficient, regular sleep (most people need between 7 and 8 hours).

Stay supple: Consider taking a glucosamine supplement to keep your joints healthy.

Ask for aid: Seek medical attention for chronic problems, both physical and mental.

■ **Make it stick:** Along with the checklist above, try this: after your next run, go for a walk. Think of it as a cooldown walk, and enjoy it. It's one of the best ways to ensure that your leg muscles don't ache the next day.

4. Don't let your running become too repetitious. We runners can be creatures of habit, which is fine. That's what this chapter is all about, after all. But we can take our running habits too far, in which case they become ruts. To keep your running from getting stale, make a habit of shaking things up on occasion – by changing your running route, your training programme and your races.

'A good way to do this is to plan one new running adventure a year,' says one endurance coach. 'Maybe it's a relay race you do with your training partners, maybe it's exploring a new trail or maybe it's a marathon in an interesting place. Whatever it is, make it something different and interesting.'

This advice can also extend to what you wear. While ours is not an accessory-driven sport, there have been tremendous innovations in running gadgets and apparel in the last 10 years. Keep your mind open to these things.

Be smart on shoes: know that the latest running gear on the market isn't always the best for you.

Walk this way

When former US Olympic marathoner and ultradistance champion Ted Corbitt ran regular 30-mile training runs in New York City's Central Park, he noticed that what he did immediately afterwards had a huge impact on how he felt. 'When I took the subway home, I'd be stiff and sore for days,' says Corbitt, now in his late 80s and still running strong. 'But when I walked home, which took me about an hour, I'd never have any muscle soreness.' OK, we're not saying you need to walk for an hour after all your runs, but even 5 minutes is a great way to cool down, mentally regroup and help those leg muscles recover more quickly.

■ **Make it stick:** Give yourself a running makeover this year – and every year thereafter. Here's how.

Invest in the best: Treat yourself. Buy a new winter (and summer) running outfit.

Mix things up: Tweak your running schedule. Do one of your weekly runs on a different day than you normally do or at a different time than you normally do.

Try something new: Run a different course each month – with someone you haven't run with for a while.

Hatch a plan: Plot a running adventure. It's easy. Check out *www.runnersworld.co.uk, www.marathonguide.com* (international listings) or *www.coolrunning.com.au* (Australian events) for interesting new places and events to try.

5. Plan occasional breaks from running. Élite runners train hard, but not all year long. After peaking for major races, Paula Radcliffe, Sonia O'Sullivan and Joseph Chebet take time off. So should you. A week or two – maybe twice a year – will enable you to rest and recharge. Use the time to do some cycling, begin a DIY project or take a holiday. You'll come back to running stronger than ever. And don't worry: you won't lose conditioning during this relatively short break. If you're worried about putting on weight, this is the time to explore the gym, start a strength-training programme (*see habit 2*) or simply get out for a brisk 20-minute walk each day.

■ **Make it stick:** Take a break from running, but stay active with a health club 'six pack'. That is, over a 12-day period, try six different activities spread out every other day. For example, take a spinning class one day, do a circuit of free weights next time, hop on the elliptical trainer, do a circuit of resistance machines, walk on the treadmill and take a yoga class. All this strengthening and stretching will be good for your body, you'll burn plenty of calories thanks to the cardio work, and you'll return to running fit, happy and energized. Also, you may just find a favourite new cross-training activity or two you'll want to continue with. (If you don't belong to a gym, many clubs sell weekly or monthly memberships.)

6. Join a training group or running club. When then-42-year-old Dick Murphy started running in 1977, he hooked up

Smooth moves: practising yoga may be a welcome break from months of intensive running.

with a group of runners who trained near the Nissequogue River in a New York City suburb. They called themselves the River Road Rats. A year after he started running with the group, Murphy qualified for the Boston Marathon, and he's done it every year since. Murphy, now 68, attributes his consistency and longevity in the sport to the Rats. 'They're a great bunch of people,' he says. 'We run together, solve the world's problems, then go out and have breakfast together every Sunday.'

While the solitude of a solo run will always remain one of the great joys of our sport, the chances are you'll stay more motivated if you join a 'running family'. That could be a local club or training group like the River Road Rats, an online runners' forum or simply a group of training partners and friends. Together, you'll help each other stay in the game for many years to come.

■ **Make it stick:** Visit *www.runnerswebuk.com* to find a running club in your area, or go to *www.runnersworld.co.uk* or *www.ausrun.com.au* and visit one of our popular forums. Or just make it a point to start getting together with a running friend or two each week at the same scenic location. It could be the start of something great.

7. Avoid injuries with quality training. When researchers studied 583 veteran runners recently, they found that the most important predictor for injuries was total mileage. Those who ran 40 miles a week or more were more likely to get hurt. This doesn't mean you should never do more than 40 miles a week in your training; some people handle the high mileage perfectly well. (Also, most marathon training plans get you doing more than 40, but only for a short period.) However, the research does suggest that over the long haul, running more quality miles may be the way to go.

■ **Make it stick:** Try the '7-8-10-Go' plan. In the first stage of this programme, you run three times a week: 7 miles on Tuesday, 8 miles on Thursday and 10 miles on Saturday or Sunday. You'll still get in 25 miles a week, while giving your body a full day's rest between runs.

After 4 to 6 weeks, begin to add a little more quality to this regime. Throw in some hills on the Tuesday run, for

THE BEST WAY

Q : What's the best way to avoid getting injured?

A : First, make sure you're wearing the right pair of shoes, and make sure you replace them as necessary, every 400 to 500 miles. Second, run on a variety of surfaces, not just tarmac and concrete. Add grass, trails, soft road verges and treadmills to your routine. Your leg muscles will react a little differently to each surface, which is better than forcing them into the pattern of overuse that results from always running on the same surface.

Why quality counts

Mike Keohane, who competed in the 1992 US Olympic Trials Marathon and is now a running coach, says his ideal training week would look like this: a long run, a tempo run and a hilly run. 'Twenty miles a week of quality running is going to beat 35 miles of plodding, hands down,' he says.

example, and pick up the pace on Thursday – even by just 10 to 15 seconds per mile.

Then, when you find yourself tempted to begin entering some races, it's time to introduce true speedwork. Now, you add a fourth day of training: interval repeats. There are lots of ways to do that, of course. One way to ease into it is to do 60-second pickups, alternating 60 seconds of hard running with 60 seconds of jogging. Do five sets of those (a total of 10 minutes), then cool down for a mile. Build up to 90-second pickups, then 2-minute pickups and so on.

The beauty of this programme is that you're getting three or four quality runs in per week, which minimizes total mileage while maximizing fitness. This also keeps your injury risk low.

8. Remind yourself of the reasons why you run. Ask yourself this question: Why do I run? To feel better, of course. To stay fit, definitely. Still, as our running lives progress, we sometimes need more than this to get ourselves out of the door. Ruth Anne Bortz started running at the age of 48. That was back in 1978, and she's still at it. In fact, she completed the Boston Marathon in 2002 with her husband, Walter, making them the oldest married couple ever to do so.

But her motivation has changed during that time. 'Early on, I ran for competition,' she says. 'Then I ran

'Each year, try to get at least one friend, colleague or family member to start running.'

Incorporating hills into your running is an ideal way to pick up the pace and 'step up a level' – literally.

THE FINISH LINE

Three things to remember about this chapter:

1. Consider your physiotherapist as the first line of defence against injuries. A good physio can help you run more healthily, recover from injuries and prevent future ones. From strengthening to stretching, a physio knows it all. Plus, experienced physios will have worked with hundreds of runners just like you, so they've gained valuable insight into runners and running injuries.

2. Introduce variety into your training programme. It's important to have a regular, consistent approach to your training – to make sure you do it three or four times a week. However, over the longer term – your whole life – it's just as important to add the spice of variety. The more different fitness activities you follow, the more you'll enjoy staying in top shape.

3. Find a training partner or partners. This is the gold standard for a successful training programme. Some people like to go it alone in their early days of running, while others are comfortable seeking a training partner from the outset. Either way, there will eventually come a time when finding a training partner or group is the best way to make sure you stick to the programme. They'll be there for you when running is the last thing on your mind – for whatever reason – and vice versa.

as an example to my children. Now, I'm running to get others started. I see myself as an apostle of running.'

■ **Make it stick:** Make this the year to join thousands of other charity runners who run and race while raising funds for worthy causes, through such programmes as the Heart Runners team who run for the British Heart Foundation (*www.bhf.org.uk*), Cancer Research UK's Race for Life series of 5-K runs for women (*www.raceforlife.org*) or the Shelter Running Team (*www.shelter.org.uk*) who raise funds for homeless people. In Australia, check out *www.athletics.org.au/ running australia/index.cfm* for details of charity events such as the annual City to Surf (Perth). Or spread the good word about our sport. Each year, try to get at least one friend, colleague or family member to start running.

Again, the idea here is to incorporate each of these 8 training habits into your exercise programme. This will take conscious effort at first – some things will work, some won't. But if you're diligent and stick to it for a few weeks, these strategies will become your standard operating procedure.

WEBWISE

If you can't afford a real personal trainer, try a 'virtual' coach. Bupa has linked up with American firm Get Fit to offer this accessible service, which tailors your workouts and tracks your progress.
www.bupa.co.uk

CHAPTER 18

Boost Your
Consistency

Proven Ways to Improve Your Workouts

You can't get in shape unless you do the workouts you're supposed to do. Here's a variety of ways to help you get past all the obstacles and make every workout count.

The key to getting in shape and staying there is consistent workouts. And therein lies the rub. Many runners have the best intentions. They'd like to work out on a regular basis, but life has a way of interfering with the best-laid plans.

You go to work, and you also have to find time to get the car fixed; you pick up the kids from school and also take them to the dentist; you get dinner ready, and you also have to take care of a thousand other things. No wonder it's tough to find time for that precious workout. No wonder it's tough to get in shape and stay in shape.

Often it's not just the lack of time, however. It's the excuses we make. They come too easily, and we accept them too readily. Until now.

Finding time to run isn't always easy, so make the most of it when the opportunity arises.

Below, you'll find a list of the most common excuses that many runners come up with and solutions to each of them. That is, practical steps that you can take to wipe them away. Then you'll be able to get in all the workouts you need.

You're too busy, there's no time (weekdays)
■ **Real life:** There's no question that the number-one problem we all face is a lack of time to run. We're all busy. You plan to run at lunchtime. Or after work. But a meeting runs late or a deadline looms. So you settle for one more zero in your log.

■ **Real-life solutions:** Be flexible. Maybe the problem isn't a lack of time as much as it's a lack of flexibility with your running. You manage to be flexible at work, obediently toiling through your lunch hour or well past 6 p.m.

Try to be equally flexible with your running, and be prepared to go whenever your busy workday allows for it. If the lunch hour disappears or you work overtime, gobble an energy bar in the late afternoon to keep you fuelled up for an evening run.

The absolutely best solution? Bypass life's craziness by running before work. Or at the very least, plan to run early on those mornings when you know your day is going to be packed and hectic. Wake-up runs take the 'if' and 'when' out of the work/run equation, guaranteeing that the run gets done. They're also a great way to start the day.

You're too busy, there's no time (weekends)

■ **Real life:** Fitting in a couple of runs at the weekend should be easy. But after sleeping late and indulging in a hearty breakfast (which rules out running for the rest of the morning), there are chores to do, kids to chauffeur around, a football match to watch and, before you know it, the day's gone.

■ **Real-life solutions:** Plan ahead and prioritize. Make your run an important element of your weekends. A little planning can go a long way towards making it happen – at least a few miles' worth. Wake up each Saturday, Sunday and holiday morning with a good idea of when and where you'll run. The earlier in the day you get going, the better. Running first thing allows some room for spontaneity later in the day, so you can take an unplanned trip to an antiques market or the beach.

Setting a date to run with a friend or joining a training group are two other good strategies. Running partners who are too busy to meet you during the week are often eager to get together at weekends. On Thursday or Friday night, agree on a time and place for that weekend's run. Or join your local running club's weekend group run. Most clubs welcome members and non-members alike, with participants going various distances and at different paces. It's a great way to meet fellow runners, too. *www.runnerswebuk.com* provides a list of UK clubs, while *www.coolrunning.com.au* has details

Setting a date to run with a friend is a simple yet effective way to ensure you'll run when you plan to.

of clubs in Australia. Or contact your local running store or health club, which probably organizes group runs on weekends.

You're too tired

■ **Real life:** Your newborn child has left you lacking sleep. Or the 12-hour-a-day demands at work are taking their toll. You're simply too exhausted to go for a run.

■ **Real-life solutions:** Don't think about whether you should or shouldn't go for a run. Just do it. Once you do, you'll get a pleasant surprise after the first few, stiff-legged minutes of running as your exhaustion melts like butter in a hot pan.

Whether you were sleep deprived, just bone tired or both, a good run will quickly awaken and revive you, pumping you full of enough energy to carry you through the day or evening. Granted, the very idea that a physical workout such as running can actually energize you is quite illogical. But all you need to do is try it, and you'll see that it works.

> *'Running reduces stress; in fact, it's one of the best stress-busters out there.'*

Stop stress in its tracks

Who upset you today? Was it a client, your mother-in-law, your teenage daughters? (Who didn't?) There are bills to pay, and trying to help your son with his maths has you grinding your teeth. After working out how to explain equations, you still need to finish the work you brought home. A run is simply out of the question. You're just trying to come up for air.

Well, you know the answer to this one. You know because you've read and heard about it, and it's worked for you countless times. But in case you're in denial, here it is again: running reduces stress, in fact, it's one of the best stress-busters out there. Many health professionals prescribe it for their stressed-out patients. Studies have proven that running works effectively to calm the frazzled mind. The president of the United States uses running every day for stress relief, and no matter how crazy your life is, it's probably not any worse than his.

The weather stinks

■ **Real life:** Go on, and pick one: it's too hot, cold, humid, windy, wet, icy. Weather is a great justification for not running because it shifts all blame to the forces of nature. It's not my fault, you smugly assure yourself. It's that annoying weatherman who predicted the brutal cold front that came along and prevented me from running. Nice excuse. But it's not going to work.

■ **Real-life solutions:** The weather is vitally important to all runners, but most runners reckon that what doesn't kill them just makes them tougher. Most runners think there's nothing more invigorating than running through freshly fallen snow. Or beating the heat before the sun comes up. Most runners enjoy an occasional duel with the harshest elements. How is this so? They prepare for it. Here's what you can do so you don't use the weather as an excuse.

■ If the day is likely to be too hot or humid or the air is too polluted, run early before it gets too bad. Also, either carry

THE BEST WAY

Q : What's the best way to run in the dark?

A : Very carefully, and with ample reflective gear. Many runners find that early morning runs, sometimes before sunrise, fit best into their daily schedule. Others enjoy running in the calm of night. Either is fine but of course demands special precautions because of the limited visibility. Always wear reflective gear – on your shoes, running shorts, vest and hat if possible. The more the better. Run sensibly and defensively, and also watch out for patches of ice and snow in the winter.

The weather is only 'bad' if you make it so – as a runner you should be prepared to head out in any conditions.

some water or a sports drink, or plan to run past several water fountains in the park.

■ If it's going to be extremely cold, try to run in the daylight hours when it won't be quite as bad. Wear gloves and a hat, make sure you invest in running clothes made of lightweight, moisture-wicking material, and dress in layers. If you get too warm, peel them off and tie them around your waist.

■ If it's raining or snowing, wear a water-resistant running top and tights over breathable inner layers.

■ If the weather is truly horrendous, and the terrain is treacherous, jump on a treadmill or seek out an indoor track (*see following section*).

It's too dark

■ **Real life:** As with the weather, there's nothing you can do about darkness. If that's the only time you can run, prepare for it. But don't use the darkness as an excuse for missing a run.

■ **Real-life solutions:** Speciality running stores and bike shops carry an array of reflective, neon-coloured shirts, jackets, vests and adhesive strips. On dark, unlit roads or even trails, powerful torches or headlamps can light the way. Night running demands more awareness of your surroundings, but it can be just as exhilarating as a daylight run. If you live in a particularly tough area or busy city where the streets are just too dangerous to run in the dark, run indoors on a health-club treadmill or indoor track. Some clubs let non-members work out for a minimal fee. Treadmills let you run any pace, on any incline, in climate-controlled comfort. If you dislike the gym, purchase a home treadmill.

You have no motivation

■ **Real life:** We all go through periods when it's hard to get the motor running. We can't seem to get psyched up for a run, and no amount of inspiration or encouragement works.

■ **Real-life solutions:** If you really don't want to run, don't. The feeling will pass in a few days. But remember also that you'll almost always feel much better once you get out of the door. Try this trick: tell yourself you're going to run for just 10 minutes. That's it. Often, that's enough to break you out of your lethargy, and you'll be amazed how quickly the time

Walk the walk: when you can't face running, at least stretch your legs and do a walking workout.

goes. Once you've been running for a few minutes, you'll probably feel good enough to keep going for half an hour or more. Or if you're truly down in the dumps and even 10 minutes of running is out of the question, walk. Just getting outside and moving for a few minutes is better than moping around, doing nothing. And often you'll end up breaking into a run.

You feel guilty

■ **Real life:** After being away from your family all day, you come home and . . . then what? Do you selfishly head right back out to get your run in? That won't score points for you. So instead of feeling guilt stricken for neglecting your family, you abandon the run.

■ **Real-life solutions:** There are two ways to avoid this dilemma. The first is to leave work a little early, then stop before you get home and run in a park or along a cycle path. This lets you get your run in before your family ever sees you and also allows you to get rid of your work and commuting stress. If your family still makes you feel guilty for getting home later, point out that the run makes you healthier and more relaxed. If they don't buy that, try this: you owe it to yourself.

■ **The other solution is even better:** Convince your spouse and kids to become your occasional running partners. They can join you on a run (or keep you company on a bike), allowing for quality family time and a nice dose of exercise. Everybody wins.

You procrastinate

■ **Real life:** How many times have you said these words – 'I'll run later' – and never did? If that sounds at all like you, join the crowd. We all suffer from this one at times. 'Later' often turns into 'tomorrow' and then 'next week'. Before you know it, you have a week of blank pages staring at you in your training log.

■ **Real-life solutions:** Pencil in a specific time on your calendar for your run and you'll be a lot more likely to do it. Meeting a friend raises the chances that you'll feel obliged to follow through. If your friend cancels at the last minute,

> *'Pencil in a specific time on your calendar for your run and you'll be a lot more likely to do it.'*

don't cave in yourself. Instead, run solo and give your partner grief about what a great run you had. Another way to fit running into your schedule is to join a running-club group run (*see page 146*) once or twice a week. If it becomes a habit you look forward to each week, you won't play truant as often.

You feel post-race letdown

■ **Real life:** You were so good and trained like a champion for so many months. On race day, you gave it everything you had and maybe even set a personal record. Congratulations! But now the necessary recovery days have stretched into weeks of infrequent runs. With the big race behind you, it's hard to gear up again.

Beat the post-race letdown that can follow a runner's high by planning early for your next race.

THE FINISH LINE

Three things to remember about this chapter:

1. Add a jolt of java to your workout. When you're feeling too tired and stressed to run, consider this two-point programme. First, meditate with deep, slow breathing for 5 minutes. Then have half a cup of coffee. The combination should spark you back to life and add some pizzazz to your workout.

2. Feel good about your workouts. Some runners feel guilty that their workouts take them away from their families and family time. But any reasonable family would agree that maintaining your health and fitness is one of the most important responsibilities of every family member. Spread this attitude through your family and among your friends. A family that encourages fitness for all is a family that wants all members to be healthy and happy.

3. Use training partners to beat procrastination. When you're worried about missing workouts, make an appointment to run with a friend, a training group or even your dog. It's much harder to miss a run when someone else is expecting you. If you and your friend can't actually get together in person, arrange to ring each other before and after your workouts.

■ **Real-life solutions:** One antidote is to find another race in the weeks that follow the 'big one'. Then pick another after that, so you're racing maybe once a month or so. To keep your interest level high, pick from a variety of races – different distances, road and trail races, big-city and small-town ones. You will probably enjoy yourself more taking this pot pourri approach than putting all your eggs in the basket of one or two races a year.

WHY IT'S EASIER TO KEEP ON RUNNING

One other thing that should keep you running (if not racing) year-round is that the alternative is so much worse. For every week you fall out of running shape, it can take a couple of weeks to get back to your previous fitness level. Ping-ponging back and forth between being in shape and out of shape is like driving along a motorway with traffic lights every couple of hundred metres: it's hard on the engine to constantly whip yourself back up to speed. That's why excuse-free running is easier, healthier and more productive. Once you jettison the excuses, running becomes as automatic as filling up the tank.

WEBWISE

Men's Health magazine is pretty much the ultimate source for articles about optimal nutrition, strength building and improved fitness. The magazine's website provides much of the same.
www.menshealth.co.uk

CHAPTER 19

Run Smoothly and Easily

How to Become an Effortless Runner

There's no way of getting round it: running is hard work. That's why it produces such big benefits. But these 10 tips will help you run smoother and easier.

Effortless running. To any non runner, or even to a beginning runner, that sounds like an oxymoron, like 'working holiday', or 'airline food'. After all, how could a vigorous activity such as running be effortless?

It can't, in a literal sense. But there are times when running feels as effortless as coasting downhill on a bicycle. When you're in this zone, time dissolves and you finish your run feeling better than when you started. Paradoxically, your pace is often faster than normal, too. That's because, while in the zone, you're physically and mentally at the top of your game: perfectly relaxed, sometimes even elated, with all moving parts in sync.

The only problem is, you don't find yourself here very often. And when you do, it seems like sheer luck.

Time to change that. Here are 10 things you can do to reach the 'effortless zone' more often.

1. Leave stress at the door. Relaxation is the key to entering the effortless zone, and stress is the deadbolt that locks you out. When you're stressed, your muscles tighten and your mind muddles.

That's why work, relationship woes and other problems should be left at your doorstep. If these thoughts come meandering back into your head later in the run, fine. Initially, though, try to flush them out.

'Stress can increase fatigue and muscle tension,' says Dr Jeffrey Martin. 'You don't breathe as deeply when you're stressed, which increases the effort of running.' The US sports psychology professor and former World Cup marathoner adds that athletes under stress, according to studies, become ill and get injured at a higher rate than lower-stressed athletes.

It may not be possible to run away from a major stressor such as a job change or divorce, but you can make your runs a mental escape from lesser irritants such as arguments, traffic jams and computer malfunctions. Inadequate sleep can also elevate stress levels, so try to get your nightly 7 to 8 hours.

2. Don't expect too much. Burdening your runs with outside stresses is bad enough, but it's even worse to get stressed about your running. Goals are great, but too-rigid expectations can sour your enthusiasm and prevent you from entering the effortless zone.

Don't expect to break 50 minutes, for example, on a particular training run or in a 10-K race. Your on-the-run anxiety about doing it will actually reduce the odds that it'll happen. Instead, settle on a broader goal, such as finishing somewhere between 48 and 52 minutes. You'll be more likely to succeed. And even if you fall outside the range, adopt the attitude that you gave it your best effort. That's all you can do.

Setting a narrow goal is a sensible approach because so many factors affect performance: pacing, weather, course difficulty, stress and so on. Sometimes you just have a bad day. You need to acknowledge that you won't always run fast, race well or improve your time.

3. Strengthen your core. A strong 'core' – which includes your lower-back, abdominal and hip muscles – makes it easier to maintain good, upright, effortless running form. 'When runners with weak cores get tired, they start leaning too far forwards,' says Janet Hamilton, running coach, exercise physiologist and author of *Running Strong & Injury-Free*. 'That's biomechanically inefficient and will even limit your lung capacity.'

THE BEST WAY

Q : What's the best way to use running as a stress reducer?

A : Run without a watch. Don't time every single workout and don't try to get faster every time you run round the block. Just go out of the door, walk briskly for a couple of minutes, jog at a comfortable pace for several minutes, then go back to a brisk walk. Alternate the two at will. Let your body be your guide. Don't push through the pain barrier. Embrace the relaxed running zone. *Enjoy* your running.

'*Relaxation is the key to entering the effortless zone, and stress is the deadbolt that locks you out.*'

Like many coaches, Hamilton considers core strength to be essential. 'It ensures an efficient transfer of power from the core to the legs and upper body,' she explains. She recommends taking a yoga or Pilates class or doing the following gym exercises at least twice a week – but not on long or hard running days. (If possible, get a personal trainer to demonstrate correct form.)

■ **Squats.** Start to sit down, knees in line with ankles; stop when thighs are parallel to the ground (before feeling pain); come back up. Do two sets of 10 reps.

■ **Side bridges.** Lie on your side with knees slightly bent. With one forearm on the floor, lift your whole body, keeping straight from head to foot. Hold for 15 to 30 seconds, and do three reps per side.

■ **Modified crunches.** Lie on your back with one leg straight and one bent. Place a hand under the small of your back for support. Lift your head and shoulders a few inches off the floor and hold for 3 seconds. Do two sets of 10 to 15, alternating left and right leg out.

■ **Ball toss.** Hurl a weighted medicine ball against a concrete wall. Do two sets of five to 10 throws, alternating between overarm, underarm and chest throws.

4. Skip a day. This one goes against the grain for lots of runners who believe that when their running isn't going right, it's because they're not running enough. The funny thing is, it could be just the opposite. Remember, effortless running can only happen when your legs are fresh, and that requires regular rest. If your legs feel tired or sore fairly often, running fewer days per week could be just the ticket. For example, *Runner's World* magazine columnist Jeff Galloway suggests that runners over 40 run only 4 days a week, runners over 50 run every other day, and runners over 60 run 3 days a week.

'Without sufficient recovery,' adds Janet Hamilton, 'you'll be fatigued and generally more prone to injury. Your glycogen stores need to be resupplied, and your muscles and tendons need repairing. If you're still fatigued after a day or two off, take a clean break from running for a week or even more. Keep active with walking, cycling, swimming or other low-impact activities. You don't have to break from exercising.'

Swimming is a great way to stay active while giving your running muscles time to recover.

Besides taking occasional days and weeks off, here are other ways to put the spring back in your step.

■ Alternate between short and long, fast and slow, and flat and hilly runs.

■ Space your races several weeks apart, especially those longer than 10-K.

■ Don't run the day before or after a short race, or for at least 2 or 3 days before and after a long race.

5. Start more slowly. Any mechanic will tell you to warm up your car's engine before driving anywhere. The body's engine works in the same way. Yet we're often too rushed to warm up. We lace up our shoes and go. That's a mistake, because a rushed start makes it unlikely you'll reach the effortless zone on that run.

'You need to gradually increase your heart rate and core temperature while warming up your muscles,' says Norm Witek, an exercise science professor and running coach. 'Otherwise, you're going to go into mild oxygen debt, strain your muscle fibres and end up with sore legs.'

Start each run by walking for a minute or two, then jogging. Barely clear the ground at first, then start lifting your knees higher and lengthening your stride as you cover the first mile. On morning runs, when your body takes longer to wake up, this gradual acceleration may continue for more than a mile. But within 10 to 15 minutes, your body should be ready for effortless running.

6. Add a little speed. Add speed to run effortlessly? It doesn't sound right, but it is. Regular doses of fast running will make the rest of your running seem comfortable in comparison, both mentally and physically.

'When you add occasional fast running to your programme, this increases muscle enzyme activity, which allows you to access energy more efficiently any time you run,' says exercise physiologist Robyn Stuhr. 'It also enhances neuromuscular function, raises your lactate threshold and, on slower runs, delays the onset of fatigue.' Regular speed training will also make your races seem easier because you'll be accustomed to the faster pace.

Adding speed to your runs needn't be scary – do short sprints with a fast, but relaxed, effort.

' Just as fast running makes your standard pace easier, long runs make your regular distance seem shorter – thus easier.'

There are several ways to inject speed into your schedule besides killer track workouts (though those are effective as well). Here are a few examples.

■ **Speed sandwich.** Run 2 miles slowly, 2 miles fast, 2 miles slowly.

■ **In-and-outs.** Do several reps of 1 to 4 minutes hard and 1 to 4 minutes easy, at mid-run.

■ **Pickups.** Periodically pick up the pace for short distances between lampposts or trees.

■ **Tempo.** For the middle part of your run – say 15 to 20 minutes – maintain a pace that's about halfway between your training and racing speed. It should feel comfortably hard.

7. Go longer. Just as fast running makes your standard pace easier, long runs make your regular distance seem shorter – thus easier. By pushing the pace on some days and lengthening the distance on others, you'll be able to cruise in the effortless zone on the rest of your runs. It can be tough at first, but the rewards are worth it.

'Long runs train the body to use fat, so you don't have to rely as much on carbohydrates for energy,' says Stuhr. 'Long runs also increase the number of capillaries, the vessels that deliver oxygen to muscle cells, and mitochondria, the structures inside the cells that convert that oxygen into energy. The result is a positive one: a richer supply of blood providing energy to your muscles.'

Psychological barriers also tumble when you run a long way. Marathoners who go the full 26 mile distance in training have a very high finish rate in the real thing. This works for shorter races as well. Prepare for a half-marathon or even a 10-K by running (or exceeding) the race distance at least a couple of times in training to boost your endurance and confidence. Nice side effect: more of your regular training runs will be in the effortless zone.

8. Hit the treadmill. It's hardly effortless to sweat through a run in 90-degree heat on polluted streets or to negotiate an icy pavement in a snowstorm. Of course, you can run in any weather you want, but unlike the postal worker, you don't have to. The best way to enter the zone during adverse

Increasing your distances has the effect of making your shorter runs feel much easier.

outdoor conditions is to head indoors, where the weather and surface are controlled.

'Once you set a treadmill on your desired speed, the machine does the work of setting the pace,' notes Sara Wells, winner of the US 2003 Women's Marathon National Championship. 'You can shut your mind off and just run. It's also less impact on your legs compared with running on tarmac, and safer than outdoor running at night.' Wells did most of her afternoon runs on a treadmill last winter, including several 20-milers.

Here's how to make treadmill running more effortless.
■ Wear headphones and pop in your favourite CD to block out any gym noise.
■ Get on the gym treadmill with the smoothest, most cushioned surface.
■ Run alongside a friend and get into a conversation.
■ If possible, visit the gym during quiet, off-peak hours, like mid-morning or mid-afternoon.

9. Eat lightly and often. Feeling full, empty or nauseous will keep you out of the effortless zone, so you simply can't afford to eat the wrong foods at the wrong time. Make sure you follow these guidelines.
■ Before a morning run, don't eat much. A light carbohydrate snack such as a banana or half an energy bar washed down with a glass of water will provide ample fuel for running without taxing your digestive system.
■ Before a midday run, eat a good-sized breakfast, plus a carbohydrate snack 1 to 2 hours before your run.
■ Before a late-afternoon or evening run, be sure you eat lunch and a mid-afternoon high-carbohydrate snack.

10. Drink up. 'Water aids in the functioning of every muscle and cell, so inadequate fluids can make you sore, weak and tired,' says marathon runner and author Lisa Dorfman. 'Even a 2 per cent reduction in your total body fluid will increase your effort level during running.' Therefore, there is no possibility of effortless running.

When you run on a hot, humid day, you sweat up to 2 lt (3½ pt) or more per hour. To keep yourself fully hydrated, try

Trust the treadmill: it's the one piece of equipment that comes to the aid of runners time after time.

Why carbs count

Having a carbohydrate snack in the last 2 hours before a run is critical to your performance. 'Besides being easily digestible, complex carbohydrates maintain your blood sugar to keep your energy level up,' says Lisa Dorfman, a marathoner and author of The Vegetarian Sports Nutrition Guide. *'The best choices are low fibre and lactose-free, to prevent intestinal problems.' Examples: bananas, energy bars, bagels, pretzels, rice cakes and sports drinks.*

THE FINISH LINE

Three things to remember about this chapter:

1. Your running gets better and smoother when you don't try to force it too much. There are days for hard running, but many more days for easy running. The body is like a battery that needs to be recharged from time to time. When you have easy days or days off, your body rebounds and gets stronger. And then your next workout is easier than you ever imagined it could be.

2. A runner needs more than just strong legs and a strong heart. All the muscles in your body contribute to your running, some more than others. Your core muscles of the abdomen and hips are particularly important. When you make them stronger, you become a smoother, more injury-resistant runner.

3. You can go further by going more slowly. If you seem to hit a wall in your attempts to build mileage, don't get angry and frustrated. Simply slow down and start again. Once you find the right pace, your body will feel better and go further. When you run too fast, you create a failure environment rather than the success environment you want.

to consume at least five servings of fruit and vegetables (for their water content); 1 lt (1¾ pt) of fluid; and 600 ml (1 pt) of fluid for each 0.5 kg (1 lb 2 oz) you lose on the run. (Determine this by weighing yourself immediately before and after a run.)

On runs lasting more than an hour, either take fluids with you or stash sports drinks along the way. Aim to take in an average of 150 to 230 ml (5 to 8 fl oz) of fluid every 20 minutes or so.

WEBWISE

The fitness world is full of special equipment that can help you reach all your aerobic, strength and stretching goals. Here's a website with an extensive selection of equipment for professionals and home users alike.
www.proactive-health.co.uk

CHAPTER 20

Train, Don't Strain

Easy Yet Effective Ways to Increase Your Speed

Everyone wants to get a little faster, but many runners are afraid to do speedwork. It sounds too hard. But not if you use these fun workouts.

Admit it: you'd like to get faster. That's OK; you're not alone. Every runner would like to get a little smoother and faster, even beginning runners.

And you can achieve your goal. Even if you weren't born with the gift of speed, you can learn to run faster in the same time-honoured way that violinists learn to play better. It's called practice.

Now, no one can deny that running fast is harder than slow running. But consider this: research has shown that you can significantly improve your running pace when you dedicate just 5 per cent of your training to speed sessions. And the results come quickly, often in just 2 to 3 weeks. So you'll be amply rewarded for your efforts.

All you need is a shift in attitude. Promise yourself not to get scared off by speedwork. Don't find reasons to avoid it. Just do it, once or twice a week, in modest doses. You might even start enjoying it.

In this chapter, you'll find a whole host of different speed-training sessions that will make you faster, and not one of them involves running circles on a track. Yes, that means these sessions are intended to be fun. In fact, all these workouts offer many variations on the theme, so you can pick and choose. Try just one or two of them for starters. And then expand your repertoire when you're ready for more.

Running faster is harder than running more slowly, but the resulting benefits are manifold.

You'll notice the results in almost no time. You'll be running more quickly, strongly, lightly and smoothly. And the variety of approaches will add spice to your training. You'll look forward to each new speed session. I promise.

STRIDES OR PICKUPS

■ **What they are:** Strides are the most basic, versatile form of speedwork. They're simple pickups or accelerations of short duration that are usually done at the end of a workout for relaxed speed training.

■ **How to run them:** At or near the end of a workout, find a smooth stretch of road or grass and gradually accelerate to almost top speed. This should take about 30 to 50 metres. Then hold the speed for another 50 to 75 metres before gradually decelerating. The entire 'stride' should take about 100 to 150 metres. Jog for 30 to 60 seconds and repeat. Be careful not to strain at any point. Strides are always done at a 'fast-but-relaxed' speed. It's important to keep them smooth and controlled at all times.

■ **The payoff:** Strides are an efficient way to maintain your speed even when you aren't doing other fast workouts. Strides are also useful as a transitional drill when you're shifting into more speed-oriented workouts. They teach you to run in a relaxed way and with good form.

■ **Classic workout:** Following your normal run, do six to 10 strides of 100 to 150 metres. Do more as you get stronger or when you're focusing on an approaching race.

OUT-AND-BACKS

■ **What they are:** Out-and-backs are runs in which you turn around after reaching a certain point (or time) on the course and retrace your steps back to the start. As a result, your 'out' run and your 'back' run should be the same distance. The goal of this workout: to run back faster than you ran out. In runner lingo, you want to run negative splits.

■ **How to run them:** For best results, select a flat course where you're not going to be interrupted by traffic and you can run an easy pace to a turning point or for a set number of minutes (like 20 minutes). Be sure to note your time at the turning point. Then run back to your starting point at a faster

'Strides are an efficient way to maintain your speed even when you aren't doing other fast workouts.'

pace. You can do out-and-backs on runs as short as 4 miles and as long as 20 miles. There's no rule about how much faster you should run the second half of this workout, but it's often possible to cover the distance at a pace that's 30 to 60 seconds per mile faster than the first part of the run.

■ **The payoff:** Running the second half of any race slightly faster than the first – negative splits – is the most efficient way to race. And out-and-back workouts are the best way to practise negative-split running.

■ **Classic workout:** Run for 30 minutes to your turning point point. Come back 2 to 3 minutes faster, for a total workout time of just under 1 hour. Out-and-backs are infinitely variable. Use your imagination.

EASY SPEED

■ **What it is:** Easy speed is a speed drill that alternates 60 seconds of fast running with 60 seconds of easy running.

■ **How to run it:** Although similar to fartlek runs (*see below*) and cruise intervals, easy speed is both shorter and faster. Here's what you do: in the middle miles of one of your normal distance runs, pick up your pace to a hard (but not sprint) effort for 60 seconds. After the 60 fast seconds, slow to a jog for 60 seconds. Repeat the 60/60 pattern six to 10 times. Don't strain. Run with relaxed form and a quick leg turnover.

■ **The payoff:** Easy speed improves your leg speed and running efficiency at one of the most important running speeds – 5-K race pace. It also helps simulate the tough miles in the middle of a race. Many runners find easy speed a relaxed way to do speed training at a time when they aren't focusing on intense speed. Bonus: easy speed makes a great tune-up run 3 to 4 days before a race when you want that last bit of sharpening.

■ **Classic workout:** During a normal, easy distance run, speed up to 5-K race pace for 1 minute. Then recover for 1 minute. Repeat four times. As you get stronger, add more repeats, but never more than one a week.

FARTLEK RUNS

■ **What they are:** *Fartlek* means 'speed play' in Swedish, and that's what fartlek workouts should be: play. Fartlek runs are

By trying different speed-training workouts, you will push your limits and improve your running.

playful because they consist of unscheduled, unrestricted fast and slow running.

■ **How to run them:** Instead of doing your normal, steady run of, say, 3 to 6 miles, run the same distance with fast bursts followed by slow recoveries. The fast bursts should last from 30 seconds to 5 minutes. Often they're based on distances between landmarks like trees, hills or telegraph poles. The more variety, the better. Running a fartlek workout is like being a child again and challenging one of your mates with a 'Race you to the house on the corner'.

■ **The payoff:** Fartlek running develops sustainable strength and speed. It's also a good way to 'sneak' speed sessions into your training programme. For more advanced runners, it teaches acceleration and fast, relaxed running.

■ **Classic workout:** By definition and design, fartlek runs should be unstructured, but many runners enjoy fartlek 'ladders'. A classic ladder workout: warm up for 10 to 15 minutes, then do fast runs of 1, 2 and 3 minutes at a time, with equal amounts of slow running between each fast repeat. Once you reach the 'top' of the ladder, work your way back down in the same manner. As you get stronger, climb higher up the ladder to fast runs that last 4 and 5 minutes.

CONTINUOUS 400s

■ **What they are:** Continuous 400s are a fartlek run in which you change pace every 100 metres in the following fashion: walk 100, jog 100, stride 100, run at a hard pace 100.

■ **How to run them:** Find a stretch of grass, trail or road that's about 400 metres long and string together four to six repeats of 400 metres as described above. Don't stop between repeats. Make the run continuous, covering 1 to 1.5 miles. When striding, emphasize a smooth glide. When you reach race pace, lift your knees and focus on a quick leg turnover without overstriding. Run fast but in a relaxed way. Visualize yourself finishing strongly over the last 100 metres of a race.

■ **The payoff:** Continuous 400s are a great way to transition to faster-paced workouts for beginners who are just starting speed drills. Continuous 400s are relatively easy because the entire workout follows a simple formula, and you are never running hard for more than 100 metres at a time.

> '*Easy speed improves your leg speed and running efficiency at one of the most important running speeds – 5-K race pace.*'

THE BEST WAY

Q: What's the best way to get faster?

A: For beginning runners, the best way to get faster is to run more, get fitter and lose more weight. You don't have to do anything special. You just have to keep on going – that is, to stick to your training programme. Over time, the simple act of running more will turn you into a faster runner. After a point, if you're not satisfied with your pace, you can try several of the specific workouts suggested in this chapter.

■ **Classic workout:** Do four to six continuous 400s in the manner prescribed: walk 100, jog 100, stride 100 and run race pace for 100. As you become fitter, add more 400s, but never more than one a week.

TEMPO RUNS

■ **What they are:** Tempo runs are fast, continuous runs during the middle miles of a regular distance run. They're done at a pace that is generally termed 'fast but controlled'. Tempo runs should leave you tired but not exhausted.

■ **How to run them:** After doing a 10- to 15-minute warm-up, do a continuous, steady run of 15 to 30 minutes at a pace that's 10 to 20 seconds per mile slower than your 10-K race pace. (If you don't know your 10-K race pace, follow the 'fast-but-controlled' rule.) Tempo runs aren't supposed to be killers. If it takes you more than a day or two to recover from a tempo run, you're either going too fast or too far.

■ **The payoff:** Tempo runs help you develop a sense of the kind of fast, even pace you'll need in races. Tempo runs can be particularly valuable when you're training for a half-marathon or marathon, as they'll help you hold a fast pace with relative ease.

■ **Classic workout:** Warm up with 10 minutes of slow jogging or walking and jogging, then run 15 to 20 minutes at a fast, steady pace. Stronger, more advanced runners can do two 15-minute tempo efforts, with 10 minutes of easy running between them. Or, on a long run, you could do 60 minutes easy, followed by 20 minutes at tempo pace, followed by 30 to 60 minutes easy.

CRUISE INTERVALS

■ **What they are:** Cruise intervals are basically short tempo runs with short recoveries. They're run at the same pace as tempo runs, but typically last only 4 to 10 minutes each. Result: you can do more of them. Cruise intervals give beginning runners a good introduction to tempo-running pace.

■ **How to run them:** After warming up with 10 minutes of jogging or walking and jogging, gradually accelerate to a hard-but-controlled pace. Hold this pace for just 4 to 6 minutes the first time you do cruise intervals, then jog for

Tempo runs are runs that start easy, build up to a steady speed and then finish at an easy pace.

'Effective hill training will greatly improve your form, endurance and overall mental toughness.'

2 minutes, then repeat the cruise interval and jog. Do only three cruise intervals the first time. Gradually increase the length of each cruise interval and the number you complete. But don't go beyond 40 total minutes of cruise intervals. You can also decrease the length of your recovery jogs to 30 to 60 seconds.

■ **The payoff:** Cruise intervals improve your ability to run more smoothly and for longer at a fast, sustained pace. They're shorter than tempo runs and include short recovery breaks, so they'll help you build up to tempo runs.

■ **Classic workout:** Run 5 to 6 minutes at cruise-interval pace and repeat five to eight times, with 60-second recovery jogs. Or run 10 minutes at cruise-interval pace and repeat four times, with 90-second recoveries.

HILL REPEATS

■ **What they are:** Hill repeats are runs of 1 to 4 minutes up a moderately steep hill.

■ **How to run them:** Find a smooth hill that has good, consistent footing. If it's a road hill, be sure it has light traffic and a wide shoulder, where you'll do the actual hill repeats. Run easily to the base of the hill, then gradually increase your effort up the hill. Don't sprint, but run at a strong, steady effort.

The hills are alive – or at least they will be when you start running repeats up them.

Emphasize knee lift and a strong, forward-and-back arm swing. Try to maintain pace all the way to the crest of the hill. At the top, turn round and jog back to your starting point to recover. Repeat four to 10 times.

■ **The payoff:** Hill repeats can be thought of as both speedwork and strength training in disguise. You don't go that fast and you don't carry any weights, but you get plenty of resistance training to develop power and leg strength. Effective hill training will greatly improve your form, endurance and overall mental toughness.

■ **Classic workout:** Pick a short hill and run it four to six times. Each repeat should take 1 to 2 minutes. Between repeats, jog back down to the bottom of the hill. As you get stronger, run more repeats or find a longer hill.

CUTDOWNS

■ **What they are:** Cutdowns are repeats that get shorter and faster as the workout progresses.

■ **How to run them:** You can do cutdowns on a loop of measured distances or by using your watch. The idea is to run a series of repeats, each of which is shorter and faster than the previous one. For example, on a measured loop, you might run four laps, then three, then two, then one, then

'Running the second half of any race slightly faster than the first – negative splits – is the most efficient way to race.'

Running cutdowns on a loop of measured distances – on a trail you know well, for example – is an ideal form of speed training.

THE FINISH LINE

Three things to remember about this chapter:

1. To increase speed, do strides. Several times a week, after your regular workout, do 'strides' where you gradually pick up your speed and hold a comfortable, fast pace for 50 to 75 metres. Strides teach you to run at a quicker pace, but without excessive strain. Always pay attention to relaxation and good form.

2. Run out-and-back courses. The simplest speed workout is one runners call 'out and back'. It means that you time yourself from a certain starting point to some other point down the road, then turn round and take the same route back to the start. On the way back, you run a little faster, and you time your 'out' run against your 'back' run to measure how much you picked up the pace.

3. Try short hill repeats. Running hills is a great way to build both endurance and speed. To improve your speed, find short uphills of 50 to 70 metres and run them at a quick pace with strong arm movement and knee lift. Don't sprint, and don't strain excessively. Run fast but smoothly.

half. With your watch, you might run 8 minutes, then 6, then 4, then 2, then 1. As the repeats get shorter, you run faster. In general, the longest repeat you'd want to do would be 1 mile, and the shortest would be 200 metres.

■ **The payoff:** Cutdowns teach you proper pacing and how to harbour your resources so you'll save something for the finish. Cutdowns also make a great race-simulation workout. You run fast from the start and finish even faster, which is what happens in a shorter race such as a 5-K. Experienced racers call this negative-split running, and it's one of the best ways for you to maximize your performance.

■ **Classic workout:** Following a warm-up, run 1 mile, 800 metres, 400 metres and 200 metres at increasing speeds. Jog 3 to 4 minutes between each repeat. Start slowly enough so you can finish faster than you start. As you become stronger and fitter, add more repeats at the 'top end' of the workout.

WEBWISE

The about.com website is an excellent place for basic information about many subjects. The Running/Jogging section does a good job of organizing training programmes, nutrition and injury-prevention advice.
www.running.about.com

5

INTERMEDIATE TRAINING

CHAPTER 21

Make More Progress with
Progressive Training

Make Great Strides with this Simple Training System

To get in better shape, you need to train a little more and a little harder. But that doesn't mean your workouts have to be complicated. They just have to follow a system.

The training system you're about to encounter has to be one of the simplest ever invented. And one of the most effective. It's as old as Pheidippides and as proven as gravity. This system works because it's built on the most basic principle of exercise science: add resistance, get some rest, add more resistance. End result – a stronger, fitter organism (you, in other words).

For lack of a better name, this system can be called progressive training (PT). Basically, it's a way of producing a superstructure from a series of small building blocks. Beginners walk and run, then walk a little less and run a little more. That's pure PT. But PT can also go further and higher. Marathon runners concentrate on building up the distance of their long runs, mile by mile, week by week. More PT.

Did you know that PT has dozens of other applications? You can use it to increase your speed (through intervals), your leg strength (through hill running), your lactate threshold (tempo training), etc., etc. The list goes on and on.

Another bonus: PT workouts are incredibly easy to grasp and follow. Every PT plan involves: (1) increasing time or distance; and/or (2) increasing numbers of pickups, repeats, intervals or whatever you want to call them; and/or (3) increasing speed; and/or (4) decreasing rest periods. That's it. Just four elements. You take the basic four, you mix and match, and you've got a winning workout plan.

Progressive training helps you become stronger, fitter, faster and leaner – through gradual change.

Because PT workouts are 'progressive', some ingredient is always changing. Your workouts are getting longer or faster or even shorter (rest periods). PT workouts are the sworn enemy of static programmes, complacency and laziness. That's why they're so successful.

PT workouts are also simple to monitor and measure. Everything goes by the numbers. Some runners will find this intimidating, but it shouldn't be. A good PT plan, like any good training programme, has to be 'doable'. The workouts aren't meant to defeat you; they're meant to reward you. And since PT workouts are so measurable, you'll get a real sense of accomplishment by completing them. You can put your improving numbers in your training log or daily calendar. Just pick the place that will do the most to keep you motivated.

Some of the following PT workout sequences are clearly intended for beginning runners. Others might seem daunting to you. That's OK. This is merely a workout menu. Pick the ones you like the most. And don't hesitate to adapt them to your own needs and circumstances.

THE GOAL: TO INCREASE LEG POWER

The workout: Warm up for 10 minutes, finishing at the bottom of a 50- to 100-metre hill. Run a series of hard but controlled repeats up the hill. After each repeat, jog back down to the bottom. Finish the workout with a relaxed 10-minute cooldown.

The rationale: Hill running builds leg strength, which ultimately improves speed, efficiency and endurance.

- **Week 1:** Warm up. Do three hill repeats. Cool down.
- **Week 2:** Warm up. Do four hill repeats. Cool down.
- **Week 3:** Warm up. Do five hill repeats. Cool down.
- **Week 4:** Warm up. Do six hill repeats. Cool down.
- **Week 5:** Warm up. Do seven hill repeats. Cool down.
- **Week 6:** Warm up. Do eight hill repeats. Cool down.

THE GOAL: TO BUILD SPEED FOR MILE TO 5-K RUNNING

The workout: Go to a track and warm up easily for 10 minutes. Then run eight laps, alternating fast 200s and slow 200s. Run the fast 200s hard but not at a full sprint. You'll

'If you concentrate on making just one weekly workout truly productive, you can add a spark to your training.'

Running hills builds muscular and cardiovascular strength, helping to increase leg power.

quickly learn how fast and slow you must go to finish the full workout. Cool down easily for 10 minutes.

The rationale: This is a tough workout. It will build your ability to run hard while tired.

■ **Week 1:** Warm up. Run eight laps with alternating fast/slow 200s. Cool down.

■ **Week 2:** Warm up. Run nine laps with alternating fast/slow 200s. Cool down.

■ **Week 3:** Warm up. Run 10 laps with alternating fast/slow 200s. Cool down.

■ **Week 4:** Warm up. Run 11 laps with alternating fast/slow 200s. Cool down.

■ **Week 5:** Warm up. Run 12 laps with alternating fast/slow 200s. Cool down.

THE GOAL: TO BUILD SPEED FOR MILE TO 10-K RUNNING

The workout: A 40-minute run punctuated by increasing numbers of 30-second pickups (also known as repeats or intervals). Pickups are fast, steady runs but not all-out sprints.

The rationale: You need to break out of the rut. Instead of doing the same old boring run all the time, add some pizzazz.

■ **Week 1:** Run for 40 minutes with a 30-second pickup at the 10-minute, 20-minute and 30-minute marks. After each pickup, ease back to a relaxed running pace.

■ **Week 2:** Do the same 40-minute workout with pickups at 8, 16, 24 and 32 minutes

■ **Week 3:** Repeat 40-minute workout with pickups at 6, 12, 18, 24, 30 and 36 minutes.

■ **Week 4:** Repeat 40-minute workout with pickups at 5, 10, 15, 20, 25, 30 and 35 minutes.

■ **Week 5:** Repeat 40-minute workout with pickups at 4, 8, 12, 16, 20, 24, 28, 32 and 36 minutes.

■ **Week 6:** Repeat 40-minute workout with pickups at 3, 6, 9, 12, 15, 18, 21, 24, 27, 30, 33 and 36 minutes.

THE GOAL: TO INCREASE ENDURANCE FOR 10-K TO HALF-MARATHON RACING

The workout: An out-and-back workout where you run slowly for the first 40 minutes to get to the halfway point.

Training on a track is ideal for building speed for shorter distances, such as 1 mile to 5-K.

After turning round, you begin to pick up the pace on the way back.

The rationale: You'll cover a good distance and also accustom your body to running strongly in the later miles.

- **Week 1:** Run at a slow pace for 40 minutes. Turn round. Run back in 38 minutes.
- **Week 2:** Run out for 40 minutes, turn round and run back in 36 minutes.
- **Week 3:** Run out for 40 minutes, back in 34 minutes.
- **Week 4:** Run out for 40 minutes, back in 33 minutes.
- **Week 5:** Run out for 40 minutes, back in 32 minutes.

THE GOAL: TO BUILD STRENGTH FOR ALL DISTANCES, PARTICULARLY 10-K TO THE MARATHON

The workout: Increasing numbers of 'Yasso 800s' (a workout devised by *Runner's World* magazine staffer and longtime runner Bart Yasso). Originally designed to help runners reach their goal time in the marathon, Yasso 800s are actually a great form of tempo training, which pays benefits across many distances.

Important definition: A Yasso 800 is an 800-metre run in the minutes:seconds time that's the same as your marathon goal time, expressed in hours:minutes. That is, if you hope to run a 3:40 marathon (3 hours, 40 minutes), you run your Yasso 800s in 3:40 (3 minutes, 40 seconds). If you don't have a marathon time or marathon goal pace, run your Yasso 800s at your 10-mile race pace.

Rationale: Like other tempo training workouts, this one forces you to run at close to your lactate threshold pace – a pace that's particularly good at building strength and efficiency.

- **Week 1:** Warm up for 10 minutes, then run three Yasso 800s. After each 800, jog for the same amount of time that it took to complete the 800. Cool down.
- **Week 2:** Warm up and run four Yasso 800s. After each 800, jog for the same amount of time that it took to complete the 800. Cool down.
- **Week 3:** Warm up and run five Yasso 800s. After each 800, jog for the same amount of time that it took to complete the 800. Cool down.

' Progressive training workouts are the sworn enemy of static programmes, complacency and laziness. That's why they're so successful.'

THE BEST WAY

Q: What's the best way to train harder?

A: Do just a little bit more every week, and wait for the weeks to add up. They will, and very quickly. For example, if you were to add just 5 minutes of extra running to your weekly workout plan, you'd find you'd achieve an additional hour a week in just 3 months. That's a significant increase, and it will definitely help you reach your weight-loss, performance and other goals. Do more each week, but don't do much more. That's the key to gradual, progressive increases.

■ **Week 4:** Warm up and run six Yasso 800s. After each 800, jog for the same amount of time that it took to complete the 800. Cool down.

■ **Week 5:** Warm up and run seven Yasso 800s. After each 800, jog for the same amount of time that it took to complete the 800. Cool down.

■ **Week 6:** Warm up and run eight Yasso 800s. After each 800, jog for the same amount of time that it took to complete the 800. Cool down.

THE GOAL: TO IMPROVE YOUR STAYING POWER LATE IN A RACE

The workout: A series of 400-metre repeats on the track with decreasing rest periods between the repeats.

The rationale: Shorter rest periods will accustom you to running hard even as your fatigue level is increasing.

■ **Week 1:** Warm up for 10 minutes at a track. Run 8 × 400 metres at your 5-K race pace. Jog for 3 minutes between repeats. Cool down for 10 minutes.

■ **Week 2:** Warm up. Run 8 × 400 at 5-K race pace. Jog 2:45 between repeats. Cool down.

■ **Week 3:** Warm up. Run 8 × 400 at 5-K race pace. Jog 2:30 between repeats. Cool down.

■ **Week 4:** Warm up. Run 8 × 400 at 5-K race pace. Jog 2:15 between repeats. Cool down.

■ **Week 5:** Warm up. Run 8 × 400 at 5-K race pace. Jog 2 minutes between repeats. Cool down.

■ **Week 6:** Warm up. Run 8 × 400 at 5-K race pace. Jog 1:45 between repeats. Cool down.

THE GOAL: TO INCREASE YOUR LONG-RUN TIME TO ALMOST 3 HOURS

The workout: This workout will prepare you for a first marathon. The following are runs of increasing duration, all based on a pattern of running at a comfortable pace for 7 minutes and walking for 3 minutes.

The rationale: The name of the game is staying on your feet for a certain period of time. The best way to do this is with an alternating run/walk system. Don't worry that you're not running all the time. Just keep moving.

' Progressive training workouts are so measurable, you'll get a real sense of accomplishment by completing them.'

■ **Week 1:** Alternate 7 minutes of running with 3 minutes of walking for 60 minutes.

■ **Week 2:** Repeat the 7/3 system for 1 hour, 20 minutes.

■ **Week 3:** Repeat the 7/3 system for 1 hour, 40 minutes.

■ **Week 4:** Repeat the 7/3 system for 2 hours.

■ **Week 5:** Repeat the 7/3 system for 2 hours, 20 minutes.

■ **Week 6:** Repeat the 7/3 system for 2 hours, 40 minutes.

(Note: To continue building endurance, don't add more minutes overall. Instead, change the run/walk ratio to 8/2 or 9/1 or whatever works for you.)

THE GOAL: TO BUILD ENDURANCE AND MARATHON CONFIDENCE

The workout: A long run that increases in length and in the number of 5-minute pickups en route. Do the pickups at approximately the same pace that you would hope to run during a marathon.

The rationale: The longer run will improve basic endurance. The pickups at marathon pace will teach your body to grow comfortable at that pace.

■ **Week 1:** Run 90 minutes easy.

■ **Week 2:** Run 100 minutes with one 5-minute pickup after 40 minutes and a second one after 80 minutes.

■ **Week 3:** Run 110 minutes with a 5-minute pickup at the 30-minute mark, the 60-minute mark and the 90-minute mark.

■ **Week 4:** Run 2 hours with a 5-minute pickup at the 25-minute mark, the 50-minute mark, the 1:15 mark and the 1:40 mark.

■ **Week 5:** Run 2 hours, 10 minutes with 5-minute pickups at the 20-, 40-, 60-, 80-, 100- and 120-minute marks.

BUILDING A COMPLETE PROGRAMME

Many runners find that it's easy to get out for several workouts a week but hard to concentrate enough to make any of those workouts particularly productive. In other words, you find the time to run whenever you can, and you run however you can on those occasions. But if you concentrate on making just one weekly workout truly productive, you can add a spark to your training. And if you change that workout every 6 weeks, you can become a better, stronger runner. Here's how.

Pushing progressive training further

Tip: Aside from a beginning running programme (such as the one described in this chapter), other PT workout sequences shouldn't be extended for more than 6 weeks. Continue any longer, and you risk staleness and burnout.

Tip: Don't do more than one PT sequence at a time. A good idea: for one 6-week period, work on endurance; for the next 6 weeks, on strength; for the next 6 weeks, on speed. In a sense, you'll be doing what élite athletes do. They call it periodization. You can call it fun. (See 'Building a Complete Programme', below left.)

Tip: If you find that you can't do a particular PT workout, scrap the whole sequence and design a new one with smaller improvement increments. The idea is to motivate yourself with workouts you can complete successfully, not to get frustrated by unattainable workouts.

Tip: Unless you've got a training partner whose speed and strength nearly match yours, consider doing your PT workouts alone. That's the best way to concentrate on your own pace and goals. There are plenty of other days in the week for social running.

Tip: You might not want to do PT training year-round, but remember, it's only 1 day a week. And no one's going to force you to set killer goals. Make them relatively easy if you want. The idea is simply to spice up your running occasionally so you avoid the ho-hum training syndrome.

THE FINISH LINE

Three things to remember about this chapter:

1. Your body adapts to increased stress, as long as you also give it rest periods. Progressive training only works if you allow your body – primarily your legs – to recover sufficiently between workouts. That's why many veteran runners like to alternate running workouts with strength training and other forms of cross-training.

2. Long runs build endurance. Whether you're training to run your first non-stop 2 miles or to complete your first marathon, it's the long runs – often expressed as 'time on your feet' – that help you increase your endurance. Speed is completely inconsequential when doing longer runs. Just focus on very gradually increasing the time you spend running or running and walking.

3. Hill runs build leg strength. You can strengthen your legs with weight workouts in a gym, but hill running accomplishes much the same. Start with a few runs up a short, not-very-steep hill, and slowly increase both the number of uphill runs you do and the length of the hill. Run hills with a short, efficient stride. Don't try to bound like a kangaroo.

1. For 6 weeks, run long and slow once a week. Increase the length of your long run by 10 minutes per week.

2. For the next 6 weeks, run hills once a week. Begin with three hill repeats and increase by one per week until you reach eight.

3. For the next 4 weeks, run four 800-metre repeats once a week. The first week, run them at your 10-K race pace. The following 3 weeks, run the 800-metre repeats 3 to 6 seconds faster each week than the previous week.

4. Run a few races now, when you're in good speed shape. Then plan a new series of PT workouts for fun, challenge and motivation.

WEBWISE

Greg McMillan has a master's degree in exercise physiology and years of experience working with runners from the middle of the pack to the front. His website includes many original articles and approaches to training.
www.mcmillanrunning.com

CHAPTER 22

56 Super
Training Tips

Words of Wisdom Guaranteed to Help Your Workouts Run Smoothly

These 'real runner' training tips will boost your motivation, help you lose weight, prevent injuries and bring you closer to all your goals.

Many of the best training tips and ideas come from experienced coaches, great scientific researchers and the best Olympic athletes. Many . . . but definitely not all. Runners like you also come up with dozens of great training tips, learned from their own unique experiences. Some of these tips will prove especially useful to you, precisely because they've come from runners who encounter many of the same situations you face in your life.

In this chapter, you'll find more than 50 such regular-runner tips. They won't all apply to you, and you won't be tempted to adapt them all. But their originality and creativity will impress you. And chances are good you'll want to try at least a handful of them.

So have fun sampling these training, nutrition, motivation, injury-prevention and racing tips. It will only take a couple of them to make you a better, happier runner.

1. 'When evaluating my training, I always step back and look at my three S's: strength, speed and stamina. As in: strength training, speedwork and long runs. When I'm doing all three consistently, I know I'm fit. If I'm behind on one of them, I get back to it right away.'
Michelle Baptie

2. 'When I turned 40, I made a vow that I'd never eat my favourite food – ice cream – before running at least 4 miles that day. Now, 13 years later, I've kept my vow: No ice cream unless I do those 4 miles. My running has been very consistent over the years.'

Hugh Smith

3. 'For years I was a consistent 3:30 marathoner, but couldn't get faster. Then I changed my long runs, adding three separate mile repeats at 10-K pace and ran 3:20 the very next time out. I also qualified for the Boston Marathon for the first time at 50.'

Mike Wearing

4. 'There comes a point in almost every long, hard race when you ask yourself, "Why am I doing this?" Work out those answers (keep them short and sweet) on your long or hard training runs, and you'll have them ready on race day.'

Michael Collins

5. 'To help me get out of the door year after year, I write the names of my three children in permanent marker on every pair of running shoes I buy. This reminds me how much I want to stay strong and healthy for the long term, so I can see my kids grow into adulthood and be there for them.'

Pam Landry

6. 'After tough runs, I get into the shower, which has a hose attachment and variable pulse, and put it on the hardest pulse and coldest temperature I can stand. This way, I get a cheap massage and ice treatment in a matter of minutes.'

Andrew Lohman

7. 'I run three times a week. On Sunday, I run alone. On Tuesday, I go with my running group. On Thursday, I join my favourite training partner. This way I get my solitude, the energy and variety of a group, and the one-on-one encouragement and feedback from my friend – every week!'

Joanne Sheesley

8. 'I like to memorize one or two monologues from Shakespeare and recite them in my head on a run. There is

Two's company: Vary running with a partner and training alone to rev up your workouts.

something about iambic pentameter that keeps me happily
cruising along.'   *Warren Miller*

9. 'Sometimes I don't plan my running route – I just follow
my dog. If he turns right, I go right. If he heads up a big hill,
I follow him. It's a great fartlek workout, because he always
speeds up when he sees something interesting (read: cats and
squirrels). This has really helped my leg speed.'

Marcia Steelman

10. 'I always had problems staying motivated – until I started
running a mile for each victim of the 9/11 atrocities. Here is
the list I use: *www.wallofamerica.com*.'   *Jan Reese*

11. 'I used to think wearing any kind of clothing was fine for
running, but not any more. There's nothing like good-looking,
high-tech, super-comfortable running gear to keep you rolling.
You'll feel like a runner and start acting like one, too.'

Andrea Weeks

12. 'Add an occasional theme run to your routine. For
example, with my "school run", I run to every school in my
area. I run a lap on the track, then go to the next school and
so on. The options are endless. I've done park runs, bus-stop
runs, petrol-station runs and church runs.'   *John Lang*

13. 'To keep running for a lifetime, simply set yourself the task
of running 15 times a month without concern for days of the
week or time of day. That works out to 180 runs a year. Since
I started this technique, I've never missed a workout – because
I've never really had one scheduled!'   *Donald Brown*

14. 'I've tried all the usual workouts, such as hills, repeats
and fartleks. But I finally noticed significant improvement
when I started doing 20- to 30-minute tempo runs at slightly
slower than 10-K race pace. These make me mentally and
physically strong.'   *Dan Tipple*

15. 'Sometimes I go out the day before my long run and drop
coins along the route, then look for them on my run the next

*'Don't compare
yourself to other
runners. The key to
staying out of that
trap is to set goals
that are realistic
and attainable
for you.'*

THE BEST WAY

Q : What are the best ways to
make sure I do my workout on any
given day?

A : Prepare for it the day before. Lay
out all the clothes you'll need for a
workout at home, or pack them in your
athletic bag to take to work or the gym.
Plan and write down the precise workout
you want to do. Also, know what time
of day you plan to run, and organize
your meals and snacks accordingly.

day. It always gets me out there – and keeps me out there – because I have to get my money back!' *Sue Kaplan*

16. 'After running regularly for about 25 years, I have only one tip: force yourself to step out of the door. Once you're outside, you're smiling.' *Jeannie McGrew*

17. 'To spice up our speed workouts, my running partner and I race buses. We run along a street where there are several stops. When there aren't passengers to pick up, the bus usually wins. But when people are waiting, look out. We never know what to expect, which makes this workout fun.' *Sian Satterthwaite*

18. 'I always brush my teeth before I run. It makes me feel fresh, energized and ready to go.' *Eleanor Bonar*

19. 'When I hit a big hill or a tough patch during a run, I pick a chorus from a favourite song and sing it over and over again until I'm past the hard bit. The trick is to match my stride to the beat of the song. Also, the lyrics keep my mind off my troubles or tired legs.' *Mandy Hill*

20. 'When faced with a tough speed session, I read up on the workout the night before, so I know exactly what benefits I'll be getting from it. This always boosts my enthusiasm and assures me that the discomfort I'll feel is worth it.' *Stuart Macdonald*

21. 'Near the end of my runs, I pass by the house and let my dog out so he can accompany me on the last few miles. This way he gets his exercise, and I have something to look forward to. And since he's fresh, he helps me finish strong.' *Angela Brame*

22. 'Last year I bought a packet of small smiley-face stickers. I have six different colours – one for each fitness achievement – and I put them on my office calendar after my workouts. A red face stands for speedwork, yellow for long runs, green for strength training and so on. This way, I can look at the

A new you: investing in some of the latest running gear will make you feel good and run better.

calendar and immediately see if I'm covering all my fitness bases each month.'   *Jill Fortune*

23. 'Everyone talks about eating bagels or bananas before a run, but I swear by pears. They're easy to digest, they don't make me full and they provide all the energy I need in a race or hard workout.'   *Holly Carrow*

24. 'Whenever I'm lacking motivation, I think about how great I feel after my runs. That in itself is the only motivation I need. (Corny, I know, but it's true.)'   *Anne Eisold*

25. 'My absolute best motivator is the astonished look I often get from people when I'm running at 5.30 in the morning or on really cold days (or both!). Non-runners just don't get it.'   *Marlene Shepherd*

26. 'If I ever have trouble getting out of the door, I tell myself I'll just walk instead. About 95 per cent of the time, I end up running. I've become much more consistent with my running because of it.'   *Francis Wallis*

27. 'I plaster quotes, magazine ads and photos of places where I've run all over a wall in my house that's totally devoted to running. Whenever I'm feeling unmotivated, I look at it and remember all the reasons I started running in the first place.'   *Danielle Wilcock*

28. 'Don't compare yourself to other runners. The key to staying out of that trap is to set goals that are realistic and attainable for you. Write down your goals and keep them where you see them often (mine are by my computer at work). More than anything, be proud! You're doing what a lot of people don't do.'   *Lara Roberts*

29. 'My favourite thing to do on a long run is to "buy" a house – a really big one – then decorate it top to bottom. This way you split your workout between the physical aspect of running and the mental side of your new abode. It usually takes me at least 10 miles to finish the decorating.'   *Ann Brennan*

Bananas? Bagels? Pears? Try different kinds of food to discover what gives you the best energy kick.

30. 'I like to do "carleks", which are similar to fartleks. I jog slowly along a road until a car passes me, then I pick up the pace until the next car passes me. This workout is fun, varied and really gets me fit.'
Donna Black

31. 'Avoid eye-irritating sweat by using baby shampoo for several days before a race. Otherwise, residue from dandruff shampoo and even normal shampoo can combine with sweat to make your run a misery.'
Scott Kent

32. 'When I feel fatigue setting in and I get out of rhythm during longer runs or races, I start repeating the words "tick tock". Invariably, after a minute or two, my rhythm and concentration return. Try it next time you feel out of step.'
Eileen Cohen

33. 'Because I run very early in the morning (5 a.m.), I lay out all my running gear in the bathroom the night before. This way I know exactly where everything is, and I don't have to stumble around in the dark and wake my husband.'
Heather Cass

34. 'During my marathon buildups, I like to do an occasional 5-K or 10-K race the day before my long runs. This teaches me to run when I am tired, and I'm always better prepared once I reach mile 20 in the marathon.'
Craig Redfearn

35. 'My tip comes in the form of a recipe. I swear by this refuelling drink: 1 handful spinach leaves, 1 handful baby carrots, few sticks celery, small handful parsley, 1 medium apple (raspberries work, too), 2 tablespoons protein powder, 1 large glass cold water and 5 ice cubes. Mix in a blender until smooth, then drink. The recipe may sound gross, but it's packed with nutrients and tastes fine. Of course, my family says I would drink pond scum if it would help my running. They're probably right.'
Sarah Cooper

36. 'Running isn't all about heading off into glorious sunsets on warm, sunny evenings. Don't ever miss an opportunity to train in really miserable weather, such as freezing temperatures,

> *To keep running for a lifetime, simply set yourself the task of running 15 times a month without concern for days of the week or time of day.*

torrential rain or strong winds. You'll feel great afterwards, and when races come along, you'll be invincible.'

Mark Stodghill

37. 'My husband and I do our long run during the week instead of at the weekend. That way, after it's over, we're sore and grumpy at work, but at the weekend, we're feeling fine and are ready for fun with the kids.'

Katherine Christenson

38. 'I live in a remote rural area, but I keep in touch with several online running "clubs" for motivation, information and encouragement.'

Karen Massy

39. 'The best way to get through a marathon? Smile as often as you can, especially during the tough parts. It is really hard to have negative thoughts if you're smiling. Plus, people watching the race will really respond to you.' *Diana Lyle*

40. 'On a run or in a race, I always count down the miles, rather than count up. When I have certain mileages left to run, I think of really fun runs that are that long, and visualize myself on those runs.' *Suzi Snowden*

41. 'Many years ago I decided I would run at least a mile a day no matter what the weather, where I was or how I felt. I haven't missed a run since, and have done several marathons along the way.' *Dave Barker*

42. 'I run home from work several times a week and always look forward to the relaxing "commute". Therefore, I'm more consistent. I'm home by 6.30 – never stuck in traffic – and can have dinner ready by 7.30.' *Barbara Morissey*

43. 'I throw 50p into a piggy bank for every 15 minutes I run. I use this money to buy CDs or other treats I wouldn't normally buy for myself.' *Charlotte Stang*

44. 'When the first really cold day of winter hits each year, I always make a point of putting on my running clothes,

Visiting running websites will help you stay in touch with the latest news, views and innovations.

heading out, and saying: "OK, Mother Nature, it's just you and me. We're either going to get on, or it's going to be a very long winter." We usually make our peace, and I get through the season very well.'   *Andy Abrams*

45. 'I'm a competitive runner, and I thought I'd seen my best times by the time I hit 40. Then I jettisoned my 50-mile weeks and went to 30-plus a week. I also incorporated lots of 400 repeats, did long runs on alternate weekends and took more recovery days. It worked. Since making the changes, I've run personal bests from the mile to the half-marathon.'   *Jo Kay*

46. 'I always used to get blisters on my feet after long runs. Then I tried turning my socks inside out so the seams didn't rub against my feet. It worked. I've been blister-free ever since. So simple.'   *Miles Tale*

47. 'I used to get blisters until I started putting sweatbands just above my ankles to keep the sweat from running down

'Force yourself to step out of the door. Once you're outside, you're smiling.'

Taking on the elements: try running in adverse weather conditions and overcoming what Mother Nature throws at you.

and soaking my socks and shoes. It looks a little odd, but no more blisters!'

David Stocks

48. 'I keep a running scrapbook that starts with my very first race at the age of 8. When I don't feel up for a run, I just get out my book. Looking at all those pictures of me in races and with my teammates reminds me how much I love running.'

Nicole Ernster

49. 'When I take my two kids in the running buggy, I often let them dictate the pace. When they say "Go!" I run fast until they say "Stop!" This is an excellent workout, as I never know when I'll start sprinting, or how long I'll have to do it. It also keeps them involved, so they're happy to let Mummy get on with her run.'

Caryn Jacobs

50. 'After I suffered from heat problems near the end of a marathon, my doctor said I needed more sodium in my diet. So what's my secret weapon? A tin of spaghetti hoops the night before a race. This way, I carbo- and sodium-load at the same time.'

Bobby Egbert

51. 'A while ago I found a great way to speed up muscle recovery after my long runs. Right after I finish, I stretch a little bit, then put ice packs on my legs and down a large recovery drink. The next day, I'm completely recovered.'

Esther Dill

52. 'Before long training runs, I like to write "15-mile training run" (or whatever distance I'm doing) on the back of an old race number and pin it to my shirt. The yells of encouragement I get are so motivating.'

Lawrence Wilkes

53. 'Whenever I start a run, I focus on one thing: making sure I'm striding properly. I think about landing softly on the heel, rolling forwards, then pushing off with my toes. Once my body takes over, my mind is free to wander.'

Mark Mitchell

'*The best way to get through a marathon? Smile as often as you can, especially during the tough parts.*'

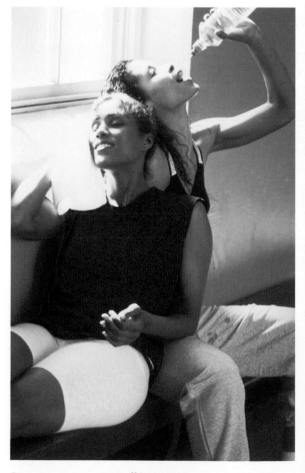

Post-race recovery: start off by stretching, move on to icing sore muscles and finish by taking on fluids to rehydrate.

THE FINISH LINE

Three things to remember about this chapter:

1. Set yourself a monthly workout goal. It might be 12 workouts a month, or 15, or 20 or even more. The benefit of the monthly plan is that it gives you room for a little error. If you miss a day or even two, it's no big deal. You've got time to make up for it and stay on target.

2. Have an ice pack available at all times. Ice is simply the easiest and best way to reduce any inflammation you feel after running. Use an ice pack, a bag of frozen peas or sweetcorn, or a paper cup filled with water and frozen to produce a 'lip' above the cup's edge. Apply the ice for 10 to 15 minutes several times a day. To avoid an ice burn, put a light piece of cotton cloth between the ice and your leg or foot.

3. Reward yourself for your successful training. There are many ways to do this, from putting money in a piggy bank for every mile you run, to treating yourself to a massage after long runs or races. The important thing is to do things you look forward to and that make you feel good about all the time you've devoted to your running.

54. 'I live where the winters are long and arduous. However, I took some pictures of the autumn countryside when the leaves were changing and my running route looked beautiful. I now have the photos taped to my wardrobe door. This winter, they're going to help me stay focused on training for next year's races.'

Kathleen Murphy

55. 'I run cross-country races, and my best racing strategy is to sleep in my team vest! I know it sounds silly, but it works. When I wake up, I'm raring to go and feel like I'm already two steps ahead of everyone else!'

Judy Mansell

56. 'When I run, I always try to remember the people who encouraged me. I think of my mum, who bought me my first pair of running shoes. I think of my college friend, who bought me new shoes when I couldn't afford them. The best tips I can offer: be thankful, work hard and remember to pass the torch.'

Angela Sales

WEBWISE

For more than 25 years, Jeff Galloway has been dispensing advice and motivation to people who want to begin fitness programmes, as well as to runners who want to improve their performance.
www.jeffgalloway.com

CHAPTER 23

Run with
Your Heart

Use Your Body's Engine to Measure Your Running Success

To train with precision, you need to know exactly how hard your body is working. A heart-rate monitor gives you that information and helps you train more effectively.

Running is a simple sport, perhaps the simplest, which is one of the reasons for its widespread popularity. You don't need lots of fancy equipment – just a good pair of training shoes – and you don't need to take expensive holidays to a ski resort or a scuba diving location in the Caribbean.

On the other hand, running is one of the most technical of sports, if you consider the basic physiology of it. No other sport provides as many health benefits as running, because no other tests the body in a consistent, continuous manner the way running does. Left foot, right foot, left foot, right foot. Your running rhythm is a bit like a rapid drumbeat.

A nd the important drumbeat in this case is your heartbeat. Your heart rate gives an unerring reflection of your running effort. That's why heart-rate monitors have become so popular among runners in the last decade. They can help you measure your training effort like no other equipment can.

At one time considered the gadget du jour for hard-core professional athletes, heart-rate monitors have gone mainstream, their telltale chest straps poking out from T-shirts on everyone from fitness runners to veteran marathoners. All these people are wearing monitors for the same reason.

And that reason is? No matter what type of runner you are, a heart-rate monitor can help you train more scientifically and more effectively.

A heart-rate monitor can set your training pace, prevent burnout and push your running forwards.

TIPS FOR BEGINNERS

Newcomers to running get some of the biggest benefits from heart-rate monitors, for two main reasons. Tracking heart rate ensures you're working hard enough to reap fitness benefits. On the flip side, setting a maximum heart rate on the monitor can keep over-zealous novices from overdoing it.

You should choose a target heart-rate zone – generally between 65 and 75 per cent of maximum heart rate (MHR) – and stay within it for most of your workouts. Runners who haven't yet developed a sense of their speed and effort can learn from their monitors. 'I love being able to keep a consistent pace without having to look at my watch all the time,' says Kerrie Hardman, 37, who started running 2 years ago. 'Nothing has helped my training more than monitoring my heart rate.'

■ **Suggested workout:** This one comes from running coach Roy Benson, a longtime advocate of heart-rate training. To do it, first you'll need to determine your MHR (see 'Finding Your MHR' on page 188). Second, take 75 per cent of your MHR, which will be your upper limit. Then calculate 65 per cent of your MHR, which will be your lower limit. Plan to run 20 minutes total (head out for 10 minutes, then turn round).

Start running until you hit your upper-limit heart rate, then walk until it's back down to your lower limit. Run again up to 75 per cent, then walk until you hit 65 per cent. Continue this way for the whole 20 minutes. 'As you progress through the weeks, you'll spend more time running than walking, because you'll take longer to hit your upper limit,' says Benson. Extend the length of your workout as your fitness progresses.

■ **Fun twist to try:** To keep your motivation high, use the monitor to track your fitness. Here's one simple way to do this. Choose a running speed that's realistic for you, and run a timed mile. Repeat exactly the same mile at exactly the same pace a month later, and monitor your heart rate all the way. It should be lower this time, because you're in better shape.

You can continue running the same timed mile on a regular basis, say every month or two. Each time, record your heart-rate figures in your training log. You should end up with a good visual reminder of your improved condition. This will also serve to motivate your continued training.

THE BEST WAY

Q : What's the best heart rate for my workouts?

A : For most runners, especially beginners, a very high percentage of your training should be done at between 65 and 75 per cent of your maximum heart rate. This is known as the aerobic training zone. If you don't exercise this hard, you don't get the benefits you want. If you exercise at a higher intensity, you risk over-training. Even Olympic runners do a lot of training in this zone. Of course, they also add speedwork and hard runs, so they can go for the gold.

Your pulse precision

'While it's important to be aware of your effort so you're in touch with your body's subtle cues, your basic perceptions don't always form a very accurate feedback system,' says Dr George Parrott, running club coach. 'A heart-rate monitor, on the other hand, gives you a precise index of the effort expended.'

FINDING YOUR MHR

For years, fitness magazines and books told readers that the best way to find your MHR is to subtract your age from 220. Newer research shows that this formula only works for sedentary, out of shape people. That may describe your fitness level before you become a runner (by following the training schedules in parts 9 and 10 of this book), but it certainly won't describe you after you can run 2 miles with ease.

Here are two newer and better heart-rate formulas for you.

> (A) MHR = 208 - (.7 × your age)
> (B) MHR = 205 - (.5 × your age)

A small group of *Runner's World* editors recently tested these two formulas and reached the following conclusions. Both seem to work almost equally well for runners under 40. For runners over 40, formula (B) appears to be more accurate. In general, (B) is the formula that will work best for most runners. It's also very simple, a nice bonus.

Keep in mind that no formula, even the most accurate, will work with absolute precision for all runners. Formulas can only give the best 'average' results.

MOVING UP THE FITNESS LADDER

Once you've been running long enough to be comfortable with your training and to want more, you'll find the heart-rate monitor a great help as you start doing more challenging workouts. One of the best ways to use a monitor is to preset a target heart rate for a tempo workout. This will keep you from going too fast (a typical mistake with tempo running). For most tempo workouts, you should be running at 85 to 90 per cent of your MHR.

Another great way to use your monitor is on longer, more relaxed runs. On these efforts, you want to avoid running either too fast or too slowly. The optimum benefit comes from workouts at 65 to 75 per cent of MHR, basically the same effort as your easy, beginning runs. The difference now is that you're going further, depending on your fitness level.

■ **Suggested workout:** This 'ladder' workout progresses through a range of heart-rate zones. After 10 minutes of

'Tracking heart rate ensures you're working hard enough to reap fitness benefits.'

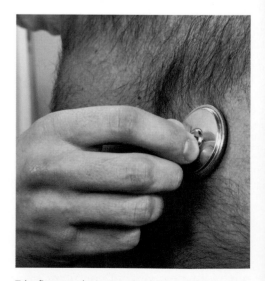

Take fitness to heart: running is one of the simplest ways to protect your respiratory system.

jogging, run 4 minutes at 70 to 80 per cent of your MHR, 3 minutes at 80 to 90 per cent, 2 minutes at 90 to 95 per cent, and finally 1 minute above 95 per cent. Finish with 10 minutes of easy jogging. For a less challenging workout, decrease the amount of time spent in each zone by a minute. For a more challenging workout, do the ladder two or even three times.

■ **Fun twist to try:** Even runners who swear by heart-rate monitors in training tend to leave them at home during races. But Benson says they're the perfect tool for learning to race at the proper pace. 'The monitor will show you if you're starting out too fast or too slowly,' he says. 'Within half-a-mile or so you should be in your desired zone, and a heart-rate monitor will enable you to stay there.'

GOING FOR THE MAX

Even the best runners can benefit from heart-rate feedback. South African training expert Bobby McGee, who coaches some of the fastest runners in the world, relies on heart-rate monitors to train his athletes.

When US distance star Colleen De Reuck moved to a mountainous region of Colorado, McGee suggested she start wearing a monitor. 'She knew how to run easy and how to run hard, but nothing in between,' he says. 'Being at an altitude, I knew she'd need something other than pace-per-mile to determine workout efforts.' De Reuck, who now wears a monitor for easy and intermediate workouts, was a quick convert. 'I stopped burning myself out,' she says. In 2004, just 10 days before her fortieth birthday, she won the US Women's Olympic Marathon Trials.

Many advanced runners also use monitors to track recovery during interval workouts. Instead of waiting a predetermined number of minutes or jogging a certain distance between repeats, you can check for your heart rate to drop before beginning the next repeat. Your recovery target should be less than 80 per cent of your MHR.

■ **Suggested workout:** Jog for 10 minutes, then run three repeats of 1.5 miles at tempo pace (about 85 to 90 per cent of MHR). Rest 3 minutes between each repeat. Note the time you run each repeat in your log. 'You'll see your times decrease as your season progresses,' McGee says. 'You're not working

What's a rest day?

Many runners forget one of the most important principles of good training programmes: you need regular easy days – days on which you give your body the chance to recover and gain strength. Too often, runners just keep trying to do more and more. Result: they get injured or burned out. A heart-rate monitor can help you prevent these problems. 'I actually found it harder to stay below 75 per cent of my MHR on my easy days than I did staying at 95 per cent of my MHR on hard days,' says Laverne Sheppard, 41, who attributes a 30-minute improvement in her marathon personal record to her monitor.

THE FINISH LINE

Three things to remember about this chapter:

1. Many beginners train too hard. No wonder they become discouraged that they can't run as far and as often as they'd like. The solution is simply to slow down – to mix running and walking to help you reach your goals. A heart-rate monitor offers another solution, as it actually beeps at you when you begin to run too fast.

2. A heart-rate monitor can also assess your basic health and your stress level. Many athletes note their morning heart rate, as it's considered an excellent gauge of your health, your stress level, and the amount and quality of sleep you got. If

you keep track of your morning heart rate, you will know early in the day if you need to be careful not to overstress yourself on this particular day.

3. As helpful as a heart-rate monitor can be, you must not become a slave to it. You don't need to wear it every day or for every workout. As you become a more experienced runner, you'll develop excellent internal feedback mechanisms to gauge your effort and your pace. At that point, you may only want to use your heart-rate monitor for special workouts.

---

any harder, but at the same heart rate you're running much faster.' By the way, tempo workouts are an excellent way to prepare for all race distances, from the 5-K to the marathon.

■ **Fun twist to try:** A rise in resting heart rate (best taken in the morning immediately after you wake up) often indicates that you're overtraining, and a monitor can help make this diagnosis. For this you'll need a monitor that stores information for later recall. 'My élite runners sleep with their monitors on,' McGee says. 'The resulting graph is a helpful indicator of form. It tells me if they're overtraining.'

According to McGee, an erratic heart rate with lots of variation throughout the night is typical when an athlete is training hard. When tapering and resting for a race, the heart rate should be steadier and more consistent. If yours is still erratic leading up to a big race, consider a longer taper, or cut your mileage and intensity during your taper.

■ **Or try this:** Test your fitness from time to time with this game on the track. Warm up well, then pick up the pace until your heart rate hits 90 per cent of MHR. Then jog very slowly until you recover to 70 per cent of MHR. See how many times you can go from 70 per cent to 90 per cent and back again in 20 minutes of running. You can increase the challenge by raising the upper limit to 95 per cent of MHR.

WEBWISE

Here's a highly technical but also very useful site created by sports scientists interested in sharing information directly on the Web. It has many good search tools to help you find what you want. **www.sportsci.org**

'*Even the best runners can benefit from heart-rate feedback.*'

CHAPTER 24

Boost Your
Endurance

How to Keep on Running Longer, Faster and Better

There are many programmes for increasing your endurance. Here are some of the best, with real-world success stories.

As runners, we all want to increase our endurance, but we're often referring to two different things. The beginning runner wants to go further – from 2 miles to 4 miles, then to 6. More experienced runners don't see much point in running further. (Isn't 26.2 miles far enough?) These runners want to improve their speed-endurance – the pace at which they can cover substantial distances.

Fortunately, you can have it both ways. You can follow training plans that build the length of your long runs and others that improve your speed-endurance.

Increasing endurance is the Holy Grail of runners, leading to greater distances and faster times.

Using such workouts, thousands of runners have dramatically improved their endurance. Craig Beesley, a beginning runner, extended his longest run from 30 seconds to nearly 3 hours. Doug Underwood, a successful marathoner, wanted to lower his best from 3:50 to 3:30 to qualify for the Boston Marathon. And Deena Kastor, the American 10-K and cross-country star, wanted nothing less than to run the marathon faster than a legend, Joan Samuelson.

All three runners achieved their goals. Each used a different method. Which raises the point that exercise physiologist Kris Berg explains in his recent article, 'Endurance Training and Performance in Runners', in the journal *Sports Medicine*. 'After decades of studying how to improve endurance,' says Berg, 'I'm leaning more than ever towards the great gestalt of mind-body wisdom, and encouraging runners to do what feels right.'

In other words, different strokes for different folks. We're not all the same. Genetic researchers refer to 'high responders' and 'low responders'. Sometimes we need to take different paths to reach our goals.

In this chapter, you'll find a variety of endurance-boosting strategies that have worked for a range of runners. Not all will work for you. But one or more will, and that should be enough to significantly increase your endurance, which means you'll run further and more easily than ever before.

BASIC ENDURANCE

1. One step at a time. If there is one overarching principle of endurance building, this is it. Call it gradual adaptation. That is, be consistent, be patient and build up slowly. This principle applies to all circumstances and all runners – the beginner who's trying to make it around the block four times as well as the 36-minute 10-K runner who's training for a first marathon with long runs that stretch to 12 miles, then 16, then 20.

Witness the success of Craig Beesley. When Beesley began running in 2001, he could only manage 30 seconds at a time, followed by 4½ minutes of walking. But he didn't let his lack of fitness discourage him. He simply repeated the cycle eight times (for a total of 40 minutes) and made sure he did three workouts a week.

Thirteen weeks later, Beesley was running 30 minutes at a time, and eventually he completed his first half-marathon in 2:12. Pretty impressive. But Beesley didn't stop there. He kept running outdoors through the winter months, and in 2003 added speedwork to his routine. By May, he was running long runs of 2:40, and doing six 400-metre repeats in 1:45. In his near future: a first marathon.

A programme can't get any simpler than Beesley's, or any more successful. 'I've increased my endurance and my speed, and I've done both without any injuries,' he says. 'My family describe me as a very patient man. Patience combined with persistence is a great combination for success in running.'

■ **What you should do:** Whatever your present endurance conditioning, build it slowly but steadily. Follow a programme that adds 1 mile a week to your weekend long run, for

Getting ready for the big one: marathon training is the ultimate endurance programme.

example: 5 miles, 6 miles, 7 miles. Every fourth week, reduce mileage by skipping the long run. Rest and recover. The next week, build again, 1 mile at a time: 8 miles, 9 miles, etc.

2. Run long and slow. Meghan Arbogast was already a successful marathoner in the mid-1990s, with a 2:58 to her credit. Only one problem: 'I was overtraining and killing myself,' she says.

No longer. Since 1998, Arbogast has been training slower and racing faster under a programme designed by Warren Finke, a well-known US coach. Finke believes marathoners should focus on consistent, easy-paced training runs that help them build endurance without getting hurt every couple of months. 'A lot of runners train too hard, get injured and never reach their potential,' he notes.

The Finke programme emphasizes 'effort-based training', and he believes in keeping the effort modest (at 80 per cent of the speed you could race the same distance) most of the time. 'Most runners are probably training at about 90 per cent of their race pace,' says Finke. 'Running 80 per cent is pretty easy, but it helps keep you injury-free.'

The programme has certainly turned things around for Arbogast. Two years after beginning Finke's effort-based training, she improved her marathon personal record to 2:45. And in June 2003, she won the Christchurch Marathon in New Zealand with another 2:45. 'To improve further I have to stay healthy and keep gaining endurance,' says Arbogast.

■ **What you should do:** Do most of your runs at 80 per cent of the speed you could race the same distance. So if you can race 10 miles at 7:30 pace, you should do your 10-mile training runs at 9:23. To convert a race pace to an 80-per cent training pace, multiply the race pace by 1.25; for more details, visit Finke's website: *www.teamoregon.com*. To find a wide range of your equivalent race times, go to *www.runnersworld.com* and click on 'Race Time Calculator' under the Tools and Calcs drop-down menu.

3. Run longer tempo runs. Runners admire other runners who refuse to give up on their goals and who keep trying various methods to reach them. By this standard, Patrick Noble,

THE BEST WAY

Q : What's the best way to build my endurance?

A : Slowly, and 1 day at a time. The world's best endurance runners often take up to 7 years to reach their peak performances, so you can hardly expect to find a shortcut. Regular, consistent training and a healthy dose of patience are the essential ingredients. Do keep at it, but don't expect miracles. Your body builds endurance by becoming more and more accustomed to the training load that you apply to it.

'If you want to finish strongly and improve your times in the marathon, you have to run hard and fast at the end of your long runs.'

a career Army man who's now retired and living in South Korea, deserves a lifetime achievement award. In 1986, Noble finished his first marathon in 3:17, feeling both proud and ambitious. 'Let's go for a sub-3,' he told himself.

Thus began the journey. Noble increased his training, and before long he had run 3:04, 3:01, 3:05 and 3:02. You can quickly see what's missing from this list. A less-determined runner might have given up. Not Noble.

He kept running marathons – dozens of them. He ran his 49th marathon. No luck. His 50th. Ditto. His 51st. Nope, sorry, not this time. But in May 2003, in his 52nd marathon, Noble broke through the 3-hour barrier with a 2:58:23 at the Camp Casey US Army base in South Korea. And it was a new approach to tempo runs, Noble believes, that helped him dip below 3:00.

The conservative view on tempo runs suggests that you cover 20 to 40 minutes at a pace that's 10 to 20 seconds per mile slower than your 10-K pace. Noble pushed his tempo runs up to 60 minutes. 'I think the long tempo runs gave me the extra strength I needed,' says Noble. 'I also made sure I ran very easily the day after the tempo runs, and watched my diet and even gave up beer for 6 to 8 weeks before the marathon.' (Joe Vigil, coach of Deena Kastor and 2003 US marathon champ Ryan Shay, also believes in long tempo runs to build endurance.)

■ **What you should do:** Do a tempo run once a week for 8 weeks. Start with a 20-minute tempo run at 10 to 20 seconds per mile slower than 10-K race pace, and add 5 minutes to your tempo run every week. Be sure to take 1 or 2 easy days before and after tempo days.

'A lot of runners train too hard, get injured and never reach their potential.'

SPEED-ENDURANCE

1. Run Yasso 800s. This amazingly useful technique comes from *Runner's World* magazine race and event promotions manager Bart Yasso, and it has been followed by literally thousands of runners. Virtually all have found that Yasso 800s work for them. With the Yasso system, you run 800-metre repeats on a track in the same minutes:seconds as your hours:minutes goal time for a marathon. (So if you're hoping to run 4:30, do your 800s in 4 minutes and 30 seconds.)

Doug Underwood is a big Yasso fan. A runner for just 3 years, Underwood completed his first two marathons in 3:55 and 3:53, and then was bitten by what he calls the Boston bug. He wanted to qualify for the Boston Marathon and was willing to train harder to get there.

The core of his programme: Yasso 800s. Since Underwood needed to run a 3:30 to reach Boston, he ran his Yasso 800s in 3:30, building up to 10 of them in a single workout, taking a 3:30 recovery jog between the fast 800s.

Underwood finished his goal race in 3:30:54, good enough for a race entry to Boston. (Boston Marathon organizers offer runners a 59-second grace period beyond the strict qualifying standards.) 'I credit the Yasso 800s with getting me there,' says Underwood, who also made sure to log plenty of long runs. 'They are tough workouts, but they do the job. If you can run 10 of them at your goal pace, you have a great chance of achieving your marathon goal time. It's a case of putting in the effort to reap the rewards.'

■ **What you should do:** Run Yasso 800s once a week. Start with just four or five of them at your appropriate pace, then add one a week until you reach 10. The first few weeks should feel quite easy. The last few will be hard, but hang in there. This workout builds focus and concentration, as well as speed-endurance. (If you're training for a half-marathon, run five Yasso 800s at a hard pace. The time you can run for those 800s, divided by 2, will equal your potential half-marathon time. That is, if you run five Yasso 800s in 3:50, you should be able to run a half-marathon in 1:55.)

2. Do plyometrics. Deena Kastor had already joined the ranks of America's all-time best female distance runners, including Joan Samuelson, Mary Slaney and Lynn Jennings, when she first paid a visit to Zach Weatherford in 2002. She asked Weatherford, the strength and conditioning coach at the US Olympic Committee's training facility in California, if he could devise a programme that would give her more leg endurance and quickness.

Weatherford said he wasn't sure, acknowledging to Kastor that he had never worked with a distance runner before. 'But let me think about it and do some research,' he said.

Make sure every workout counts

Exercise physiologist Bill Pierce has an advanced degree in exercise physiology and has been running marathons for 25 years. At 53, Pierce still runs marathons in about 3:10, not much slower than when he first stepped up to the starting line more than 2 decades ago.

His secret? The 3-day training week. Pierce follows the usual advice to alternate hard days with easy days, but he takes it to the extreme. He runs only hard days – 3 of them a week. On the other 4 days, he doesn't run at all, though he lifts weights several times a week and also plays tennis.

In stripping his training programme to its essence, Pierce runs each of his three workouts at a specific target pace and distance. One is a long run, one is a tempo run and one is a speed workout. 'I run at a higher intensity than some others recommend, but I have found that this programme has worked well for me for many years,' says Pierce. 'It reduces the risk of injuries, improves long-term adherence and still lets me enjoy the gratification that comes with intense efforts.'

What Pierce does: interval training on Tuesdays, tempo training on Thursdays and a long run on Sundays. For interval repeats, he runs 12 X 400 metres or 6 X 800 metres at slightly faster than his 5-K race pace. On tempo days, he runs 4 miles at a pace that's 10 to 20 seconds per mile slower than 10-K race pace. On Sundays, he runs 15 miles at a pace that's 30 seconds per mile slower than his marathon race pace. You can easily adapt these workouts to your own 5-K, 10-K and marathon race paces.

Weatherford returned with several ideas worth testing, and the two have been working together ever since. 'We started with core strength and progressed to explosive leg plyometrics, always focusing on the basics, and doing quality sessions, not quantity. Runners already do enough quantity,' he says. 'In her first plyometrics workouts, Deena hit the ground like a big, flat-footed person, but we kept emphasizing, "Get your feet up fast. Get your feet up fast."'

Kastor did plyometric (or 'bounding') exercises such as jumping over a rope, skipping, box jumps and even high-knee sprints through the 'rope ladder' that you often see at football or rugby training camps. And then she ran the London Marathon in April 2003 in 2:21:16, a personal best by more than 5 minutes and a new American record. 'I really felt a difference in London,' says Kastor. 'I've noticed a considerable change in my running mechanics. My feet are spending less time on the ground, and I've increased my stride frequency. At London, my legs did not fatigue at all during or after the marathon.'

■ **What you should do:** Instead of running strides at the end of several easy runs a week, do a 'fast-feet' drill. Run just 15 to 20 metres with the shortest, quickest stride you can manage. You don't have to lift your knees high; just lift them fast and move forward a few inches with each stride. Pump your arms vigorously as well. Rest, then repeat six to eight times. Once or twice a week, you can also do 5 minutes of single-leg hops, two-legged bounding and high-knee skipping, all on a soft surface such as grass or packed dirt.

3. Run long and fast. This is the opposite of the Run Long and Slow approach on page 193. But it works for some runners. A perfect example of the high-responders versus low-responders principle.

A recent convert to long-fast training: American Scott Strand. In February 2003, Strand improved his marathon personal best by more than 4 minutes with a 2:16:52 in the National Championship Marathon in Birmingham, Alabama. And it was his longer, faster long runs that got him the PB, Strand believes.

'I covered 18 to 23 miles in my long training runs,' says Strand, 'and I did the last 9 to 14 miles at marathon pace or

In it for the long run: endurance training isn't an easy option, so don't be put off if you hit a plateau.

THE FINISH LINE

Three things to remember about this chapter:

1. Add a mile a week to your long run. Even if you start with just 2 miles at a time, you will soon increase your long run to a respectable distance. Remember that the early miles are the hardest; once you get past them, the later and more impressive miles come more easily. If you stick to a gradual programme, you'll be rewarded.

2. Run less often, but longer distances. If you only run three times a week, your body will recover from workout to workout, and you'll find it easier to cover more distance on the days when you do run. On your non-running days, do strength training, swimming, cycling, walking or whatever other activities you enjoy most.

3. Don't expect constant progress. No one can keep running further and stronger week after week, indefinitely. In fact, you'd soon reach the point of diminishing returns. And, after that, an overtraining breakdown. Instead, plan your training in cycles. Every month, take an easy week when you substantially decrease your training. Run a shorter long run, or none at all. Let your batteries get completely recharged before you renew your best training efforts.

faster. That was much faster than my previous long-run efforts of 17 to 22 miles at whatever pace I felt like running.'

This kind of endurance programme, based on long, hard runs, has been popularized in the last few years by marathon world record holder Khalid Khannouchi. Khannouchi does ferocious long runs – so fast and sustained that he gets nervous for several days before them. Old school: the only thing that mattered was spending 2 to 3 hours on your feet. New school: if you want to finish strongly and improve your times in the marathon, you have to run hard and fast at the end of your long runs.

■ **What you should do:** On your long runs, pick up the pace for the last 25 per cent of the distance. Gradually accelerate to your marathon goal pace, or even your tempo-run pace. You don't have to attack your long run the way Khannouchi does, and you shouldn't collapse when you finish. But you should run hard enough at the end to accustom your body to the late-race fatigue of the marathon.

WEBWISE

The Serpentine Running Club, based in central London, organize a monthly 5-K race around Hyde Park, and their friendly website includes detailed maps of London routes as well as advice for runners everywhere.
www.serpentine.org.uk

'Sometimes we need to take different paths to reach our goals.'

6
INJURY
PREVENTION

CHAPTER 25

Beat Aches
and Pains

Most Running Injuries Are Preventable, but Some You'll Need to Treat

*All runners encounter aches, pains and outright injuries at
some point in their training. In this chapter, you'll find surefire
remedies for six of the most common running injuries.*

*In this age of managed health care, many doctors don't
spend enough time working out why your knee, shin or heel
hurts. So you often end up with cursory advice you either
don't want to hear ('stop running') or you've already tried
('put some ice on it').*

*And that's a shame, because there are so many good doctors
and new treatments out there. Doctors and treatments that can
give you solutions to your problems. Yes, you might have to
search for them. You might have to talk to a number of your
running partners and check out a few different practitioners
(particularly those who run themselves and/or see plenty of
runners in their practice), but you can and will find them.*

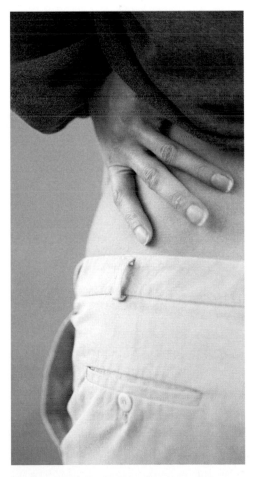

Here's proof. In the following pages, you'll find half a
dozen of the injury problems that runners face most
frequently, as well as doctors who treat them and solutions
that work. These people might not live close to you, but
others do. And the prevention practices outlined here will
help you avoid injuries, no matter where you live.

When you embark on an injury-healing programme, don't
expect miracles. You need to be consistent in doing the
treatments, and patient in waiting for results. But they will
come; you will get better. Also very important: when you have
a serious injury, don't run. You'll get better quicker and more
completely if you give your body and legs a complete rest.

Pain is a sign that something is wrong – just
ignoring it will affect your running performance.

ACHILLES PAIN

Experts used to think Achilles pain was an inflammatory condition. Today, many think the pain results not from inflammation but from degeneration of collagen fibres. This new understanding has brought forth new treatments.

■ **Best new alternative remedy:** Available over the counter, glucosamine supplements, which are commonly used to treat osteoarthritis, may also halt collagen degeneration.

About two-thirds of the people who try the supplements feel improvement, says Karim Khan, a sports medicine doctor at the University of British Columbia in Vancouver. 'Some people benefit greatly, while others see no effect, and right now we don't know why,' he says. Take a daily dose of 1,500 milligrams of glucosamine.

■ **Best new mainstream treatment:** In one study, Swedish researchers asked 15 runners with chronic Achilles pain to do the following exercise for 12 weeks. At the end of the study, all were running strongly. Here's what to do.

1. Stand with your toes on the edge of a step. Use your uninjured leg to push yourself up on your toes.

2. Shift all your body weight on to your injured leg, and slowly lower your injured heel while keeping your knee straight.

3. Use your good leg to rise up again on your toes. Repeat the exercise.

4. Work up to three sets of 15 repetitions of this exercise. Then add weight by holding dumbbells or wearing a backpack stuffed with books. Repeat twice a day 7 days a week for 12 weeks. Expect some mild soreness during the first 2 weeks. If the exercise is too hard, first strengthen your Achilles by repeatedly standing on your toes for 10 seconds at a time.

Also try these excellent ideas.
■ Buy quarter-inch heel lifts for your shoes.
■ Wear a heated ankle wrap throughout the day to improve circulation.

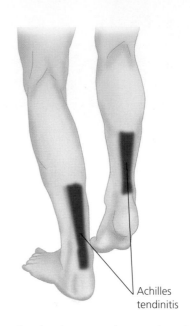

Achilles tendinitis

When placed under too much stress, the Achilles tendon tightens and becomes inflamed.

'Shinsplints are especially common among beginning runners and those who dramatically increase their mileage.'

■ Massage your Achilles with ice to prevent poor-quality blood vessels from forming.

■ Have a weekly massage to break up scar tissue.

■ Do the push-against-the-wall stretch regularly, with your rear knee straight and then with it slightly bent.

HAMSTRING PAIN

Many hamstring strains heal slowly as long as you avoid offending activities such as hill repeats, bounding from one leg to the other (often called plyometrics) and speedwork. On the other hand, if you've been hurting for months, the real problem may be your back. Even if your back doesn't hurt, get it checked by a doctor, especially if you have chronic hamstring problems. Your problem may be degenerative disk disease or an abnormal pelvic tilt. The following treatments may help.

■ **Best new alternative remedy:** Cross-fibre friction massage will help break up scar tissue, encouraging your hamstring to heal faster. See an experienced sports-massage therapist once a week until you can run pain-free. If your injury is mild, one session may be all you need. For best results, combine massage with a comprehensive programme that includes icing, gentle stretching and strengthening.

■ **Best new mainstream treatment:** You have to focus on well-rounded strength. 'Many runners think they have strong legs because of the distances they cover when in fact they don't,' says Dr Robert Wilder, director of sports rehabilitation at the University of Virginia. 'Runners often have excellent endurance, but not necessarily strength.'

When you strengthen your hamstrings, work them concentrically and eccentrically. Those are fancy words that simply mean your hamstrings need to be strong when you bend your legs as well as when you straighten them. They also should be strong at the bottom, where they attach to the backs of your knees, and at the top, where they attach to your hips.

Try the following exercises with ankle weights.

1. Lie on your belly. Slowly raise one foot until your knee is bent at a 90-degree angle, then slowly lower your foot. Do eight to 15 repetitions with each leg three times a week.

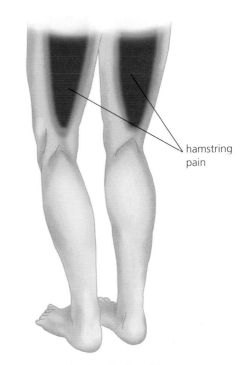

hamstring pain

Sprinting, speedwork or back problems can cause a strain in the muscles at the back of the thigh.

2. Lie on your stomach and slowly raise one foot without bending your knee. Do eight to 15 repetitions with each leg three times a week.

Also try these excellent ideas.
■ Stretch, but only gently. Vigorous stretching can make your injury worse.
■ Wear compression shorts or a neoprene sleeve around your upper leg when you run.
■ Ice your hamstrings for 15 minutes after each run.

ILIOTIBIAL BAND (ITB) SYNDROME

Extending along your outer thigh from your hip to just below your knee, your ITB stabilizes your knee and absorbs a lot of the impact of running. When it becomes tightened, your ITB can rub against the outside of your knee or hip joint, injuring and inflaming your knee tendon.

■ **Best new alternative remedy:** Before you can correct the cause of your ITB pain, you have to reduce the inflammation. To do so, see an experienced physiotherapist, athletics trainer or massage therapist, who will press trigger points in your quadriceps and buttocks and stretch your ITB. 'This really helps people get through the acute phase,' says Michael Fredericson, head doctor for the US Stanford University track and cross-country teams.

See your physiotherapist every other day until you can climb up and down stairs without pain (usually within 2 weeks). You can speed the process along by buying a foam roller that you lie on to stretch and massage your ITB area.

■ **Best new mainstream treatment:** In theory, your gluteus medius – a muscle in your buttocks – keeps your hips aligned so your ITB doesn't rub against your knee or hip joints. That is, if the muscle is strong enough to do the job. Often it isn't, says Dr Fredericson. To strengthen your gluteus medius, try the following exercises once the inflammation has subsided.

1. Lie on your side with your legs, buttocks and back against a wall and with your injured leg on top. Tighten the muscles on the side of your hip and slowly raise your heel along the wall about 30 degrees. Hold for 1 second. Lower and repeat

'Stretching your calves and Achilles tendon in multiple directions will release pressure on your plantar fascia.'

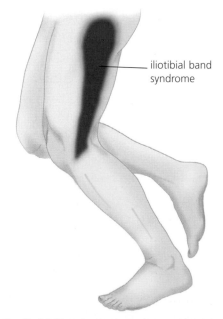

iliotibial band syndrome

The iliotibial band runs down the outside of the leg and can become inflamed at the knee.

10 to 20 times. Work up to three sets of 20 repetitions three times a week.

2. Stand on your injured leg in front of a mirror (so you can check your form). Slowly lower yourself into a one-legged squat. Keep your hips level and your knee pointed forwards, centred above your foot. Lower yourself only 30 degrees from the starting position. Repeat 10 to 20 times three times a week.

3. Stand on a step. Put all of your weight on your bad leg, letting your good leg dangle off the step. (You may use a wall for balance if needed.) With both legs straight, lower the hip of your free leg towards the floor as you shift your body weight to the inside of your standing foot. Then rise back up. Build up to three sets of 20 repetitions each day.

Also try these excellent ideas.

■ When you return to running, start with strides and sprints, suggests Dr Fredericson. The quicker pace forces you to bend your legs more as you run, which reduces the risk of too much stress on your ITB.

■ Stretch your ITB after every run. Stand with your right leg crossed behind your left, and place your left palm against a wall. Keep your right foot planted while allowing your left knee to bend. Hold for 30 seconds. Repeat on the opposite side.

■ If you run on slanted roads or banked tracks, run so your injured leg is on the higher side of the road.

■ See a sports medicine specialist for orthotics.

PLANTAR FASCIITIS

Your plantar fascia, the thick band of tissue that connects your heel to the base of your toes, can get torn, inflamed or overstretched during running. You will often feel the pain at the base of your heel when you step out of bed in the morning. This injury can be very troublesome; it can prevent you from running for weeks, sometimes months.

■ **Best new alternative remedy:** In one study, acupuncture reduced pain for 18 people who had been unable to recover from plantar fasciitis for a year. At first, practitioners needled traditional meridian points. When some runners didn't

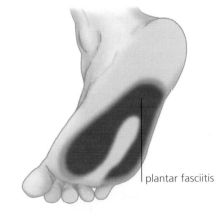

plantar fasciitis

Repeated microscopic tears of the plantar fascia can lead to a bruising sensation at the base of the heel.

respond, the acupuncturists focused on trigger points in the runners' calves and arches. This reduced pain completely within 6 weeks. Experts aren't sure why acupuncture heals, but some believe it signals your brain to release pain-soothing chemicals.

■ **Best new mainstream treatment:** Stretching your calves and Achilles tendon in multiple directions will release pressure on your plantar fascia, says physiotherapist and chiropractic doctor Gary Mascilak. Here's how to do it.

1. Get in the push-against-the-wall position, with one foot 60 cm (24 in) in front of the other and your palms pressed flat against the wall.

2. Slowly lean forwards while pressing the heel of your rear foot into the ground. Keep your toes pointed forwards and your back knee straight. Curl your toes to accentuate your arch as you shift your weight to the outside of your rear foot. Alternate between this curled-toe position and the starting position for 30 seconds.

3. While still pushing against the wall, bend your rear knee until you feel your heel wanting to rise off the floor. Again curl your toes to accentuate your arch, putting your weight on the outside of your foot. Alternate back and forth between the curled-toe and starting position for 30 seconds. Repeat the whole sequence as often as possible.

Also try these excellent ideas.
■ See a sports medicine specialist for orthotics, which work within 6 weeks for most runners.
■ Before you get out of bed, wrap a towel around your toes and gently pull them towards you. Do this with your knees straight as well as bent.
■ Make an appointment with a physiotherapist, podiatrist or chiropractor for ultrasound treatments to break up scar tissue and encourage healing.
■ Ask your podiatrist or physiotherapist for a night splint, a device that you wear on your foot while you sleep to keep your Achilles tendon and plantar fascia lightly stretched.

'Experts aren't sure why acupuncture heals, but some believe it signals your brain to release pain-soothing chemicals.'

■ Massage your arch often by sitting on a chair and rolling a marble, a frozen cola bottle or another massage device under your foot. Progress to a standing position.

RUNNER'S KNEE

You know you have runner's knee (sometimes called chondromalacia) when you feel pain beneath your kneecap while running. Sometimes you can feel pain even when you're not running, especially when walking down stairs. Runner's knee is often caused by improper tracking of the kneecap. This makes the undersurface of your kneecap rub against your femur. To get back on track, try the following:

■ **Best new alternative remedy:** In one study, a group of athletes who took the gelatine supplement Knox Nutrajoint for 8 weeks reduced their knee pain more than a group that took a placebo. The amino acids in gelatine may repair mild cartilage damage, says Dr David Pearson, the researcher who led the study.

■ **Best new mainstream treatment:** A great number of runners have a weak inner quadriceps muscle (in the inner thigh) and stronger outer quadriceps. This imbalance tends to pull your kneecap out of alignment, says Dr Fredericson. Leg extensions, often prescribed for weak quads, actually put too much pressure on your kneecap and may exacerbate your injury.

Instead, strengthen your quads with the following exercises.

1. Do exercise number 2 listed under those already recommended for ITB syndrome.

2. Use a leg-press machine, but only work one leg at a time, and lower your leg only 30 degrees from the starting position.

3. Cross-train by cycling, which strengthens your inner quads.

Also try these excellent ideas.
■ Cut back on hill repeats and stairclimbing.
■ See a sports medicine specialist for orthotics if you overpronate or have knock-knees.
■ Ice your knee for 15 minutes after you run.

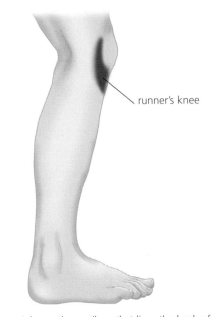

runner's knee

In runner's knee, the cartilage that lines the back of the kneecap becomes damaged and causes pain.

Strengthening your inner quads by cycling is a good way to ease the symptoms of runner's knee.

■ Have regular massages that emphasize your quadriceps and ITB area.

SHINSPLINTS

More of a catchall term than an actual medical condition, 'shinsplints' refers to any swelling of muscles, tendons and even the covering of the bones in your shins. Shinsplints are especially common among beginning runners and those who dramatically increase their mileage.

■ **Best new alternative remedy:** A thin tissue called fascia envelops all of your muscles and tendons, including those in your shins. When injured, the fascia can become restricted. A form of massage called myofascial release can improve mobility and enhance circulation and healing of the fascia. Try the following self-massage.

1. Sit in a chair. Place one thumb in the groove between the shinbone and shin muscle of the leg that hurts. Place your other thumb on top for support.

2. Rub down your leg. Then move your thumb about 2.5 cm (1 in) to the outside and rub down your leg again. Next, move 2.5 cm (1 in) to the outside again, and so on. Do this as often as possible, lightly at first and more deeply as the injury begins to heal.

■ **Best new mainstream treatment:** When you have shin-splints, the muscles, tendons and nerves in your shins become tightened. To elongate all of them, do the following three stretches. Hold each stretch for 30 seconds and repeat several times a day.

1. Lie on your back with your right leg in the air. Wrap a towel or belt around the ball of your foot. First, pull on the towel with your left hand (as if you're making a horse turn left), bringing your toes down and to the left. This will stretch the outside of your lower leg and ankle.

2. Pull the towel with your right hand, so your toes come down and to the right. You'll feel this stretch deep in your calf.

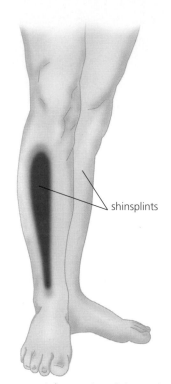

shinsplints

Shinsplints are an inflammation of the tendons on the inside of the front of the lower leg.

Anti-inflammatories such as aspirin can be taken to ease the swelling caused by shinsplints.

THE FINISH LINE

Three things to remember about this chapter:

1. Regular massage can work wonders. It's difficult for researchers to prove that massage helps runners, but it's easy for runners to feel it themselves. After a massage, you'll feel more relaxed, and your muscles will feel looser. You can have a professional massage, or you can use a variety of self-massage tools to get almost the same results.

2. The same goes for stretching. No one has been able to prove that stretching is the wonder cure that runners would like it to be, but most athletes and sports medicine specialists continue to believe in stretching. The key: go gently, a little at a time. If you overdo stretching, you could actually injure yourself, the same as when you overdo anything else. So breathe deep and slowly, take your time and enjoy the gentle benefits of stretching.

3. Always remember the RICE formula – Rest, Ice, Compression, Elevation. This is one of the best ways to treat injuries and prevent minor ones from getting worse. The rest prescription is especially important, though sometimes hard to follow. A couple of days away from workouts won't hurt your fitness programme, however, and the rest will help you get back into training as soon as possible.

3. Sit on the front edge of a chair with your feet flat on the floor and legs as straight as possible (without raising your toes). Turn your toes inwards and heels out. Lean forwards from the waist, keeping your chest and head up and your back straight. This stretches the outside of your shins.

Also try these excellent ideas.

■ Reduce inflammation with ice, elevation and anti-inflammatories such as aspirin, ibuprofen or naproxen sodium

■ You should see a sports medicine specialist for orthotics, and try stability or motion-control shoes if overpronation is a problem.

■ Strengthen your shin muscles by walking around alternately on your heels, then on your toes, with your toes pointed out as well as pointed in. Progress to doing all four of these in a squatting position.

WEBWISE

The foot is the foundation of every runner's training programme. Without healthy feet, you can't reach your goals. This website has plenty of advice to keep your feet happy and healthy.
www.drfoot.co.uk

CHAPTER 26

Your Friend,
the Physiotherapist

Put Your Injuries in the Hands of a Specialist

A physiotherapist can't order prescription drugs for you. But the things physiotherapists can do for you might be just what you need.

A couple of years ago, US Ironman triathlete and marathoner Charlie Suthard heard the words that every injured runner dreads. You know, the ones that begin with, 'You'll never . . .' Ugh. But don't worry: with luck and good prevention, you can escape ever hearing these words.

The cause of Suthard's knee problems was clear. One of his legs was measurably longer than the other, and after years of running, the leg-length discrepancy had taken its toll on one knee. The kneecap was scraping and rubbing painfully instead of tracking smoothly.

Don't let injuries hold you back: get back to full fitness with the help of a physiotherapist.

With the Hawaiian Ironman just a few months away, Suthard was desperate to find a cure so he could get back to training. But after visiting a host of doctors, he hadn't improved and was told it was time to give up his Ironman plans. 'They told me I would never be able to finish the marathon,' Suthard recalls, 'that there was just no way.'

In a last-ditch effort to find a cure, Suthard called physiotherapist Mark Plaatjes. 'I'd heard through the runners' grapevine that Mark was really good at what he did and knew his stuff,' says Suthard.

Plaatjes, of course, isn't just another physiotherapist. During the '90s, he was one of the top marathoners in the world, winning the World Track Championships in 1993. When not running, he could often be found working on other runners before or after races. After retiring from competitive racing a few years ago, Plaatjes established a physiotherapy practice.

Suthard went to see Plaatjes four times for his injured knee. 'After Mark finished with my treatments, I was ready to run,' he says. 'The knee pain disappeared and never returned. I was able to get back into training for the Ironman, and 3 months later, I finished it.'

Plaatjes used one of the most common treatments in the physiotherapist's arsenal by digging his well-trained fingers into the tendons and ligaments surrounding Suthard's knee. He smoothed out the knots in the scar tissue so the kneecap could track properly. That was all Suthard needed.

This type of massage is nothing like the full-body, relaxing massage that many athletes enjoy. This was painful, tough love. 'I have this horrible reputation that I hurt people,' says Plaatjes. 'But with some injuries, that's what gets them better.'

Certainly, not all physiotherapy hurts – most of it doesn't – but physiotherapists (or physios, as they're commonly known) often provide the critical hands-on treatment that can cure even the toughest injury.

MEET YOUR NEW BEST FRIEND

The building blocks of physio training are anatomy, physiology, kinesiology and biomechanics. Physiotherapy is studied over three years at degree level in the UK, with master's and doctoral degrees also available.

But physiotherapists are not medical doctors, so they can't prescribe medication or give injections. In most cases, physios also can't order diagnostic tests such as MRIs, bone scans or X-rays. They can – and certainly should – let you know when such tests are warranted and suggest that you see an appropriate specialist.

Many physios specialize in one area or another, but most runners need physiotherapy for common running injuries that haven't responded to self-treatment and/or rest. The normal runner's woes – Achilles tendinitis, runner's knee, shinsplints, plantar fasciitis, iliotibial band syndrome and muscle strains and pulls – all fall under a physiotherapist's practice because they usually require non-invasive treatment and rehabilitation techniques. But if you have a serious injury that requires

In physios we trust

Physiotherapists take a two-pronged approach to their work: first, they treat the injury and get the runner back on the road. Second, they look at the body as an entire, functioning unit, root out the primary cause of the injury, then correct it. Their treatments range from high-tech modalities such as ultrasound and electrical stimulation to no-tech, age-old solutions as simple as ice, rest and stretching. In short, physios are the runner's pit crew, a one-stop shop for whatever ails you.

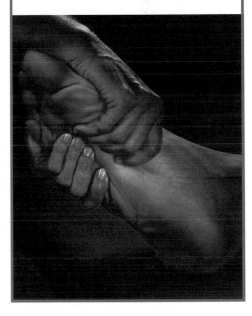

surgery, you can bet you'll be doing your rehab under the supervision of a physio.

WHO TO SEE?

As the law currently stands, anyone can work in private practice as a physiotherapist (or 'physical therapist'). If you opt for private treatment, make sure you see a chartered and/or state registered physio. This will guarantee that their qualification is properly recognized; they are governed by a professional code of conduct; and they are covered by professional liability insurance.

Chartered physios work in a variety of settings including hospitals, health centres, GP practices, schools, work places, private clinics and also by visiting people at home. There are three main treatment routes if you are resident in the UK and wish to see a physio.

■ **Via the NHS.** You will first need to make an appointment with your general practitioner (GP), and then ask him or her to be referred to a physio. Onward referral will be at the discretion of the GP.

■ **Via private practitioners.** If you are in a position to pay for your own treatment, there are a large number of physios across the UK offering treatment in dedicated physiotherapy and sports injury clinics as well as many who will treat people in their own homes. To find a local private practitioner within the UK visit *www.csp.org.uk/physio2u.cfm*. The Organisation of Chartered Physiotherapists in Private Practice (OCPPP), an occupational group of the CSP for private practitioners, also have a listing service of private practitioners working in the UK.

■ **Via the independent sector.** Some large employers run occupational health schemes for their employees that may include provision for physio treatment. Check with your human resources or personnel department to see if you're eligible.

Private medical insurance schemes for individuals through the independent healthcare sector will often include physio treatment too. Check with your scheme providers.

RUNNERS: WE'RE DIFFERENT

Injured runners are not like injured skiers. That's because running injuries, for the most part, are not caused by traumatic

---

THE BEST WAY

Q: What's the best way to avoid running injuries altogether?

A: There is no such way. All runners eventually experience some aches and pains, though these aren't always serious injuries to bones or joints, and they generally go away in several days. You can make sure you don't develop serious injuries by stopping your training for 3 days at the first sign of persistent pain. Also, ice the area that's sore twice a day for 10 to 15 minutes at a time, and take over-the-counter anti-inflammatory treatments. Then restart your training slowly and gradually.

Injury expertise

The most important factor when choosing a physiotherapist is to find someone who is familiar with running injuries. You need to consult someone who can put themselves in your shoes. 'It's like any kind of speciality,' says Dr Irene McClay Davis, director of research for Joyner Sports Medicine Institute. 'The more cases practitioners see, the better they become.'

accidents, such as falling at 30 miles per hour on a steep, icy slope. Instead, running injuries are usually due to a slow accumulation of stresses on a muscle or bone over a period of time. When a runner tips the delicate balance – typically, he or she runs too far or too fast – painful symptoms of overuse flare up somewhere in the body, usually the lower legs.

In order to fully cure such overuse injuries, a good physio will not only treat the symptoms but will try to determine the original cause of the problem. 'Physiotherapists have in their army of knowledge probably the best understanding of the mechanics of human movement,' says exercise physiologist Janet Hamilton. 'They are also one of the best sources for understanding the "why" of injury onset. Just about any overuse injury will respond to rest and ice, but when you resume running, you may get injured again unless the factors that led to the injury are corrected.'

That's why visits to a physio typically involve a lot of detective work. Once the initial healing treatments reduce your pain enough, the physio will probably watch you run on a treadmill (and videotape it) in order to analyse your stride and biomechanics. Physios will also measure muscle strength throughout the body in order to detect imbalances that can pull a stride out of alignment.

After determining the cause of the injury, a physio can prescribe various steps to correct the problem. The correction may be as simple as a customized stretching and strengthening programme for certain muscle groups. A physio might also check the runner's shoe and if necessary add arches, heel lifts or customized orthotics.

THE DO-IT-YOURSELF APPROACH

There are a number of physiotherapy approaches and treatments that you can practise on your own. Perhaps your Achilles is starting to groan. Or you feel a twinge in your knee with every step. Or the bottom of your heel is sending out warning signals.

Not to worry. Here are some healing tips from physios that you can use on yourself.

■ 'The first thing the runner needs to ask is, "What am I doing that's different?"' says physio Bruce Wilk, who also owns a

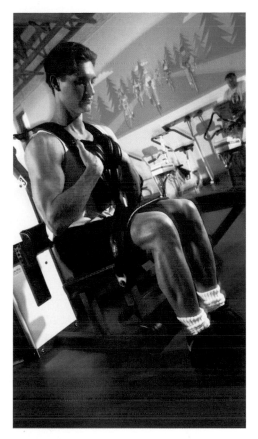

Suffering from a running injury? A physio may suggest cross-training while you recover.

'Physiotherapists are the runner's pit crew, a one-stop shop for whatever ails you.'

running store. 'Did you change your footwear? Increase your mileage? Do too much hill training while on holiday?' If you can pinpoint a change, your first step should be to try to correct it: cut down your mileage, change your shoes, back off the speedwork, reduce hill training.

■ Treat the problem with ice and gentle stretching. 'Whether it's a muscle strain, Achilles trouble or plantar fasciitis, the treatment is all pretty much the same,' says Dr Irene McClay Davis, director of research for Joyner Sports Medicine Institute. Your goal, she explains, should be to calm the area down, reduce muscular inflammation and relieve stress to the site – this means relaxing so as not to exacerbate the injury.

■ Ice the injured area several times a day for about 10 minutes, especially after running, stretching or cross-training.

> *' When choosing a physiotherapist, find someone who is familiar with running injuries.'*

Going Deep

Physiotherapists use an array of techniques to keep runners healthy. Deep-tissue massage is just one of the many options. Your physio will discuss your condition with you, examine you for postural and biomechanical problems, and then devise a recovery plan designed to reduce your pain and inflammation and speed the healing of your injured tissues or joints. Effective options include:

Ultrasound. The use of sound waves to produce a deep heat to warm muscle tissues. A wand attached to the ultrasound machine is gently massaged over the tissue around the affected area for several minutes, delivering the heat therapy. The warming effect promotes healing by relaxing muscles and increasing range of motion.

Electrical stimulation. Sometimes called 'e-stim' for short, this treatment sends low-voltage electrical impulses to the injured area via electrodes. It sounds scary, but the runner only feels a mild twinge when the muscle contracts. E-stim relieves pain in the injured area and can also help heal bone and tissue.

Cryotherapy. A fancy term for ice or other cold treatment, cryotherapy is used in the initial injury phase to relieve pain and swelling by reducing blood flow and nerve conduction. Ice is often used after other physio rehab treatments, such as manual manipulation and stretching, in order to reduce the ensuing swelling.

Iontophoresis. Since physiotherapists are not doctors, they can't give injections. Iontophoresis is a non-invasive method of delivering healing medication. The drug (usually an anti-inflammatory) is transmitted to the tissues via an electrode with an absorbent pad.

Deep-tissue massage. A rigorous hands-on stroking and kneading of muscles and connective tissue. Some physios eschew deep-tissue massage in favour of less painful treatments, but others, like Mark Plaatjes, swear by it. 'When you injure your tissue, collagen is like a superglue that heals it,' explains Plaatjes. 'But sometimes the body can do too good a job, and the collagen can bind the healthy fibres with adhesions. Then every time you move, it hurts, even though the original injury is healed. The purpose of cross-fibre deep massage is to break up the adhesions. It hurts like hell, but it works.'

THE FINISH LINE

Three things to remember about this chapter:

1. Don't run through pain. Runners often pride themselves on being tough and being able to deal with the occasional aches and pains of running. But toughness has its limitations, particularly when it causes you to ignore the onset of an injury. At the first sign of real pain, take several days off. If that doesn't help much, consider seeing a doctor.

2. Trust your physio. While doctors are trained to diagnose injuries, physios are trained to heal them through active strengthening, stretching and other techniques. Find out who's the best in your area and use him or her (after getting a doctor's recommendation) whenever you need help getting back on the road.

3. Not all massage is blissful. Some physiotherapists will use deep-fibre friction massage to help you work out muscle adhesions deep in the muscle tissue. This massage, applied with considerable tension, sometimes feels more like torture than the more common and gentler forms of massage. But it can be very effective, and your physio can use ice to limit the pain.

■ Take an over-the-counter anti-inflammatory (such as naproxen sodium, ibuprofen or aspirin) to reduce any pain and inflammation.

■ Stretch the nearby area gently. It's important to focus on stretching the surrounding and connecting muscles, not the area that's already sore. For example, if your Achilles hurts, stretch your upper calf area. If there's any pain while stretching, don't continue.

■ Cut back on your training. If your injury is the result of overuse, it should respond quickly to rest or easier running. If it doesn't improve within 10 days, then it's time to seek advice from a medical professional.

■ Never run through pain or take medication to mask pain. Any attempts to do so will only delay recovery time. Instead of running, try some cross-training activities that won't aggravate the injury.

■ Don't continue running even if the pain decreases during your run. Some injuries will feel better with the increased blood flow that exercise provides, but, Wilk warns, that's false security. 'Tendons, for example, hurt more when they are cold,' he says. 'You start moving and they feel better, but the next day they feel worse again.'

Icing an area of soreness on a daily basis can soothe inflammation and accelerate recovery time.

WEBWISE

The Chartered Society of Physiotherapy is the professional, educational and trade union body for the UK's 40,000 chartered physiotherapists, physiotherapy students and assistants. Visit the website to find a practitioner in your area.
www.csp.org.uk

CHAPTER 27

The Mental Side of Injuries

Heal Yourself by Putting Mind over Matter

To deal with injuries and recover to full strength, you need more than just a bottle full of pills. You also have to understand the psychology of injury and how you can use it to cope with your layoff time.

Most runners have a reasonable idea about what to do first when their knees moan or their hamstrings groan: Apply ice. Gulp a couple of ibuprofens. Have a massage. Maybe start some cross-training.

So why don't all runners do that? Why is it that some running injuries drag on for so long? Why do so many runners ignore the signs, disregard their better judgement and try to continue running while injured?

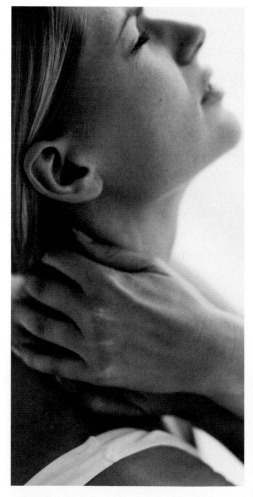

The reason is simple. Too many runners overlook the most important part of injury recovery: the mental part. And that's a big mistake. To make sure it doesn't happen to you, here's advice from a cross-section of top sports psychologists. Their experience and professional expertise gained from decades of running and training give rise to a simple, effective injury-recovery programme. Follow it, and you'll feel better when injured and return to action faster and more healthily.

'Having this kind of mental road map can be extremely helpful for injured runners,' says psychologist Dr James Prochaska, a renowned expert on behavioural models used to help people give up smoking and lose weight. 'It really helps people identify where they are on the map, where they are heading and how to get there. It will also help you rein

When stretching just isn't enough: acknowledging that you have an injury is the first step to recovery.

in your worst fears and provide reinforcement that you're on the right path.'

So if you're sitting there this very moment thinking you're never going to heal, remember that a big key to recovery is your attitude. Make the following attitude adjustments, and get better faster.

Acceptance. Psychologists often say that acceptance is the most difficult step, especially if you're talking about such things as serious illness, death or extremely large tax bills. But this is running, and your running injury is not the end of the world. Having said that, you still have to acknowledge the problem before you can solve it. If the pain you feel is sharp, persistent, lasts more than a couple of days and is compromising your running, don't ignore it, and don't try to wish it away or run through it. Accept the fact that you are injured and move on.

Adherence. During your rehab, you need to show the same discipline you've demonstrated as a runner. If that means no running at all, so be it. If the prescription calls for physio-therapy three times a week, make the appointments and do the exercises. If it's a certain series of stretches your doctor wants you to do twice a day . . . well, then, down on the floor with you. Whatever the prescription, stick to it, even if it's not as much fun as a leisurely 5-miler. The longer you delay, the longer you mess around, the longer until you're back running.

Encouragement. Yes, it's nice if your friends and family rally round and offer their support when you run, but we're talking about self-encouragement here. 'Injured runners often tend to think and talk to themselves in ways that limit them,' explains psychotherapist Dr Deborah Lee Greenslit, a keen marathoner herself. 'If you're constantly feeding yourself discouraging messages, it's going to be difficult to stay with the recovery plan.'

So give yourself a pep talk now and then. 'Look for some concrete evidence to substantiate your comeback capabilities,' says Dr Greenslit. 'This might be that you

Start researching

You're injured. You know you shouldn't run yet, but you also know you should take action. Look at some running-injury books, look at back issues of Runner's World *magazine, or better yet, go to www.runnersworld.co.uk, click on 'Health', then 'Beating Injury'. You might also look at the injuries forum. Many of the veteran runners on the forum will be eager to share their experiences with you and to explain how they coped with injuries exactly like yours.*

Also, ring your coach, a veteran runner you know or a sports medicine professional. There's plenty of information out there about running injuries and plenty of experts who can offer informed opinions. These people and resources will help you plot your course back to healthy, pain-free running.

overcame an injury in the past or that you were able to solve other vexing problems in your life.'

Or it could simply be that you, unlike a lot of people, were able to start and stick to running in the first place. 'That is a very big accomplishment, and now is a good time to acknowledge it,' adds Dr Greenslit.

Another important message you can send yourself is that you can control your situation. 'Rather than say, "How long is this going to take?", think about what you can do today to further your recovery,' says Dr Greenslit. On this day, at this moment, you can make a difference. Maybe it's a session in the gym or simply making an appointment with your doctor to get a better handle on your injury. Whatever it is, get to it. Which brings us to . . .

Redirection. What do you do with all that pent-up energy now that you're not running? Channel it elsewhere. Harness that aggressiveness you had on the track by taking it out on the elliptical trainer in the gym. Instead of pushing the pace on a tempo run, push those weights in the gym for a while. All these activities will burn calories, make you stronger and help maintain your fitness until you're back on the roads. Perhaps most important, they'll keep you from going mad.
■ **Another option:** Redirect your energy back into the sport. Maybe this is the time to heed the perennial call from your local race organizer. Sign up to volunteer at a water stop, registration table or the finish line. (Just resist the temptation to stick out your tongue at the runners because they can run and you can't.)

Separation-Engagement. These may sound contradictory, but they're not. First, separation: it's Sunday morning, and you know your usual training partners are out enjoying a long run . . . while you're at home, sitting around bored. You may be tempted to join them. Bad move. Peer pressure – real or imagined – is a force to be reckoned with. Chances are, you'll be sucked into trying to keep up with them, which could aggravate your injury. Instead, separate yourself from your normal training environment. You'll be back soon enough. Now is not the time.

THE BEST WAY

Q : What's the best way to avoid depression when you're injured?

A : First, do what you need to do to get over the injury – icing, medication stretching, strengthening and so on. Don't become lazy. Second, work on other areas of your fitness. Introduce a couple of new, nutritious foods into your diet, for example. Or read a great book about an inspirational athlete.

'Too many runners overlook the most important part of injury recovery: the mental part.'

But while you're keeping your training partners at arm's length during your injury recovery, you also need the support of others in your life to help you through.

'Be aware of the helpfulness and contributions of others in your social sphere as you move through these recovery steps,' says Dr David Pargman, a professor of education psychology and sports psychology. 'Stay engaged with your friends and loved ones, and ask for their support.' Just don't dip into this well of support too often. Even your own mother will get tired of hearing about your plantar fasciitis after a while. 'There is a fine line between sharing problems with others and whining,' says Dr Pargman.

Patience. This is the common thread that underlies every step thus far. 'The importance of patience can't be overemphasized,' says university sports psychologist Dr Michael Sachs. 'Injury recovery takes time.' Yes, it does. The diagnosis takes time. The healing effects of the icing, anti-inflammatories and stretching take time. Getting fitted for orthotics takes time. The swelling, the microtrauma, the strains, the sprains . . . they all take time to heal and they shouldn't be rushed.

The good news is that there's a cure for practically every running injury, and most injuries heal with time. Unfortunately, no magic pill will instantly cure you. Nor is a simple change of shoes the likely answer. Instead, be confident that regardless of how bad your injury may seem, it's only temporary. You will run again, if you're patient enough to allow the healing process the time it needs.

Persistence. You can't run your usual weekly miles, but you can do something every day to get your running health back. While injuries can be markedly different, most of them respond extremely well to rest and self-treatment. If there are things you can do – see a chiropractor or podiatrist, have a massage – make a point of doing them.

If all you need is a few days of icing the injury and taking anti-inflammatories, don't get lazy and forget to do these things. Stick to the programme. Make it a priority. Similarly, your injury might have resulted from a lack of flexibility. If

Eat yourself fit

When you're not running and burning the number of calories you normally do, you have to concentrate even harder on good nutrition. Don't start bingeing just because you can't run. Instead, organize a specific injury-nutrition plan that fits well into your lifestyle. Often, grazing is the best strategy – eating five or six mini-meals throughout the day. You won't go hungry, and you can eat healthy amounts of fruit, vegetables, low-fat dairy products and other low-fat protein foods.

Don't attempt to diet while you're injured. The loss of your regular exercise programme is enough stress to deal with. You don't need more stress. On the other hand, if you decide to use your extra time to learn new cooking techniques and to sample new foods, that's a great idea. You'll particularly enjoy the new choices when you have returned to your normal training and can eat without worrying so much about your daily calorie burn.

THE FINISH LINE

Three things to remember about this chapter:

1. Listen to your body. You can avoid many running injuries if you simply take several days of rest at the first sign of an unusual pain or soreness. Bear in mind that you wouldn't have the pain if something weren't wrong, so acknowledge this as soon as you feel the first twinge or two. You know the old saying: an ounce of prevention is worth a pound of cure. This certainly applies to running injuries.

2. Injuries go away. Most running injuries resolve themselves in a week or two if you allow your body to heal itself. Take whatever time you need, and then spend a day or two walking instead of running. When you can walk without pain, you're ready to step up to running again.

3. Learn from your mistakes. The bad news: all runners get injured eventually. The good news: 99 per cent of injured runners return to healthy, pain-free running after some rest, recovery and rehabilitation. When you get injured, make sure you understand how and why you got injured, and then plan to avoid the same problem in the future.

so, be sure to do gentle stretching exercises twice a day. They aren't as much fun as running, but they will help get you back where you want to be.

Here and Now. Focus on today. Don't set an arbitrary deadline for when you'll be ready to run again and then start whether you're healthy or not. With any luck, you'll only be out of action for a few weeks, but you never know how quickly you'll heal. An injury that took 4 days to heal last time won't necessarily take 4 days to heal this time. The older you get, the longer it takes your body to heal.

You may also have to forget about that approaching race (particularly if it's a marathon) you'd planned to run in. Just because you signed up for it doesn't mean you'll recover by then. And if your injury does heal before the race, be prepared to lower your expectations on race day.

Reaffirmation. Once you're back to running – and you will be back – embrace it for all it's worth. Savour the simple act of being able to put one foot in front of the other. Revel in the ability to run 2 miles, or 4 miles or 6 miles pain-free. You did the hard work of recovery. Now it's time to celebrate. One last thing before you go: promise yourself that you won't repeat the actions that got you injured in the first place.

WEBWISE

An assortment of health news items from UK newspapers collated and analyzed by the *British Medical Journal*. Use the search engine to find running-related stories, medical breakthroughs and more.
www.bmj.com/uknews

'During your rehab, you need to show the same discipline you've demonstrated as a runner.'

CHAPTER 28

New Rules of Sports Medicine

The Latest Scientific Discoveries in the World of Running

The following list of advances in sports medicine will improve your running, your health and even your mood. Give each of them a try.

We live in a high-tech, progressive world, so it's natural to expect new scientific breakthroughs that will help your running. And indeed, the studies keep coming. Medical researchers are constantly investigating new ways to build strength, speed, endurance, injury prevention, heart health and much, much more. Some of the results point the way to new practices you should consider adopting as a regular part of your fitness lifestyle. Others reveal hyped-up claims for the empty promises they are.

In this chapter, you'll learn about a variety of sports medicine breakthroughs that have been proven effective in research-based studies. Think about them, and decide which ones could make you a healthier, happier runner. Remember: it often takes just one or two changes to make a dramatic improvement in your running and overall fitness.

You'll also learn about a trio of products you don't need to waste your hard-earned money on – you'd be better off walking (or running) away from these as fast as possible. Focus on what has been proven helpful, ignore the empty hype of other products, and you'll have more time and energy for the workouts that should be the cornerstone of your training programme.

Kill pain with massage. Runners have long believed that massage helps their muscles rebound from tough workouts. Only recently, however, have researchers tried to prove this. In a study at the University of Montana in the US, 18 men did 100 leg extensions, which induced muscle damage. One hour later the men either rested, cycled or had a massage for half-an-hour. All the men did the same thing again 24 hours later. Then the researchers tested a specific area of the men's sore leg muscles. Those who had received massage treatments were able to withstand more pressure than those who had not; their legs had apparently recovered better from the 100 leg extensions.

'I was very surprised by the results,' says former massage sceptic Dr Brent Ruby, associate professor and director of the Human Performance Lab at Montana. While massage may speed healing by increasing circulation, Dr Ruby suspects that it mostly masks pain in much the same way as taking a painkiller would. 'Massage tends to treat the symptom, but probably doesn't alleviate the actual muscle damage,' says Dr Ruby.

So don't assume that massage will completely erase the effects of a hard workout. It probably won't. But massage can help, and it can certainly help you feel better after hard efforts.

Lower blood pressure by running for just 10 minutes.
New findings show you need only 10 minutes of exercise to have a positive effect on blood pressure. Researchers at McMaster University in Ontario, Canada, asked people to cycle for 10, 15, 30 and 45 minutes, then monitored their blood pressure for an hour after exercising. All the exercise sessions lowered blood pressure, even the 10-minute one. Exercise was especially beneficial for people with borderline hypertension (high blood pressure), says study co-author Duncan MacDougall. So next time you try to talk yourself out of a run because you don't have a spare 30 minutes, remember that even 10 minutes of exercise is better than none.

Use an elliptical trainer when you're unable to run.
We've known for some time that you can use an elliptical trainer to cross-train while you're injured. But does using this exercise machine really burn as many calories and give you as good an aerobic workout as the real thing? Yes, say a pair of studies from the University of Oregon and Indiana State University in the US. Researchers at both universities monitored heart rate, oxygen consumption, perceived exertion and blood pressure of people who exercised on a treadmill or on an

> '*Remember that even 10 minutes of exercise is better than none.*'

THE BEST WAY

Q: What's the best kind of massage you can have?

A: The one that feels best to you and produces the greatest overall benefits. The range of massage types keeps getting wider. Some runners prefer a relaxing, calming massage that gives the whole body a light going-over. Others want their massage therapist to attack them with a painful ferocity. It might depend on whether or not you have a specific, chronic injury (in which case, you might need the attacking kind of massage). Anyway, try different types of massage to find out what they're like and what they can do for you.

elliptical trainer. Both machines offered similar benefits, as long as the runners worked out at similar intensities.

Prevent heart disease with vigorous exercise. Despite what you may have heard, vigorous exercise boosts health more than moderate exercise for just about every heart disease risk factor, including cholesterol and insulin levels. On the other hand, if you have high blood pressure, research shows that moderate exercise may do you more good, says Dr I-Min Lee, an assistant professor of medicine at Harvard, who recently reviewed the available research.

Strength train to improve running performance. Some runners shy away from weight lifting because they fear the practice will bulk up their muscles and make running feel harder. According to a new study, though, it doesn't. In fact, in addition to preventing injuries, weight training may even improve your running. New Zealand researcher Robert Nicholson asked runners to do a series of weight-lifting exercises two or three times a week. The runners lifted a weight that was heavy enough to prevent them from doing more than eight repetitions of each exercise.

After 21 weeks, the weight lifters had significantly improved their lactate threshold, max VO$_2$, running economy and 10-K times. 'At the beginning of the study, the group assigned to weight lifting had a faster 10-K time than the group that didn't lift weights,' says Nicholson. 'But the weight-lifting group improved by a greater amount than the running-only group by the end of the study.' He believes the weight lifters would have improved even more if most of the study participants hadn't caught flu at the end of the study.

To beat muscle soreness, avoid alcoholic drinks. Researchers from Kent State University in the US asked a group of men to drink enough alcohol for their blood alcohol level to reach 0.15 – about eight beers for a 76-kg (12-st) man – while another group of men abstained. Twelve hours later, researchers asked both groups to run 9 X 5-minute repeats. The men who drank the night before had longer-lasting, more intense muscle soreness than the group that abstained.

Try stretching to build your speed

The results of this study could add a little more incentive to your stretching programme. Researchers from Adelphi University in New York put 12 men and women through a battery of tests, which included a 40-yard dash. Then they asked the men and women to run downhill, making their legs tired and sore. Two days later, researchers asked half of the study group to stretch, while the other half did not. Both groups then repeated the initial series of tests. Those who had stretched improved their times in the 40-yard dash, while those who hadn't stretched did worse.

Stay hydrated, especially if you have asthma. Here's one more reason to make sure you drink up, particularly if you have asthma. A study from the State University of New York found that asthmatics are more sensitive to dehydration. Researchers tested 16 people, once while hydrated and once while dehydrated. Dehydration decreased the asthmatics' resting and post-exercise pulmonary function, which makes it more difficult to breathe in enough air. Make sure you're hydrated by sipping water or sports drinks throughout the day and consuming 150 to 230 ml (5 to 8 fl oz) of liquid every 20 minutes during exercise.

Boost motivation with carbohydrate. Eating or drinking calories while you run a marathon can do more than just keep your muscles fuelled. A new US study has found that carbohydrate can keep your brain energized as well. Researchers from the University of South Carolina asked 10

' It often takes just one or two changes to make a dramatic improvement in your running and overall fitness.'

Sorry, but These Don't Work

With more and more people jumping on the fitness bandwagon every year, it's inevitable that lots of unproven-but-highly-promoted products will follow them. Here are three that don't work. They won't hurt you, but you'd be much smarter to sink your money into quality running shoes and clothing.

Magnets. Plenty of runners are already using magnet therapy in the hope of reducing joint and muscle pain, but only a few studies have tested its effectiveness. Other studies have shown that magnets may reduce the discomfort of painful health conditions such as diabetic neuropathy, a burning sensation caused by nerve breakdown. So it seemed logical that magnets would reduce muscle soreness as well.

Apparently they don't. In a study done at Adelphi University in New York, researchers asked 13 people to run downhill for 10 minutes to induce muscle soreness. Some of the runners then had 500-gauss magnets placed on their sore muscles 2 hours a day for 3 days, while the other runners used fakes. The magnets didn't reduce muscle soreness.

Ginseng. Some runners take the herb ginseng to boost their energy. But a growing number of studies are calling ginseng's bluff. One done on cyclists at the University of Southern Mississippi found that 1,200 daily milligrams of Siberian ginseng didn't boost performance. Another study done at the University of Detroit found that 400 mg of panax ginseng didn't improve anaerobic power or delay fatigue.

Cellulite creams. You probably suspected they didn't work. Now there's research to back you up. Scientists at the University of North Carolina asked 11 women to use a cellulite cream on one thigh and a placebo cream on the other. The creams did not reduce thigh size, but interestingly, both the cellulite and placebo creams made the women think their thighs were smaller.

THE FINISH LINE

Three things to remember about this chapter:

1. You can't go wrong with the good carbs. If you want to exercise regularly, you need to eat ample amounts of carbohydrates, because the body is designed to burn carbs more efficiently than other fuels. That said, you should eliminate as many 'simple' carbs (sugars) as possible, and concentrate on fruits, vegetables and whole grains. Also, eat a little protein at every meal to make your body feel full.

2. Strength training is the perfect yang to the yin of running. Running builds your cardiovascular system – your heart and blood vessels. Whole-body strength training builds your muscles. You need both to live a healthy, balanced life, and you should include both in your workout plan. Spend about 80 per cent of your workout time on running and other aerobic activities, and about 20 per cent on strength training.

3. Live longer with exercise. People are concerned, as they should be, when they read about runners who die during a race or workout. But the facts are crystal clear: greater fitness leads to a longer, more vibrant life. Still, vigorous exercise temporarily increases your risk of a heart attack. That's why it's important to arrange regular checkups with your doctor.

men and women to drink a sports drink or water before and during vigorous exercise that lasted more than an hour. Those who consumed the sports drink not only were able to run longer – they also had better hand-eye coordination, moods and concentration than those who drank water. Carbohydrate may work by maintaining levels of the brain chemical dopamine, which boosts energy, motivation and awareness, says Dr Mark Davis, director of the exercise biochemistry lab at the University of South Carolina.

Eat protein to control your cravings. As a runner, eating too much protein can tax your kidneys, increase your risk of dehydration and hamper calcium absorption. Yet there may be a kernel of truth to all the high-protein diet hype. Recent studies show that unlike carbohydrate, protein may take a long time to digest, which could increase the number of calories your body has to burn to break it down. Protein also may help you feel fuller than carbohydrate can. To use protein to your advantage without limiting muscle-fuelling carbs, forgo the high-protein diets; instead, simply include in every meal a protein-rich food such as fish, peanut butter, beans, a low-fat dairy product or egg whites.

WEBWISE

Thanks to the Web, it's easy to do your own medical research. The PubMed site allows you to input one or several keywords and then to search the same medical-text abstracts that doctors use in their research.

www.pubmed.org

CHAPTER 29

Stay
Flexible

Learn the Secrets of Stretching to Run Your Best

Running builds strength in certain muscle groups, but not flexibility.
To promote flexibility and prevent injuries, you need to practise a
gentle stretching routine.

To stretch or not to stretch? That's the question for many runners.
The answer: yes, do stretch. But do your stretching after a thorough
warm-up, or after your run. Most experts (and runners) believe that
regular post-run stretching decreases injury risk, which allows you
to run more consistently.

Stretching also can eliminate tightness throughout your body. This
translates to better workouts and greater range of motion, which
makes you a healthier, happier runner.

To that end, here are 10 simple, effective stretches to
do in the sequence shown. Each targets a different part
of your body. Best of all, the whole routine takes 10
minutes, max. If you haven't stretched before, start
gradually and progress slowly. You don't have to
do all 10 of the stretches; pick the ones that target
muscle groups you'd like to work on.

When doing the stretches, don't bounce
into or out of any of the positions.
Breathe deeply and slowly – don't hold
your breath. Also, don't overstretch to the
point of pain. The idea is to stop
stretching as soon as you feel a light
tension in the muscle. If you continue
further than this, you risk injury.

Hamstrings (1): Lie on your back with your right leg straight out. While keeping your right leg extended, bend your left knee and pull it into your chest by clasping your left leg. Breathe deeply, hold for five breaths, and release. Then switch legs. Repeat twice on each side.

■ **Benefits:** Stretches hip extensors and glutes. Also relieves lower-back tension.

Hamstrings (2): While still lying on your back, extend your right leg straight out and bring your left knee into your chest. Hook a skipping rope, long towel or belt around the bottom of your left foot. Slowly straighten your left leg and extend upwards to the limit of your stretch, and hold steady. Breathe deeply, hold for five breaths and release. Switch legs and repeat three or four times on each side. If the stretch feels too intense, slightly lower the leg you're stretching until you find a comfortable but challenging position.

■ **Benefits:** Relaxes and stretches hamstrings.

Outer hips (3): Continue lying on your back. Bend both knees and place the outer side of your left foot over your right thigh, just above your knee. Wrap your hands around your right knee or on top of the shin and draw it towards your chest. Keep your head relaxed and flat on the ground. Hold for five breaths and release. Switch sides and repeat three or four times on each side.

■ **Benefits:** Opens and loosens hip and glutes. Also relieves lower-back tension.

Outer hips (4): Still lying on your back, extend both legs straight out. Pull your left knee into your chest. Grasp the outer side of your left knee with your right hand and pull the knee across your body towards the ground. Try to keep your left arm extended with your shoulders and head flat on the ground. Hold for five breaths and release. Switch sides and repeat three or four times on each side.

■ **Benefits:** Stretches hip extensors, glutes, and iliotibial bands. Also relieves lower-back tension.

Quadriceps muscles (5): Roll over onto your stomach, and prop yourself up on your right forearm. Reach back with your left hand and grab your left foot. Press your left foot down towards your buttocks, while keeping your left hip on the ground. Don't arch your back or twist your pelvis. Hold for five deep breaths and release. Alternate sides, repeating twice on each side.

■ **Benefits:** Stretches quadriceps and hip flexors.

Quadriceps muscles (6): You can also do the quadriceps stretch while standing. For balance, rest your right hand on a wall, tree or fence. Grab your left foot with your left hand. While keeping the thigh muscles of your right leg tight, pull your left knee back and up towards your buttocks. Don't tilt forwards. Repeat twice on each side.

■ **Benefits:** Stretches quadriceps and hip flexors.

Lower back and shoulders (7): Stand with your feet 15 cm (6 in) apart and about 1 m (3 ft) away from a wall, tree or other supporting surface of about shoulder height. Place both your hands about shoulder-width apart on the supporting surface and flex forwards at your hips. Press down on the surface, flatten your back, and lower your head between your arms. Hold for 10 breaths. Repeat a few times.

■ **Benefits:** Stretches and relieves tension in your shoulders, lower back and hamstrings.

WEBWISE

Bob Anderson wrote one of the first books on stretching, and it has remained popular for a quarter of a century. Here's his headquarters on the Web, and a good place to learn more about stretching.
www.stretching.com

THE FINISH LINE

Three things to remember about this chapter:

1. Don't stretch before running. Instead, do a very gentle warm-up at the beginning of your workout.

2. The muscle groups along the back of your body tend to get stronger (but also tighter) when you run regularly. The increased muscularity needs to be balanced by flexibility exercises.

3. Never rush or push to the point of pain. Stretching should be like Zen meditation. You get into a relaxed position, and then you simply hold it.

Calf muscles (8): To stretch your upper calf muscles, stand facing a wall or tree. Place your hands on the wall or tree and slide your left leg back 1 m (3 ft) or a little more. Lean forwards and shift your weight onto your right leg with the knee bent. Straighten your left leg and press your left heel into the ground. Make certain to point the toes of both feet forwards, not out to the side. Switch sides and repeat twice on each side.

■ **Benefits:** Stretches upper calves and Achilles tendons.

Calf muscles (9): To stretch your lower calf muscles, assume the same position against the tree, but this time slide your left leg back 1 m (3 ft) or a little less. Bend your left knee while keeping your left heel anchored to the ground. Bend your right knee to about the same position as the previous calf stretch. Alternate both sides twice.

■ **Benefits:** Stretches lower calves and Achilles tendons.

Calf muscles (10): Finish your stretching routine with an all purpose yoga pose called downward-facing dog. First, crouch on all fours with hands and feet placed shoulder-width apart. Move your feet back another 15 cm (6 in) or so. Press down into your feet, lift your knees off the ground, and straighten your legs. Lift your buttocks high. Press firmly into the ground with your hands. Lower your heels towards the ground. (Don't worry if they don't touch it.) Lengthen your back. Allow your head to hang freely. Breathe evenly while trying to hold this pose for 30 seconds. Gradually work up to 1 or 2 minutes.

■ **Benefits:** Stretches calves, Achilles tendons, hamstrings and shoulders. Also builds strength and relaxes lower back.

CHAPTER 30

Core Training

How to Develop Power, Balance and Functional Strength

Runners run with their feet and legs, but not only with the feet and legs. By developing the core muscles of the stomach, back and hips, you can prevent injuries and improve performance.

As runners, we tend to focus on building a stronger heart (cardiovascular system) and stronger legs, but we too often neglect the in-between areas. That's a mistake. A mechanical structure (read: your body) is only as good as its weakest link, and weak core muscles can lead to injuries and below-par race efforts.

In recent years, core strength training, which develops the muscles of the stomach, back and hips, has become one of the hottest areas in the fitness field. Increasing numbers of athletes in all sports have come to realize that core training gives you more than just gorgeous washboard abs. It also improves your performance and reduces injuries.

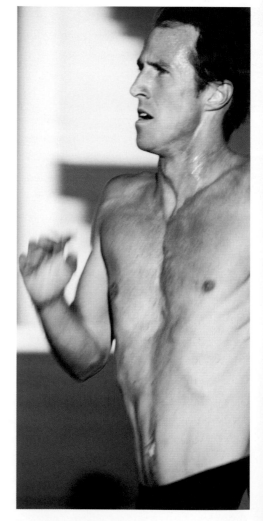

Take your pelvic area, for example. 'When your pelvis is not aligned properly while you run, you become prone to injury,' notes Mark Fidel, the director of Sports Medicine Institute International in California, who designed many of the exercises in this chapter. 'You can suffer hamstring pulls, Achilles problems, and lower-back pain.'

In other words, you need strong core muscles to keep that pelvis where it's supposed to be. A well-balanced core also improves your running economy. Result: faster times.

'The stronger your core, the more solid you are as you hit the ground,' explains exercise physiologist Dr Jack Daniels.

Enough legwork: developing the upper body will make you a stronger, quicker, more efficient runner.

'That reduces your need for unnecessary stabilization and allows you to be a more economical runner.'

Two top American marathon stars both swear by core training. Clint Verran, who has a master's degree in physical therapy, improved his marathon time to 2:14:17 in the LaSalle Bank Chicago Marathon in 2002. 'I believe muscular endurance of the core plays a key role in producing faster times and preventing injuries,' he says.

US Olympian Marla Runyan has used a core strength programme to produce great times at every distance from the mile to the marathon. In November 2002, she ran 2:27:12 to finish fifth in the New York City Marathon, her first 26.2-miler. 'I follow a core-strengthening programme for two reasons,' she says. 'First, I believe it prevents injuries to the iliotibial band and lower back. Second, it improves my running mechanics and efficiency.'

Each of the exercises that follows is designed to help you develop a strong and stable core. Mark Fidel suggests doing the exercises in the order shown, spending 60 seconds on each. Rest for 15 seconds before moving to the next exercise. After completing all six, take a 3- to 5-minute break, and repeat the whole series. Try to do this routine three times a week.

While doing each exercise, move slowly and aim for total control. If you get tired and lose form, stop for the day. It's more important to maintain quality than quantity.

' By developing the core muscles of the stomach, back and hips, you can prevent injuries and improve performance.'

1. Step downs: (A) Lie on your back with one hand under your lower back. Lift your legs so your thighs are at a 90-degree angle to the floor, and bend both knees to a 90-degree angle. (B) Tighten your lower back so that it doesn't move up or down, and slowly lower your right foot to within 3 cm (1 in) of the floor. Keep your right knee bent at a 90-degree angle, and maintain the position of your left leg. Hold your right foot 3 cm (1 in) off the floor for 2 seconds, then return it to the start position next to the left leg. Repeat the same action, but this time lower the left foot. Repeat both sequences three to five times.

2. Prone Stabilizer: (A) Start on your stomach, and raise yourself into a modified press-up position, with all your weight balanced on your forearms and toes. Keep your back as straight as possible. (B) Slowly raise your left leg until it lines up with your back. Hold this position for 4 seconds, then lower the left leg and repeat for 4 seconds with the right leg. Repeat both sequences three to five times.

3. Bridge: (A) Lie on your back with your arms behind your head and your feet planted on the floor directly below the knees. Press down on your feet, and lift your torso and upper legs until they form a straight line. (B) With your weight on your shoulders and your feet, slowly extend the right leg by straightening the knee. Make sure you keep your back straight. Hold for 4 seconds, then repeat with the left leg. Repeat both sequences three to five times.

4. Side Stabilizer: Lie on your right side with your right elbow under your shoulder and your left foot resting on your right foot. Press down with your forearm and foot until you lift your body off the ground. Keep your body as straight as possible; don't allow your hips to sag. Hold this position in a controlled fashion for 30 seconds. Repeat on your left side.

5. Fire Hydrant: (A) Start on your hands and knees. (B) Maintaining the 90-degree angle of your left knee, lift your left leg until the thigh is parallel with your upper body. Hold for 4 seconds, then lower. Repeat the same motion, but this time continue it by forcing the knee and thigh as far to the left as possible. Hold for 4 seconds. Repeat the motion again,

THE FINISH LINE

Three things to remember about this chapter:

1. Build better abs. Surprisingly enough, your running stride begins high up in your stomach muscles, and strengthening your abs will make you a better, more injury-resistant runner.

2. Stop injuries before they start. For too many years, runners paid little attention to their abs and back muscles, because they didn't get injuries there. But building a strong core makes you a more stable runner, and that helps prevent injuries to the hips, knees and lower legs.

3. Check your posture. Good running form demands good posture, and so do core-training exercises. Get a friend to check you out while you're doing these exercises to make sure you're maintaining the correct alignment.

but this time force the knee and thigh as far as possible to the right, crossing over your body's midline. Hold for 4 seconds. Repeat with the right leg. Repeat both sequences three to five times.

6. Supine Stabilizer: (A) Lie on your back with your legs fully extended. With your elbows under your shoulders, lift your whole body onto your forearms and heels. Keep your legs, hips and back as straight as possible. (B) While maintaining this position, lift your left leg 10 cm (4 in) off the floor. Hold for 4 seconds, then repeat with your right leg. Repeat both sequences three to five times.

WEBWISE

For a simple website with tons of information about getting stronger without drugs, you can't beat this 'home of physical culture'. Answers to many of your basic questions.
www.naturalstrength.com

6A

6B

'A well-balanced core also improves your running economy. Result: faster times.'

CHAPTER 31

Run to
the Water

Not Just for the Injured, Pool Running Has Many Benefits

When you have too many aches and pains to run on land, jump in the water.
Pool running helps you stay in shape and recover from injuries at the same time.

Runners get injured, at least in part, because running requires a movement
where you jump from one foot to the other. It's a small jump – and even a
smooth and graceful one, if you run with good form – but nonetheless
it's a jump. And when you come down on the next foot, that foot, leg
and hip have to work together to absorb all the shock forces that
accumulate when a jumper lands.

Result: it's easy to develop heel, ankle, shin, knee and other
aches and pains.

On the other hand, if you could run without jumping
from foot to foot, you would easily avoid all these
pains. Most of the time, of course, the Earth's gravity makes it
impossible for you to run without jumping. But if you get in
a pool or another body of water, everything changes. All of a
sudden, your body is supported by the buoyancy of the water.

Now, you can run without jumping. You can run without
injuries. Which is why pool running is such an excellent
cross-training alternative for injured runners. It's even a great
way to train when you're not injured. You can increase your
weekly training miles (or minutes) without increasing your
chances of getting injured.

POOL RUNNING IS SIMPLE

And there's almost nothing to it. You need to realize this from
the start: pool running is as simple as land running. You jump
into the water and start running. If you know how to run,
you know how to pool run.

Use pool running either to get a great workout or
to stay in shape while recovering from injury.

Granted, it looks a little odd, but so what? Thirty years ago, people used to think running looked pretty odd, too, and look how wrong they were.

TWO BIG REASONS TO POOL RUN

1. To boost fitness: 'Without exaggeration, every single one of the runners who takes my pool-running classes gets faster on the roads,' says coach Doug Stern, who conducts classes for the New York City Road Runners Club. And they do so without increasing their injury risk one bit, as pool running is a no-impact activity.

2. To recover from injury: Pool running is the best cross-training exercise for runners because it's hardly cross-training at all. It's running – in a pool. A whole host of injuries – stress fractures, shinsplints and plantar fasciitis among them – won't keep you from pool running. Therefore, you won't lose one bit of fitness during your healing period.

What's more, research has shown that injured runners who pool run can reach the same positive mood state as when they run on land. No surprise here. You're not sitting around sulking; you're staying fit and recovering from your injury.

For years, world-class runners have used pool running to maintain their conditioning when they can't run. Former marathon world record holder Khalid Khannouchi ran in the pool to stay in shape when a recent foot injury prevented him from doing his normal training. Janis Klecker, a 1992 US Olympic marathoner, has done twice-a-week pool runs for years. 'If I'm too tired to run,' says the dentist and mother of six, 'I jump in the pool. It always re-energizes me.'

IN THE WATER

You'll find that running in the pool has some differences from land running, but you'll master all you need to know in a matter of 5 to 10 minutes.

■ The first thing you're going to notice is that the water makes it impossible to move your legs as fast as you would on land. That's not a problem. If you can run at about 50 per cent of your normal cadence, the effort will approximate your dry-land running. The faster you run, the greater the resistance, the tougher the workout. Just like on land.

> *' Think like a runner when you're creating workouts – you can duplicate just about any type of running workout in a pool.'*

THE BEST WAY

Q: What's the best exercise to do in the pool?

A: If you're a runner who wants to get faster and stronger, pool running is the best exercise to do in a pool. However, the pool is also a terrific place to get in other kinds of workouts. Many runners enjoy swimming as an aerobic, upper-body-strengthening exercise. Swimming provides a great workout to alternate with running once or twice a week. The supportive buoyancy of the pool also makes it a great place for resistance training and stretching exercises. It's the perfect water gym!

■ Your running form in the pool is important. Don't lean too far forwards, which is the natural inclination. Instead, try to stay as vertical as you can, using your arms. Stern suggests 'sweeping' your entire leg forwards, with minimal knee bend. This form, similar to what you do on an elliptical trainer, uses the whole leg to drive against the water, which builds strength in key muscles such as the quadriceps, hamstrings and glutes.

■ The waterline should be about shoulder level.

■ Your arm swing should be natural, just like running.

■ Breathe as you do when running. Don't hold your breath like a swimmer.

■ Don't bob. Try to maintain a steady cadence, and keep your head above water.

■ Wear goggles. Even if your face isn't constantly in the water, the pool chemicals can be strong (especially early in the morning), which can irritate your eyes.

■ Take breaks. The first few times you pool run, you'll probably need to stop and rest. Run for 2 or 3 minutes, then grab the side for 30 seconds or so, then go again. Aim for 15 to 20 minutes of running your first time out.

■ Finish off each pool-running workout with an easy swim. It's a great way to cool down, stretch out and work the upper body.

FOUR GOOD WORKOUTS

Think like a runner when you're creating workouts – you can duplicate just about any type of running workout in a pool. Because it's more difficult to judge workout intensity with a pool run, Stern suggests you think in terms of 1 (easiest) to 10 (hardest). He says most pool running should be in the 4-to-8 range, with 6 to 8 being the speed range and 4 to 5 the easy run or recovery range.

Looking for an even simpler system? Just go with 'hard' or 'easy'. After a 5- to 10-minute warm-up of easy pool running, try one of these workouts (or do parts of all four of them).

1. Tempo. A classic tempo run on land is 5 × 5 minutes at slightly slower than 10-K race pace, which is sometimes described as 'comfortably hard'. This is about midway between your easy run pace and your speed-training pace.

Getting started

It couldn't be easier. Find a nearby pool, and keep the following in mind. First things first.

• *You need deep water, as you must be able to run without touching the bottom of the pool. Look for one with a diving board; this area will be at least 2.4 m (8 ft) deep. Plus, the diving end is usually separated by buoys from the swimming lanes.*

• *If the pool doesn't have a diving end, find an open lane and just go back and forth lengthwise in the deep water. Make sure you let a lifeguard know what you're planning to do, so swimmers can avoid your lane.*

• *Public pools get crowded, so try and go at off-peak times, such as close to opening or closing or during the lunch hour.*

• *Many pool runners use some type of buoyancy belt or vest that makes it easier to float – and therefore run. If you're fit and at ease in deep water, a vest isn't necessary. But if you're not a strong swimmer and are uneasy in deep water, you'll need a flotation device. (Note: many running stores now sell flotation devices for pool running.)*

Wear goggles when you pool run – they'll protect your eyes and build your confidence in the water.

THE FINISH LINE

Three things to remember about this chapter:

1. The water is your friend, especially when you're injured. Not all running injuries result from the impact forces of running, but the vast majority do. And when you run in the pool, you reduce those impact forces to zero. So you can often do workouts that would be impossible to do on land, and you won't feel any pain. Result: you stay in shape and heal from your injury at the same time.

2. Proper pool running technique is easy to learn. It looks strange at first, but you'll work it out in your first 5 to 10 minutes in the pool. Try different arm strokes and different leg strokes. When you find what feels comfortable to you, stick with it, relax and put your effort into the workout. You'll be rewarded with a great training session and a wonderfully refreshed feeling afterwards.

3. When pool running, do the same workouts you do on land. Instead of worrying about your pace and the number of miles you're running, focus on your effort and the total minutes of your workout. You can do long runs in the pool, speed workouts, tempo workouts – anything that comes to mind, really. You'll also get some great strength training from the natural resistance of the water, and you can add a few minutes of stretching at the end of your workout as a bonus.

It's the same in the pool. After warming up in the pool, pick up the pace and maintain tempo intensity for 5 minutes, with a 1- or 2-minute recovery. Do one or two more sets, eventually working up to five.

2. Free form. On tracks or on roads, it's easy to pick up the pace and run at a faster tempo to the next telegraph pole, tree or up a hill. In the pool, there aren't any hills or telegraph poles, so pick up the pace and run to a ladder, diving board or lifeguard chair. Or simply go for varying segments of time.

3. Follow the leader. Find some company for this one, and get in a single-file line. The person in front picks it up for a certain length of time, then slows down and moves to the back of the line. Everyone recovers for a specified length of time. Then the next leader picks it up, and so on.

4. Steady state. Everyone's favourite. Hop in the pool and run at an easy, conversational pace for 30 to 45 minutes. If you can't keep up your end of the chatter, you're running too fast.

WEBWISE

For more information about the healing and fitness-enhancing benefits of running in water (a pool, lake or even the sea), check out this helpful and informative website.
www.aquarunning.com

'If you know how to run, you know how to pool run.'

7
WEIGHT
LOSS

CHAPTER 32

Eat Well
All Day Long

Learn What to Eat, When to Eat and How to Eat

*A healthy eating plan has to get you through 16 hours a day.
Anything less than that, and you're likely to fall off it at any
point. So here are eight steps that will keep you eating well
from sunrise to long past sunset.*

*Many runners eat healthy foods for much of the day. Then
something goes wrong. It can be almost anything. Suddenly
you find yourself reaching for one of those salty, sugary, fat-
filled foods. Afterwards, you feel silly and guilty that you went
down the wrong path. You might hear yourself saying: 'I know
what I should eat. It's just that I go wrong at some time during
the day. What's wrong with me?'*

*Most runners are far from nutritionally ignorant. Quite the
contrary. They know far more about healthy nutrition than
the average person. Many, in fact, are perfectly happy with the
way they eat for most of the day.*

You can give in to temptation once in a while, but
try to follow a healthy eating plan at all other times.

But if you sometimes fall off the wagon, this is the nutrition
information you've been looking for. It presents a simple
step-by-step plan that will help you eat better all day long –
not for just 4 hours, not for 8, but for the full 16 hours of
your waking day. It tells you how to eat, what to eat and
when to eat.

Result: you'll feel better, run better, have more energy all
day long and control your weight more successfully. Recent
studies in to diet and running have shown that the leanest
runners are those who match their calorie intake and
expenditure on an hourly basis. Which is exactly what you'll
be doing soon. Here's how.

1. Don't get too hungry. The first and most important secret of better daylong nutrition is not to let yourself get too hungry. Hunger is an abnormal physiological condition that creates internal chaos, including a strong drive to eat the wrong kinds of foods (the sugary, fat-filled ones). Hunger stimulates the taste buds to want carrot cake, not carrots. And apple pie, not apples. If you want to eat more of the right foods and less of the bad ones, you need to realize that hunger is enemy number one.

As a runner, you can do this by remembering that food is fuel, and you need it to run your best. In other words, eating is good and valuable, and you need to consume premium foods all day long.

2. Make time to eat. Most runners live very busy lives at home and work, and as a result, they feel they have no time to eat. But that's simply not true. It only requires an attitude correction. Making time for meals, for the most part, is a matter of choice. You choose to make time to work, sleep, run and do things with your family, after all. You can also be more responsible about good nutrition, and make more time for it.

In a busy day, meals don't just happen. That's why it makes sense to schedule breakfast, lunch and dinner in your daily diary, in the same way you do other important events. Then you'll stick to them.

3. Surround yourself with wholesome foods. And make sure they're available at the right times of day. To do this, you have to understand that good nutrition begins in the supermarket. You can't eat a breakfast of orange juice, whole grain cereal, bananas and skimmed milk if you don't have those foods in your kitchen when you wake up. In the same way, you're less likely to finish off the tub of artery-clogging ice cream after your next long run if you have several pots of low-fat, fruity yogurt in the fridge.

4. Eat breakfast. When you start your day with a nutritious breakfast, you refuel your body after the nightlong 'fast', prevent hunger and increase the chances that you'll make sensible food choices the rest of the day. Many studies have

Start off right: by eating a wholesome, nutritious breakfast, you're fuelling up for the day ahead.

shown that people who start each day with breakfast live longer and more healthily than those who don't.

Some runners believe, however, that skipping breakfast increases their fat-burning ability. This supposedly enhances both their endurance and their loss of body fat. Well they're wrong. For endurance, you need to fuel yourself appropriately before every run, and not run on fumes. For fat loss, you have to end the day with a net calorie deficit. And you'll rarely achieve this net calorie deficit unless you eat healthily all day long and have plenty of energy for your workouts. Those who cut calories in the morning are also the ones most likely to binge later in the day.

5. Eat before you run. Some runners fail to eat in the right way all day long because they worry about suffering stomach problems during and after their workouts. For the most part, this is more urban legend than reality. (If it's a reality for you, make sure you read point number 6 closely.)

In fact, studies have shown that you should try to eat 200 to 300 calories in the 60 to 120 minutes before your workout or race. This pre-exercise food not only puts fuel in your tank, it also keeps you from feeling starved post-run.

6. Try creative meal planning. Especially if you're one of those unfortunate runners with a delicate stomach who finds that food 'talks back' to you during your workouts. In that case, you'll have to experiment with eating different types and portions of pre-run foods at different times before your runs. If you're creative enough, you can always come up with a successful regime to ensure you never suffer during workouts or a big race.

Here's a good example: let's say you're a runner who has stomach trouble during many of your morning runs. You begin to think you need to eat something before your run, but you don't want to get up any earlier than you do now. The solution: eat your breakfast the previous evening before you go to bed. An hour before you hit the sheets, have a bowl of milk and cereal and a banana. The next morning, you'll run with more energy and won't be as likely to have those sugary food cravings after your workout.

> '*Many studies have shown that people who start each day with breakfast live longer and more healthily than those who don't.*'

THE BEST WAY

Q: What's the best way to stick to a weight-loss programme?

A: Combine exercise with a diet plan that includes plenty of foods you like. You have to cut back your daily calorie intake to lose weight – that's obvious. And the best way to stick to a calorie-reduced diet is to make sure you actually like the foods on the diet. Don't pick a diet full of foods you despise – it's destined to fail. Second, exercise (and running is the best one for weight loss) is hugely important. It will add to your calorie burn while you also decrease your calorie intake. Result: significant weight loss that will keep you highly motivated to stick to the programme.

7. Don't aim for perfection. No one ever achieves it, and you're not likely to be the first. Besides, you don't have to eat perfectly to eat better all day long. You can have the occasional biscuit, bag of crisps or even a quarter pounder with cheese.

All foods can fit in to a good diet. The trick is learning to eat smaller portions of the less-nourishing foods (you don't have to eat all the chips that come with your burger), and more of the nutritious foods. Some runners have improved their diet (and lost weight) by allowing themselves to have a chocolate croissant for breakfast every day. After a favourite-and-slightly-sinful breakfast, these runners were content to eat healthily the rest of the day.

Other runners might think they are approaching diet perfection because they eat lots of fruits, salads, vegetables and whole grain products throughout the day. Unfortunately,

' Those who cut calories in the morning are also the ones most likely to binge later in the day.'

Lose weight 1 pound at a time

If you want to lose weight, aim for a small calorie deficit every day. Don't follow an overly restrictive diet. As mentioned in point number 1 on page 238, if you let yourself get too hungry, you're almost certain to start making poor food choices. Even dieters will be most successful in reaching their goals if they keep themselves from getting too hungry.

When you look at weight loss mathematically, you see how simple it is. Let's say you establish a meal plan that allows you to knock 100 calories a day from your overall food consumption – that's a mere two jaffa cakes or a small bowl of frozen yogurt in the evening. Not so hard to imagine, is it?

Yet with this small adjustment, you'll lose 10 pounds of fat in the next year. Here's the maths: 100 calories per day multiplied by 365 days equals a deficit of 36,500 calories – slightly more than 10 pounds of fat.

On the other hand, if you try to cut 1,000 calories a day from your food consumption, you'll almost certainly fail. You'll end up getting hungry, eating too many of the wrong foods and probably putting on 10 pounds in a year.

Always remember that food is your friend, not your enemy. It's healthy, filled with vitamins and minerals, and provides fuel for your workouts. When you regard food as your enemy, you tend to eat skimpy or 'diet' meals (Special K, Lean Cuisine, salads), but then are likely to succumb to chocolate bars or biscuits 2 hours later. So change your thinking to this: 'When I eat satisfying portions of healthy foods throughout the day, I'm less likely to crave fattening portions of the wrong foods.'

THE FINISH LINE

Three things to remember about this chapter:

1. **Make eating a priority.** When you eat 'on the run', you probably consume too many unhealthy snack foods that add pounds without adding nutrients. Plan a meal routine where you can sit down and focus on your foods while you eat them. Try to have a little protein, a little fibre, and some fruit, vegetables and fluid at every meal. Variety is important.

2. **Eat before and after your workouts:** a light pre-workout snack will boost your energy, guaranteeing that you exercise as long and as hard as you want. If you don't eat, you might fail to finish the workout. Eating right after your workout increases your muscle-glycogen replenishment. In other words, your muscles are literally 'hungry' in the hour after your run, and they are particularly eager to refill the fuel tank in this period.

3. **Eat more to lose more.** This is a very hard principle for dieters to grasp, but it has been proven many times over. The thinnest people often eat the most. They eat the most because they are on a healthy exercise programme that requires them to constantly stock up, but also because they recognize the importance of small meals and snacks throughout the day.

these individuals are sometimes wrong. A diet that lacks high-quality proteins and calcium-rich dairy foods is far from perfect. A simple daily goal that will work wonders for many runners: eat a variety of foods from a variety of food groups.

8. Live and learn. You're going to make food mistakes on occasion, because working out how to eat well requires a good deal of experimentation with food choices and meal times. Don't worry about your mistakes. Just learn from them.

At the end of the day, ask yourself: What went well with my eating today? What went wrong? How could I have eaten better? What can I do differently and better tomorrow?

Here's what you'll probably discover: you make bad food choices when you fail to eat on schedule, get too hungry and reach for the nearest junk food. However, you'll also start to see that you eat healthiest when you shop sensibly at the supermarket, surround yourself with nutritious foods and eat on a regular schedule to prevent hunger pangs.

It's not rocket science. That's the best news of all. Eating better all day long is so simple that every runner should be able to get it right. No excuses!

WEBWISE

For the latest news stories about weight loss, the best website is Yahoo, specifically the Yahoo news pages. Once you're on the main Yahoo news page, click on 'Health' and then 'Weight Issues/Nutrition'.
http://uk.dir.yahoo.com

CHAPTER 33

The Nearly Perfect
Weight-Loss Day

A 24-Hour Schedule to Help You Keep the Weight Off

Nutritionists all agree: there's no such thing as a perfect weight-loss plan. If there were, everyone would be following it, and no one would be overweight. No, perfection doesn't exist and never will. Having said that, it still makes sense to come a little closer to perfection than the nutrition plan (or lack of plan) that you're probably following right now.

An editorial in a recent issue of the American Journal of Clinical Nutrition *asked, 'If humans represent the most intelligent form of life on this planet, why is it that they find it so difficult to make the apparently small adjustments in daily behaviour that we calculate would halt the continuing rise in obesity?' Or, to be blunt: if we're so clever, how come we're so fat?*

When you ease into your day and stay stress-free, you're less likely to overeat.

Good question. Perhaps it's because we're looking for weight loss in all the wrong places. Like so much else in life, the biggest threats aren't always as clear as they seem. It's the little things that'll do you in: take the escalator here, grab a cola there, miss a run and before you know it you're being forklifted out of bed while a TV-news camera crew captures the whole thing on tape.

OK, that's an exaggeration. The point is that every day, from the time your clock radio rouses you to the moment you turn off your bedside light, you face a hundred tiny weight-loss choices. Some are more significant than others, but all of them add up. Over time, your choices shape you. Literally.

Nobody expects you to make intelligent choices all the time. But if you did, just for 1 day, it might look something like the following. And the results would almost certainly help you achieve your weight-loss goals.

THE MORNING ROUTINE

06:45 Wake up . . . slowly. Frazzled is no way to start your day. 'Many people overeat in response to stress,' says Penn State University professor of nutrition Dr Barbara Rolls. Give yourself a 30-minute buffer in the morning to relax and ease into your day. Rolls suggests spending 15 minutes doing yoga or meditation, or relaxing with the newspaper and a cup of tea as you get your head together. A stress-free morning will help set the tone for the rest of your day.

07:00 Milk it. In a study of 54 people, those who consumed at least 1,000 mg a day of calcium (about 3 glasses of skimmed milk) put on 6 to 7 fewer pounds over 2 years than those who were on low-calcium diets.

07:20 Walk the dog. Anybody who can't get motivated to walk obviously doesn't have a dog. A lively hound will certainly motivate you when he parks himself beside your bed every morning, yapping and staring at you with those . . . well . . . puppy-dog eyes.

07:45 No breakfast? Don't even think about it. 'Overweight people skip breakfast more than any other meal,' says Dr Rolls. Have raisin bran or porridge; both are high in fibre. 'Studies show that when you eat a filling high-fibre breakfast, you'll eat 100 to 150 fewer calories for breakfast and lunch,' explains Dr Rolls.

08:10 Perform a bypass. If the shortest route to work passes a cake shop and two fast food restaurants, then don't take the shortest route to work. Why tempt yourself?

08:20 Walk to work. Even if you drive most of the journey, park several streets away, then hoof it. Walk 10 minutes to the office every morning (and 10 minutes back every evening), and you'll burn an extra 20,000 calories per year. That's more than 5 pounds of flab!

08:30 Step right up. Lifts are for cargo and not for you. Walking up two flights of stairs per day will burn 1,100 calories per year – another ⅓ pound of fat. Besides, when you take the stairs, it's impossible to get stuck between floors with your boss.

08:35 Arrange a still life in your office. Place apples, oranges, bananas, grapes or whatever fruit you like on your desk and vow to eat them all before you leave work. You'll be eating yourself slim. 'The single easiest thing people can do every day to lose weight is to eat more fruits and vegetables,' says Dr Kelly Brownell, director of the Yale University Center for Eating and Weight Disorders.

09:00 Leave the caffeine out. Instead of coffee, go for a mug of green tea – it has compounds called polyphenols that may increase calorie burn, according to the *International Journal of Obesity*

09:15 Can the spam. Is your e-mail inbox crammed with offers for miracle weight-loss products? Delete them. Quickly. Among the 'miracles' recently for sale on the Web: (1) A weight-loss patch made of seaweed. Wear it on your backside, and the pounds will just melt away; (2) Weight-loss essential oils. 'Blended under a full moon . . . (for) added energy from the tidal pull'; and (3) Weight-reducing herbal tea. It 'tonifies the spleen qi' to chase away fat.

Ignore these claims. They're nonsense, and you know it. Focus your time and energy on the simple, realistic steps that will, when added all together, help you get your weight where you want it to be.

09:20 Log off. Close your e-mail programme, at least for a couple of hours. Have to talk to colleagues? Then go and talk to them. 'We're growing fatter as a society partly because our everyday activity has declined due to modern technology,' says Dr James Hill, director of the University of Colorado Center for Human Nutrition.

10:15 Break potty ranks. When nature calls, instinct tells you to make a beeline for the nearest lavatory. Ignore instinct for once, and use a more distant toilet – even if it's on another floor. You'll burn a few more calories.

10:20 Stay sated. Snack time is key for runners, says Dr Dan Benardot, author of *Nutrition for Serious Athletes*. 'Never let yourself grow hungry,' says Dr Benardot. 'Athletes who put themselves in an energy deficit – even a subtle one – will have lower metabolisms and won't

perform as well.' Have a wholemeal English muffin with a knob of butter. In one study, men who ate a little fat in the morning had fewer fat cravings later in the day. You just have to find a balance.

10:30 Have an ice day. Follow that snack with some iced water, and don't be stingy with the cubes. Your body will burn 31 calories warming 1 litre (2 pints) of icy water to 37°C.

11:50 Break into a sweat. Researchers have found that people who lose weight and manage to keep it off burn an average of 400 calories per day exercising – equal to about 4 miles of running. However, 'how you reach that number isn't as important as simply reaching it,' says Dr John Jakicic, assistant professor at Brown University School of Medicine in the US. The key is to develop the habit of being active every day, whether that means running, walking, cycling or simply chasing your kids around the garden for a while.

FROM NOON TO 18:00 HRS

13:00 Pack it in. It pays to bring your lunch from home. A recent study found that people who eat in restaurants six times a week consume 300 more calories a day, on average, than those who prepare their own grub. Start off with chunky soup (you'll eat 20 per cent less at lunch when you eat chunky soup first, researchers say), then have a small sandwich made with lean meat. (Use mustard instead of mayo, and you'll save 80 calories a day. Over a year, that's about 5½ pounds of fat.)

13:05 Just look at yourself. If you can, have lunch in front of a mirror – you'll eat less fat when you watch yourself, two studies have found. Likewise, you may benefit from eating alone. A study in the journal *Appetite* found that people who dined in a group ate nearly twice as much,

Develop the habit of being active every day, whether it means cycling with friends, running after work or lifting weights.

on average, as those who ate alone – even if the 'group' consisted of only one other person.

13:35 Chew on a stick of gum. Not only will it mask the onions on your breath, chewing gum will also burn about 11 calories an hour. Make sure you buy the sugar-free variety though or all your hard graft will be for nothing.

14:30 Nose around. Take a sniff of that banana on your desk. Because taste and smell are closely linked, it will actually dampen your appetite, says Dr Alan Hirsch, of the Smell and Taste Research and Treatment Foundation in Chicago. Green apple and peppermint are also particularly effective scents. 'We found that the more frequently you sniff, the more weight you'll lose,' says Dr Hirsch.

15:00 Skip the cola. Heading to a long staff meeting? Grab a bottle of water. A large bottle of cola can pack 250 calories. And if you think that bottle of fruit juice is a lower cal option, check the label: many have sugar added to them and a large bottle can weigh in at up to 260 calories. Quaff one of these every workday, and you'll rack up 1,300 calories a week. You'd have to run a half-marathon to burn that off!

16:30 Zap your snack. It's been about 3 hours since lunch; time for a bite. Try a veggie-laden slice of leftover pizza – and take the extra 60 seconds to microwave it. 'About 90 per cent of what we call taste is really smell,' says Dr Hirsch. 'And heating food intensifies its smell.' This is a good thing, because as noted earlier, smelling your food before you eat it will dampen your appetite. By the way: blot your hot pizza with a napkin, and you'll soak up 20 calories' worth of grease.

17:30 Scan your desk. Did you eat all your fruit today? Good! Now you earn a reward. Which brings us to . . .

THOSE CRUCIAL EVENING HOURS

18:00 Go for the grape. Janet from payroll is retiring, and you want to raise a toast to her at the local pub after work. That's fine. But watch out for sneaky calories: a medium glass of wine has just 85 of them, whereas birdbath-size drinks like daiquiris may have 400 calories or more.

Cut yourself off. Here are three reasons why you should limit yourself to one drink: (1) you're driving home; (2) because drinking encourages mindless munching (at a bar, that means peanuts and maybe thin fries); and (3) the more you drink, the harder it is to stay on your feet. Standing up burns 1.7 times more calories than sitting down.

18:20 Skip the smorgasbord. If you must munch at the bar, have some hard pretzels, plain or seeded breadsticks or plain popcorn – all crunchy, low-calorie foods that satisfy your appetite prior to a meal. Eat anything to keep you away from the happy-hour buffet table. Remember this simple warning: when you have more food choices, you eat more.

18:35 Walk down the aisle. On your way home, drop in at the supermarket and whip out your list (you do have a list, don't you?). Tip: buy as much as you can in small packets. You'll eat more from a huge packet than a smaller packet of the same food – up to 44 per cent more, according to one study.

Here's what to toss in your trolley.
• Fruits and vegetables (duh). 'They're high in water and fibre, so they fill you up without a lot of calories,' says Dr Rolls.
• Stock-based soups. Another filling choice.
• Lean meats. Calorie for calorie, protein is more filling than carbohydrates or fat.
• Fat-free yogurt. 'I spoon some on my breakfast cereal,' says Dr Rolls. 'That way the cereal seems more substantial.' Yogurt is also

great for making smoothies, another way to fill your stomach with relatively few calories.

• Vegetable juice. It tastes good and it'll make you feel full. In one study, men who drank 400 ml (14 fl oz) of vegetable juice – equating to 88 calories – before lunch ate 136 fewer calories during the meal.

18:45 Stare at the magazines. Not at the chocolate bars. Some supermarkets, in a nod to parents, have sweet-free checkout aisles. Find one and use it, even if it means waiting in the queue behind a grumpy 2-year-old.

18:55 Get tanked up. When you pull into the petrol station to fill up, pay at the pump with your credit card. Otherwise, you'll have to deal with the cashier, who is probably surrounded by snacks and crisps, placed there to catch you in a moment of weakness.

19:05 Use counter intelligence. When you put away your groceries, leave your fruit out on display on a table or worktop – not tucked away in the fridge or pantry. You're more likely to eat food when it catches your eye every time you walk into the room. This is why glass biscuit jars are bad news.

19:15 Have the surf, hold the turf. One study found that overweight people who ate fish every day lost about 20 per cent more weight than a fish-free group. Go for varieties rich in omega-3 fatty acids, such as salmon and tuna. And eat a regular-sized portion: A serving of fish should be about the size of a computer mouse. The same principle applies to meat and poultry.

19:30 Go for sax and violins. Pop in a jazz or classical CD. Studies show that people listening to relaxing music at mealtimes chew more slowly and eat less than people who play more frantic tunes. (Save those for your treadmill workouts.)

19:35 Savour the flavour. You'll enjoy each bite more and eat less because there's a time-lag between being full and feeling full. 'Eating slowly gives your body the opportunity to signal to the brain that you've eaten enough,' says Dr Brownell.

20:00 Fill the sink with suds. Wash your dishes by hand and you'll burn about 25 calories.

20:10 Bag it. Pack your lunch for the following day. Don't feel guilty about including a few biscuits or a small chocolate-bar indulgence. They are not only allowable, they're advisable. Without the occasional treat, your cravings will only intensify until you snap in a moment of weakness and devour a whole tub of ice cream. (Double whammy: loads of calories and an ice-cream headache!)

20:15 Be afraid. Be very afraid. In the mood for a movie, but can't decide between *Scream* and *Sense and Sensibility?* Go for the scary one. Only because you're less likely to eat when you're frightened.

21:00 Intermission. If you're hungry, it's perfectly OK to snack after dinner. The 'no eating after 8 p.m.' rule is a myth, says Dr Rolls. 'What you eat is more important than when you eat.' And you don't want to go to bed peckish.

21:40 Brush up. Brush your teeth immediately after your snack, even if you're not ready to turn in. You'll be less likely to eat again before bed.

22:15 Hit the sack – the same time every night. A chronic lack of sleep may contribute to weight gain, says Dr Pat Kendall, a food science and human nutrition specialist at Colorado State University in the US. 'When people stay up later, they tend to eat more,' says Dr Kendall. 'Also, when you're rested, you're less likely to rely on food to give you energy.' And besides, you have to wake up early tomorrow morning . . . to do your yoga.

THE FINISH LINE

Three things to remember about this chapter:

1. Breakfast is the essential meal. When you get your day off to a good start with a healthy, filling breakfast, you dramatically increase your chances of eating healthily throughout the day. You also put a full tank of fuel in your engine, so you feel happy and energized throughout the day.

2. Make soups a cornerstone of your nutrition plan. They're filling, good for you and contain lots of water, essential to runners. Many studies have shown that eating soups at the beginning of lunch or dinner will help you eat less for the whole meal, including dessert. Try as many different kinds of soup as you can find, and have fun with your own unique combinations of ingredients.

3. Eat plenty of fish as a healthy protein food. Fish is a high-protein, low-calorie food that also contains omega-3 fatty acids, shown to decrease inflammation (including your knee pain), to help your weight-loss efforts and to improve your heart health. You could hardly ask for more from a food. Eat salmon and tuna two or three times a week.

THE URGE TO SPLURGE

It strikes everyone at one time or another – that craving for a forbidden food. Perhaps it's chocolate . . . or ice cream . . . or a favourite cake or pie. We all have our food weaknesses, and we all have appetites that don't always obey the good nutrition plans we're trying to follow.

So what's a runner to do when he or she feels overwhelmed by one of these cravings? Well, give in to it. Life has to include the occasional guilty pleasures. But give in only a little bit. Enjoy a piece or two of chocolate, but not the whole box. Or allow yourself a scoop of ice cream, and then stop. Don't binge on a whole container of ice cream. Learn to exercise control over your cravings.

And keep exercising, of course. In fact, for your next two workouts, go an extra 5 minutes each time. That will almost cancel out the extra calories you consumed, and it will teach you to live a life in balance.

WEBWISE

The BBC's health and fitness website has lots of useful pages on such things as weight loss, nutrition, fitness and eating for energy.
www.bbc.co.uk/health/fitness

'A serving of fish should be about the size of a computer mouse. The same principle applies to meat and poultry.'

CHAPTER 34

Take It Off,
Keep It Off

Maintaining Weight Loss Is Easier than You Think

These runners have lost between 2½ kg (5 lb) and 32 kg (5 st) and managed to keep the weight off with a combination of sensible eating and regular running. Read their advice and learn how simple it is to achieve weight loss with exercise.

When US chat-show legend Oprah Winfrey finished the Marine Corps Marathon in 1994 (after losing 32 kg (5 st) during training), a lot of people got the simple message: running and good nutrition make perfect weight-loss partners. Many of these runners sent their e-mails and personal stories to Runner's World, *or posted them on the* Runner's World *website.*

And the mail has kept coming non-stop. Every year, the editors receive hundreds of letters and e-mails about your slimmed-down bodies, increased energy, improved health and ever-improving race times.

These are weight-loss strategies that work. And they keep on working. They've been proven effective by the runners who use them. If they work for one runner, they can work for you. Don't hesitate, and don't procrastinate any longer. When you want to get in shape and win the battle of the bulge, the time to start is right now.

The words are plain and simple, because they are the words of the successful weight-loss runners themselves. And the tips are guaranteed by the results they've already provided.

Choose a goal. 'Pick a major race to train for, and do it. Last year I trained for my first triathlon. With the extra workouts I had to do, I burned enough calories to lose those extra 3.6 kg (8 lb). I also gained the satisfaction of completing a big race.'
Katherine Cheney

Keep a food journal. 'I lost nearly 1¼ kg (2 st) by keeping a food journal. I found that I was much less likely to eat something if I knew I had to write it down first. The journal helped me eliminate my habit of constantly grazing on unhealthy foods. Even now that I've reached my goal weight, I still keep the journal. It helps me maintain control over what I'm eating.'
Aileen Sanders

Eat more carrots. 'I struggled with losing my post-pregnancy weight, but then discovered the benefits of carrots. I eat a handful of baby carrots while preparing dinner to help me resist second helpings. Not only do I stay away from seconds, I'm guaranteed an extra portion of fresh vegetables a day.'
Jessica Smith

Say no to sweets. 'Cut back on sweets. Instead, snack on pretzels or bananas. If you have to satisfy your sweet tooth, eat low-fat muffins with blueberries or chocolate chips in them.'
Charles Edwards

Exercise more, drink less alcohol. 'Exercise for 30 to 40 minutes a day, stop drinking alcohol and keep your fat intake below 30 grams a day. I lost 32 kg (5 st) in 7 months by following this advice.'
Steve Copeland

Eliminate butter and mayo. 'Get rid of all the butter and mayonnaise in your fridge. Instead, substitute mustard for mayo and soya margarine for butter. Both are lower in fat and calories.'
Michael Branch

Eat dried fruit. 'Keep low-fat snacks such as dried fruit and rice cakes at your desk to nibble on throughout the day. That way you won't be tempted to raid the vending machine.'
Kathryn Trotter

Keeping a journal of your eating habits can help you determine which of them needs breaking.

' *Replace soft drinks with tea, grapefruit or tomato juice.* '

Say no to seconds. 'Eliminate second servings. Also, eat four small meals a day instead of three big ones. And for dessert, eat fruit salads instead of sweets. I lost 5 kg (12 lb) in 2 months doing this.'
Amir Sanchez

Don't skip breakfast. 'Eat your big meal early in the day. If I eat a large breakfast, or even a large lunch, I'm less likely to snack in the afternoon and evening.'
Rita Flaherty

Don't forget protein. 'Eat a high-fibre breakfast with some protein, such as a bowl of raisin bran with milk, or wholemeal toast with peanut butter. This filled me up and reduced my food cravings. I lost 9 kg (1½ st) by starting my days this way.'
Dave Cooper

Find a way around fat. 'Sweets are not a problem for me, but bingeing on fatty foods is. At weekends, I used to enjoy a fry-up using lots of fat. Now I grill everything instead. That, combined with consistent exercise, helps me keep my weight down.'
Becky Young

Discover the benefits of tea and honey. 'All my good diet intentions were foiled each night by a post-dinner sweet tooth. But then I discovered that drinking a cup or two of caffeine-free herbal tea with a dab of honey or sugar-free sweetener curbed my cravings for dessert – enabling me to lose those last stubborn few pounds. As an added bonus, my nightly routine of drinking my favourite soothing tea relaxed me for a restful night's sleep and a better run in the morning.'
Mary Turner

Go ahead and snack after work. 'Far from starving myself before dinner, I learnt to eat something healthy on the drive home from work. I found that if I ate a piece of fruit or drank a low-calorie drink such as V-8, I could resist inhaling the contents of my fridge before dinner.'
Lorraine Story

Avoid junk food. 'Cut down on the biscuits and sweets. When you eat them, you crave more of them, and pretty soon you're carrying extra weight!'
Bryan Herbert

Drinking tea and honey can be an effective way to curb those cravings for dessert.

Run in the evening. 'I usually do my bad munching in the evening. But if I run at night, that urge disappears and I go to bed (and wake up) feeling great.' *Melissa Swaney*

Say goodbye to starch. 'I've had a weight problem all my life. Along with taking up running, I recently cut back on all forms of starch, refined sugar and flour (such as white bread, sweets and white rice), and I've lost 9 kg (1½ st) without really "dieting". I now have more energy, less fatigue and fewer migraines.' *Brenda Brown*

Add more quality workouts. 'I lost 3.6 kg (8 lb) in 5 weeks by training harder and eating better. I added one quality workout per week – such as speedwork or a long run – and stopped eating junk food in the evenings. My 5-K PB is now 45 seconds faster.' *Roy Brennan*

Eat your veggies. 'For dinner, I eat a whole pack of frozen vegetables. I spice them up by topping them with tomato pasta sauce or reduced-calorie salad dressing. Adding garlic or other herbs gives the veggies more flavour and variety, too.' *Mary Clement*

Brush your teeth. 'Immediately after eating dinner, I brush my teeth. This discourages me from snacking again because it cleanses the taste buds, leaving me feeling full.' *Glen Ponder*

Drink skimmed milk. 'If you're a milk drinker, switch from semi to skimmed – a difference of 16 calories per glass. I did this in combination with my running programme, which helped me lose 22 kg (4½ st).' *Suzanne Booker*

List your bad habits. 'Make a list of your worst dietary problems, such as fondness for sugary, salty or fried foods. Then phase them out of your diet one by one. These changes will eventually mean weight lost.' *Matt Allen*

Take a walk. 'Walk before bedtime. It acts as a great appetite suppressant. If hunger strikes at other times during the day, take a walk then as well. If you feel the need to go to the

> *' Running and good nutrition make perfect weight-loss partners.'*

THE BEST WAY

Q: What's the best way to lose 4.5 kg (10 lb)?

A: Write down everything you eat, and maintain your regular exercise programme. The simple act of writing down everything you eat, whether in a fancy journal or on simple notecards, will make you so much more aware of the food you consume that it will almost automatically nudge you to exactly the weight loss you want. It's a simple behavioural trick, but it has worked in thousands of cases.

vending machine, walk to the one furthest from your office. When you reach it, give it the evil eye and walk back satisfied.'

John Johnson

Get enough sleep. 'At college, I wasn't getting enough sleep, and as a result I relied on food to provide the energy I lost from not being rested. I've lost 4.5 kg (10 lb) since college, just by sleeping more.'

Mark Gordon

Snack on popcorn. 'If you're hungry for a night-time snack, eat microwavable popcorn. It's low in calories, and you'll feel very full.'

Robert Blackburn

Eat bananas. 'I lost 2¼ kg (5 lb) and improved my 5-K PB by replacing sweets with bananas.'

Gordon Tellinger

Go for the juice. 'Replace sugary soft drinks with tea, grapefruit or tomato juice. Just one can of fizzy drink has 150 calories, but a glass of tomato juice has only 30 calories.'

James Crabtree

Lift weights. 'Beginning a strength-training programme was the biggest factor in helping me lose 5 kg (12 lb).'

Amanda Merchant

Drink more water. 'Find a large bottle and take it to work. Fill it up with water and drink while sitting at your desk. Finish and fill it several times a day.' *James Cooper*

Get a dog. 'A few years ago I was struggling with health problems and had trouble even getting out of bed in the morning. As a flat dweller, I reasoned that having a dog would make me go outside several times a day, so I adopted a labrador called Jack. Over the next year I lost 9 kg (1½ st) just walking him around the local streets.' *Debra Fordham*

Drink green tea. 'Drink green tea every morning, before and after you run. Some studies have shown that green tea increases energy and helps burn fat.' *Nick Moore*

' When you want to get in shape and win the battle of the bulge, the time to start is right now.'

Starting a strength-training programme could be the key to unlocking your weight-loss potential.

Chew gum. 'To avoid snacking throughout the day, I chew sugarless gum. It stops me from munching and takes my mind off snacking. As an added bonus, you burn 11 extra calories per hour by chewing!'   *Bruce Atkins*

Talk to yourself. 'The best thing I ever did was to start asking myself if I was really hungry. It seems silly, but often it leads me to think, "No, I don't need this".'   *Leah Kinney*

Cut the cream. 'Instead of drinking coffee with cream each morning, I switched to drinking tea with no milk and lost 3.2 kg (7 lb).'   *Maureen Larson*

Munch on gherkins. 'I had a habit of snacking at 8 p.m. To cut back on calories, I started eating one or two pickled gherkins when I felt hungry at night. Their tart flavour satisfied my taste buds with only a few calories.'   *Rich Derry*

Think small. 'In 6 months I lost 3.6 kg (8 lb) by eating the same size portions that my toddler eats. I use a child's plate to control my portions.'   *LeeAnne McNicoll*

Have fun. 'The important thing to remember when trying to lose weight is to have fun. I did this by deciding to have my belly button pierced. I wouldn't have the piercing done until I had the stomach to show it off. A year later, I enjoyed some new jewellery and a love of running.'   *Elizabeth Potts*

Keep the cupboard bare. 'I wanted to lose 9 kg (1½ st), so I cut back on the number of food choices I stocked at my house. By limiting my variety, I cut down on impulse eating. It helped me lose that spare tyre.'   *Justin Williams*

Eat more fruit. 'What helped me lose so much weight was eating more fruit – specifically oranges and apples. They became my low-calorie snack fix, and I found them very filling as well as delicious.'   *Meredith Faulkner*

Cross-train. 'Recently I added 3 days of weight lifting and spinning to my running programme. That extra 2½ kg (5 lb)

For goodness' sake

Make a list of good versus bad. 'I made a list of every food I was eating,' explains Brian Jackson. 'Then I wrote a list of what I should be eating. I gave up one bad food and added one good food at a time. As this became more comfortable, I'd give up one more bad food and add one more good food. I lost more than 13 kg (2 st) eating this way.'

WEBWISE

There are numerous dieting websites. If you'd like a personalized plan and 24-hour support, you may find the ediets website useful. You can even have the latest diet and fitness news e-mailed to you directly.
www.edietsuk.co.uk

THE FINISH LINE

Three things to remember about this chapter:

1. Substitute protein foods for carbo snacks. Runners love and need carbohydrates for quick energy, but you don't need to eat every flour-and-sugar snack that the food industry produces. Instead of biscuits, try yogurt, a handful of nuts or a modest piece of cheese. The protein might give you a greater sense of fullness than a carb snack, so you won't be hungry for another one in 30 minutes.

2. Take some fat out of your dairy consumption. By all means, keep eating low-fat dairy foods such as milk, yogurt and cottage cheese. Simply buy dairy products with less fat in them. Switch from full-fat milk to semi-skimmed, or from semi-skimmed to skimmed milk. Instead of eating ice cream, try fruit sorbets, but be careful that they're not loaded with sugar.

3. Add another activity to your exercise schedule. It can be a simple 20-minute walk that you take several times a week, or a strength-training session in the gym, or a cycle ride with your friends or kids. Chances are you'll increase your calorie burning for the week without increasing your food consumption. In fact, getting out of the house a little more might be the best way to *decrease* those trips to the fridge.

---

slid off in 6 weeks. I also dropped my 5-K time from 20:15 to 19:50, which was a welcome bonus.'   *Dale Hinton*

Eat rabbit food. 'I eat a big salad every night before dinner. It helps curb my appetite. I experiment with different low-calorie and low-fat dressings, too.'   *Lisa Miller*

Just say no. 'Pass on those "Let's go out to dinner" invitations. Invite friends over instead. When you're the cook, you're in control and you know exactly what goes into your food.'   *Robert Patten*

Run to work. 'Commute to work by walking, running or cycling. You'll burn calories every journey.'   *Jane Merrin*

Eat Japanese. 'I'd been exercising for 2 years with little weight loss. Then I moved from London to Japan and started eating Japanese-style meals. After 7 months at the same exercise level, and eating smaller, more healthy meals, I lost more than 9 kg (1½ st).'   *Alasdair Gordon*

Savour your food. 'If I eat my meals slowly and take the time to enjoy them, I don't eat as much.'   *Shauna Stewart*

Japanese dishes are healthy and low in fat, making them ideal for those watching their weight.

CHAPTER 35

The Truth about
Fat Burning

Debunking the Myths about Weight-Loss Methods

Of course, you want to lose weight and lose body fat. But don't fall prey to all those unproven 'fat-burning' products. Here's what you really need to know to take off the extra weight (and the flabby inches).

We live in a time of fat desperation and fat obsession. We all want to eat less fat and carry less of it around on our bodies. To achieve these goals, many people are willing to try all manner of foods, systems and exercise routines.

The problem is, nothing seems to be working. In the last decade, we have lowered our average daily fat intake from 38 per cent of total calories to 34 per cent. That's the good news (though that percentage could still come down a bit more). Unfortunately, surveys tell us we're consuming more total calories, so 34 per cent as fat means we may actually be taking in more total fat than ever. Result: up to a quarter of Westerners are now obese.

Obesity has become a national health crisis, with new headlines appearing almost every day. Of course, that just makes us more desperate for programmes that claim to work, no matter how unproven they may be. The fat battlefield is a major industry in the Western world, and confusion and misinformation run rampant.

This chapter aims to set the record straight. It takes a look at some of the more persistent fat-burning claims made in the last few years and analyzes them in the clear light of scientific scrutiny. Then it concludes with recommendations that will help you win the fight against fat.

Food is energy: understand how much to eat and how much to burn – then you'll lose weight.

BIG FAT MYTH NO.1

If you take away nothing else from this chapter, remember this one fact: if you routinely consume more calories than you expend, you will put on weight regardless of the dietary composition of your intake. Even if you eat less than 30 per cent fat calories a day and limit saturated fat to 10 per cent (both are standard recommendations), you'll still put on weight if you take in more calories than you burn.

Surprised? You're not alone. Many of us believe the myth that as long as we eat low-fat or fat-free foods, we won't put on weight. Not true. If you put away a whole bag of low-fat pretzels in one sitting, you're consuming several hundred calories. Of course, most of them are carbohydrates, but carbohydrates can be stored as fat, too, if you eat enough of them. So can protein. Obviously, so can fat.

Which is not to say that carbohydrates, protein and fat are all the same. Clearly, fat is the real baddie if you get too much of it, and for lots of reasons. High-fat diets are associated with obesity, high cholesterol, cardiovascular disease and cancer. Also, fat is much higher in calories than carbohydrates or protein (9 calories per gram for fat versus 4 calories per gram for carbohydrates and protein). And dietary fat is stored as body fat more efficiently than either protein or carbohydrates.

BIG FAT MYTH NO.2

In essence, myth number 2 goes like this: the optimal exercise intensity for fat burning is low intensity – comparable to something like, say, walking.

Wrong. The physiological fact of the matter is that running burns more fat (and calories) than walking. Exercise physiologist Dr Edward Coyle of the University of Texas has found that running at 65 per cent of max VO_2 (easy running pace), you burn significantly more fat calories per unit of time than you do at 25 per cent of maximum (walking).

A final point about fat-burning exercise: running will make you a better fat burner. The reason is that habitual endurance exercise increases the activity of certain muscle enzymes involved in fat burning. These enzymes enable you to spare glycogen (which is what helps you finish a marathon) while you burn more fat. In other words, endurance exercise

Take it to the max

A recent study performed at Laval University in Quebec, Canada, showed that an aerobic exercise programme that included occasional 90-second interval bursts at 95 per cent of maximum heart rate burned three-and-a-half times more body fat than a steady-state, moderate-intensity programme did. Furthermore, the interval trainers achieved this high rate of fat loss while expending less than half the calories of the steady-state group.

One explanation for this startling result: resting metabolic rate can stay elevated for hours after a bout of intense exercise. A 1991 Norwegian study showed that for 15 hours after a 70-minute bout of exercise at 70 per cent of max VO_2, significant fat burning was still occurring. Low-intensity exercise does not cause a comparable boost in metabolism.

teaches your body to burn more fat at a given exercise intensity than a sedentary person burns.

PROTEIN PROTEST

Strange but true: in recent years, 'King Carbo' has found itself in the hot seat. Popular books like *Dr Atkins' New Diet Revolution* and *The South Beach Diet* have led millions of people down the path to eating fewer carbs and more protein. What's more, the diets appear to work for many who follow them. While it's not totally clear *why* they work, the diets have helped many who thought they would never be able to shed the extra pounds.

A similar book called *Enter the Zone* by biochemist Dr Barry Sears has also attracted many fans. Dr Sears argues that the reason Westerners are getting fatter is because they eat too many carbohydrates – and too little protein.

Dr Sears and his followers put insulin at the centre of this problem. They believe that high-carbohydrate diets raise insulin levels higher than they should be. And that high insulin levels inhibit fat burning. The answer, says Dr Sears, is to get more protein and less carbohydrate, which will keep insulin levels down and promote fat burning. To help you do this, Dr Sears created the 40-30-30 diet, whereby you consume just 40 per cent of total calories from carbohydrates, 30 per cent from protein and 30 per cent from fat.

Is he right? No, say the vast majority of sports nutritionists and exercise physiologists. Dr Glenn Gaesser, a fat-burning expert at the University of Virginia says, 'Sears has misconstrued the facts. He says there are more fat people than ever because of high-carbohydrate diets. The real point is, they're simply eating too much.'

Scientific debate notwithstanding, the fewer carbs and more proteins approach has attracted many proponents, ranging from six-time Hawaii Ironman winner Mark Allen to Canadian 2:11 marathoner Peter Fonseca to Dr Peter Snell, US 800- and 1500-metre gold medallist in the 1964 Olympic Games and now an exercise physiologist. In the late 1990s, Dr Snell began following a diet programme that utilized an energy bar with a 40-30-30 ratio of carbohydrates, proteins and fats. He quickly lost 9 kg (1½ st). His wife, a serious orienteer, also had some

THE BEST WAY

Q : What's the best way to cut out the fat from my diet?

A : Concentrate on switching from unhealthy fats to healthy ones. The unhealthy fats are the full-fat dairy products, butter, fried foods, chicken skins and cuts of beef that are marbled with highly saturated fat. Instead, switch to olive oil, fish and low-fat dairy products. Peel the skin off chicken and turkey. Don't slather your potatoes with butter and sour cream, and experiment with more vegetarian meals.

' Running will make you a better fat burner.'

luck with the product. 'We've been enjoying our success,' Dr Snell enthused. 'I'm nearly back to my racing weight. A high-carbohydrate diet clearly doesn't work for everyone. I think we may need food choices that allow us to be reasonably satisfied.'

FAT-LOADING CONSIDERED

Take a look at the list of studies on the right, and it may change your views on eating for energy. After all, carbo-loading has been around so long in the running and fitness world that it's difficult to fathom an alternative. Should you be attending pre-race fat-loading dinners instead? A plate of steak and fries the night before your next hard workout?

No. The results of the two New York studies are intriguing to say the least, but many question their validity. 'A major flaw in the design for this research was that the order of the diets was not random for each subject,' says Dr W. Michael Sherman, an exercise physiologist at Ohio State University in the US. Dr Coyle adds: 'The runners knew when they were on which diet, and they knew what the researchers were looking for in terms of performance.'

But in fairness to the New York researchers, their work does indicate that more fat may benefit some runners – highly trained ones, at least. Two of their studies awaiting publication will show that a high-fat diet among 35- and 40-mile-a-week runners not only improved several performance parameters but also increased 'good' HDL cholesterol and improved immune function.

As for the South African study, Dr Noakes maintains that a period of fat-loading may improve the body's ability to burn fat, though he still believes in carbo-loading during the last 3 days prior to an endurance activity. However, plenty of other studies have shown performance gains with high-carbohydrate diets not accompanied by fat-loading. Above all, a high-carbohydrate diet ensures that you'll have plenty of carbs in storage when you need them.

Another point about these studies: it's possible that the subjects got a performance boost simply from eating more calories. (The New York researchers admit this.) The reason: serious, high-mileage runners exercise so much that they

---

The facts about fat

In 1994, a couple of well-publicized studies seemed to show that high-fat diets could improve exercise performance and, in the process, not cause weight gain. (Don't worry. No one will ever say that high-fat diets are a good way to lose fat.)

In a study at the State University of New York, physiologist Dr David Pendergast and associates found that six well-trained runners significantly increased their max VO$_2$ and time to exhaustion on a treadmill following a high-fat diet (38 per cent fat, 50 per cent carbohydrate) compared to when they followed a typical training diet (24 per cent fat, 61 per cent carbohydrate). The researchers theorized that more dietary fat may boost fat burning, which would enhance performance.

Also in 1994, Dr Tim Noakes and colleagues at the University of Cape Town in South Africa found that 2 weeks of fat-loading (at 70 per cent fat calories!) improved performance for five trained cyclists exercising at moderate intensity (comparable to walking), compared to a regime of carbo-loading for 2 weeks. At high intensity (comparable to running), there was no difference in performance following the two diets; fat-loading did just as well as carbo-loading.

The New York lab has since completed another study showing that 4 weeks on a high-fat diet (43 per cent fat) produced performance gains among well-trained runners. Again, the researchers conclude that for performance purposes among well-trained individuals, fat-loading may be the way to go.

THE FINISH LINE

Three things to remember about this chapter:

1. Your body fat doesn't come from fats in foods. It comes from eating more calories than you expend in exercise and daily activities. If you increase your exercise level, you will burn off body fat even without changing your diet. For maximum benefit, exercise a little more and eat a little less – especially less of saturated fats.

2. You don't burn more fat when you walk or exercise at low intensity. Low-intensity exercise causes your body to burn a higher percentage of fat, but less total fat, than high-intensity exercise.

Confused? You're not the first. Here's all you need to remember: your goal is to burn as many calories as possible, and the higher the intensity of your workout, the more calories (including fat calories) you burn per minute.

3. Protein and carbohydrates are both good for you. Don't eat one to the exclusion of the other. Carbohydrates are the best source of readily available energy for exercise. But protein gives you a greater sense of 'fullness', which prevents bingeing. A good rule of thumb: have some protein and carbohydrate at every meal.

struggle to meet their energy needs. When they switch to a higher-fat diet, they may finally meet their high caloric demand (remember: each gram of fat constitutes 9 calories).

THE SMART APPROACH TO FATS AND FAT BURNING

■ If you're looking to lose a few pounds – and perhaps improve your running in the process – you must create a calorie deficit. That is, you have to burn more calories than you consume.

■ Just because you eat low-fat and fat-free foods doesn't mean you can eat lots of them and not put on weight. Read nutrition labels so you can keep track of total calories as well as fat calories.

■ High-protein diets such as the 40-30-30 protein plan won't hurt you, but there's no fat-burning magic to the ratio. A 40-30-30 diet will help you lose weight only if it helps you decrease total calorie intake.

■ Do some strength work. One, it's a good caloric burner. Lifting with the legs can burn up to 12 calories per minute, a rate comparable to running. And two, muscle tissue burns more calories than fat tissue, so your resting metabolic rate will increase as you increase muscle mass.

WEBWISE

Prevention magazine has a long history of supplying research-based medical, nutrition and fitness news. The website has a special Walk Off Weight section.
www.prevention.com

Run faster, get fitter: you don't burn more fat when you walk or exercise at low intensity.

8
ESPECIALLY
FOR WOMEN

CHAPTER 36

The Women's Running Boom

Boys, Step Aside – Women Runners Are Leaving You in Their Wake

Take a look around next time you're out on the running track. Or the race course. Or even on a treadmill at the health club. Notice anything new? How about this: chances are that the runner next to you is a woman.

That might not sound like a shocker, but it wouldn't have been the case just 5 years ago. Men have dominated running since the days of Pheidippides, the Greek messenger who ran from the Plains of Marathon to Athens in 490 BC to announce the great Greek victory over the Persians. As recently as the early 1990s, when the second running boom was taking shape, men runners outnumbered women by a wide margin. But no longer.

Consider the following statistics, and you'll soon realize how quickly women's running has advanced.

■ By the early 2000s, 19 of the 20 largest 5-Ks in the US were 'women's' races: 16 Race for the Cure events, two Revlon Run for Women races and the Idaho Women's Fitness Celebration. While in the UK, the Race for Life series of women-only 5-K races numbers 150 events throughout the summer. The UK's biggest female-only race is the Flora Light Challenge 5-K, with 25,000 participants in 2003.

■ When US organization Team In Training began coaching marathoners in 1991, 70 per cent of the participants were men. Today, the numbers are reversed. Women made up a full 70 per cent of the 34,000 TNT participants in 2000.

■ Sales of women's running shoes and apparel now equal those of men's and, in some cases, even surpass them.

A bright future ahead: women's running is growing all around the world.

■ The readership of *Runner's World* magazine, the world's largest-circulation running publication, reflects the same trend. As recently as 1992, women accounted for just 25 per cent of *Runner's World* subscribers. By 2003, that figure had jumped to 46 per cent, and it's still climbing.

The list goes on and on. Women have been entering the sport in unprecedented numbers – in races, running clubs, on the track and in shoe shops. And the groundswell has forever changed the face of running, not to mention the women who are participating.

WHY WOMEN? WHY NOW?

All this leads to two obvious questions: Why, and why now? Here are the answers.

There have never been so many entry points into running for women. Races, running clubs, running stores and health clubs are just some of the places women now can find introductory classes on running. Websites and e-mail lists have sprouted up specifically to encourage beginning women runners to get out there.

'Many women missed the fitness train the first time and are desperate to get out there,' says Kathrine Switzer, director for Avon Running in the US. That's why Avon's global women's race series, brought back to life in 1998 after a 12-year hiatus, offers clinics for beginners starting weeks before a race.

'Some of them come out overweight, wearing flip-flops or pushing a pram,' Switzer says. Within 12 weeks, most are able to complete a 5-K. 'Once they cross the finish line and earn a medal,' she says, 'they are changed.'

The same phenomenon has occurred in running clubs, says Road Runners Club of America president Freddi Carlip. 'A lot of women want to start but feel uncomfortable doing so in a mixed group,' she says. That's why many clubs have introduced beginning running programmes just for women.

IT WASN'T ALWAYS THIS WAY

Women runners also seem quick to understand that running isn't just another sport centred on fast performances. But it wasn't always this way. 'When I started running in the 1970s, we didn't run for fitness,' says nine-time New York City and

' An ever-growing stack of research backs up the health benefits of aerobic exercise for men and women of all ages.'

Weight loss, bone strength, muscle tone, the social scene – just a few of the reasons why women run.

twice London Marathon winner Grete Waitz. 'Nobody jogged. The health aspect of running didn't exist in those days.'

Now running is as much for the tortoise as for the hare. No matter what your size, shape, age or ability, you'll find a place in the sport, and you might find someone like Waitz standing at the roadside cheering for you. She started a women's race in Norway that attracts more than 25,000 runners annually. 'I wanted to encourage all women by downplaying the competition and by letting them know that it's not embarrassing to go slowly,' says Waitz.

'Women are more time-constrained than ever,' says Switzer. 'Despite talk of equality, the bulk of work falls on women's shoulders – child rearing, household management and, yes, we go to the office every day, too. So women are looking for an accessible means of fitness.'

And running is it. No sport is simpler: it requires no partner, no instructor, no court reservations. No long years of learning special skills, no carload of expensive equipment. You can do it anywhere, any time of day, any time of year, in any part of the country.

'I'm just discovering how hard it is to find time to work out,' says five-time US Olympian Francie Larrieu Smith, who now coaches college track and cross-country. 'It's a lot easier just to run out of your door for 30 minutes than to drive to the gym, change, go to a class for an hour and drive back.'

Running is both convenient and efficient, providing one of the best workouts for your time and money. Half an hour spent running will burn more calories and provide a better cardiovascular workout than 30 minutes spent doing almost anything else. It strengthens muscles and bones and builds endurance. For women seeking fitness benefits in a limited amount of time, running can't be beaten.

OLD MYTHS EXPOSED

If you're old enough, you might remember hearing this warning: 'Your uterus will drop.' Or: 'Your breasts will sag.' Those myths about running being harmful to the female body were left behind miles ago, along with plenty of others.

Today, not only is running not considered dangerous, it's recommended as one of the healthiest activities for an

THE BEST WAY

Q: What's the best way to find a woman running partner?

A: Become one. Find a friend who wants to begin a walking and running programme with you. Tell her that you're both going to succeed, because you'll have each other as motivation. You'll call each other, you'll e-mail each other and you'll get together several times a week for side-by-side workouts. There are millions of women who want to begin a programme but are afraid to start. Tell a friend that you'll supply the courage for both of you. Then, just do it.

increasingly overweight, inactive population. An ever-growing stack of research backs up the health benefits of aerobic exercise for men and women of all ages. Here's just a partial list of proven benefits: running combats breast cancer, diabetes and heart disease; it helps manage body weight and reduces body-fat percentage; and it maintains bone density, minimizes uncomfortable symptoms of menopause and elevates mood.

The good news extends even to pregnant women, who used to be discouraged from running. Research has shown that aerobic and weight-bearing activities such as running are fine for pregnant women within reason (though overheating and over-exertion should be avoided). The fact that women today have the go-ahead to exercise during pregnancy means there's one less myth to keep women from running.

RUNNERS AS ROLE MODELS

Grete, Joan, Paula, even Oprah – the heroines of running are recognizable by their first names. 'The pioneers showed us this is a sport that women can enjoy and benefit from,' says Joan Samuelson, who won the first women's Olympic Marathon in 1984. 'They gave women the opportunity to go out and do what they want to do. They opened the doors for all the rest of us.'

Today, those doors are being held open by thousands of less-well-known role models. Call it critical mass. As women began running, they attracted other women to the sport. As their numbers and power grew, they took on leadership roles: running club chairs, race directors, shop owners, coaches. Their presence now ensures, whether intentionally or not, that other women will give running a try.

'Now women who may have been afraid to try running see so many other women as examples,' says Carlip, who adds that she was considered an oddity when she began running in the 1970s. 'The enthusiasm among women is contagious. It just continues to grow,' she says.

RUNNING, THE GREAT STRESS RELIEVER

Meditation, stress relief, empowerment – running has always provided these emotional lifesavers, but women now place more value on them than ever before. That's because the

Women as lifetime runners

Even after having a baby, women can now continue their running. That's due to both new technology and new attitudes. Have a newborn at home? A treadmill in the spare room enables you to jump on for a workout while baby is sleeping. Or you can take your child to a creche, a service increasingly common at health clubs.

Have a toddler? Take her for a spin in one of those terrific running pushchairs, or invite her to cycle alongside while you run. And when your child is old enough to run, you can enter her in children's races. Bottom line: running is a sport that welcomes the whole family, which helps new mums return to their training programmes.

Finally, races have become increasingly festive. With music on the course and parties afterwards, running events have become a new form of weekend family entertainment.

This secure and fun-filled atmosphere wins over many women who may begin running for fitness, but continue running because of the friends they make. In a world become ever less personal – with anonymous neighbours and computers that talk to each other more than people do – running has become more valuable for its sociability. It's a way to make new friends and to spend time with old ones. Women can squeeze in a visit while they're working out, a healthy alternative to coffee and pastry.

And as a dating service, running clubs and races are unbeatable: you know from the first footstep that you and your potential partner share a healthy pastime.

THE FINISH LINE

Three things to remember about this chapter:

1. Training takes time. There's no way around it. And time away from kids and family has a way of making many women feel as if they're shirking their responsibilities. But the truth is closer to this: anything you do to get fitter and healthier is good for your family. What's more, the emotional release you get from running will help you focus more clearly and productively on all your other responsibilities.

2. Something as simple as running can help you inspire your friends and family. We live in a society that's inactive and overweight. And women, as the family and social leaders, have the ability to turn this worldwide problem around.

When others see you running and taking care of yourself, they'll be motivated to do the same. This includes your kids, your spouse, your friends and your colleagues.

3. You can enter a race without worrying about the pressure. The boom in women-only 5-K races has made it possible for beginning women runners and walkers to find out that races aren't nearly as fearsome and competitive as they might have imagined. In fact, the races are hardly competitions at all. They're much more like celebrations – celebrations of life, of women, and of good health and fitness. As a result, the energy and enthusiasm that you feel in races can help motivate your continued training.

more harried our lives become, the more important it is for us to take care of our whole selves. Running provides a one-step emotional cleanser.

'I don't think anything makes you feel as empowered and as full of self-esteem as running,' Switzer says. 'The sense of accomplishment carries over to everything else in your life. When you get your run in during the day, you feel as if you have a little victory under your belt, no matter what else happens at work, college or home.'

WEBWISE

If you're looking for inspiration, advice on getting started or improving your performance – or simply a list of forthcoming UK events – the running4women website is very useful.
www.running4women.com

CHAPTER 37

Be Safe
Out There

Keep Your Wits about You Wherever You Run

The world is a big and exciting place for running, but you'll want to take certain steps to make sure you're always safe. Here they are.

As a runner, the chances are pretty good that you're slimmer, stronger, happier and more confident than your sedentary peers. True? Glad to hear it. All good so far.

Unfortunately, plenty of runners take this confidence thing too far – with potentially dangerous results. In effect, some runners suffer from what could be called the Invincibility Complex. You're strong, you're capable, so you think you can run anywhere, any time and no one is going to hurt you. Even on a deserted trail or street. At night. Alone.

A *Runner's World* magazine poll revealed that many of you routinely ignore the basic safety rules of running. For example, less than half of you said you wear reflective clothing when you run at night. Only 23 per cent have taken a self-defence class. And a measly 6 per cent always run with a partner.

So what are you supposed to do to stay safe while you run? Basically, you want to decrease the chances of getting into trouble in the first place.

To that end, integrate the following strategies into your routine. And don't worry, before long they'll be just that: routine. At which point your running will be safer and more enjoyable than ever.

Plan ahead. Know exactly what route you're taking before you head out. Evaluate it for potential danger spots (unpopulated or poor-visibility areas) and have a plan for where you'll go and what you'll do if you run into trouble. Think about having 'safe houses' along your route (places to go if you need help) and play out possible scenarios in your head. Ask yourself: 'What if this happened? How would I react?' This way, you'll be ready if trouble comes.

Go online. Visit *www.timeoutdoors.com/clubfinder* to find a running club in your area with potential partners for you. Or pop into a local recreation centre or specialist running store and enquire if they organize group training runs.

Tell a friend. Your running partner can't meet you for a run? What a shame, but you can still call. Call her (or someone) before you leave, tell her where you're going and what time you'll be back. Make contact with her again when you return. Get her to do the same when she goes for her run.

Keep your ears open. Everyone knows this one, yet 13 per cent of our poll respondents said they always run wearing headphones. Unless you're on a treadmill, headphones are usually unacceptable because they prevent you from being fully aware of your surroundings. Better alternative: find a running partner who sings. Or sing to yourself.

Make eye contact. Making eye contact with other runners or people on your route shows that you're confident and that you're aware of them. Ergo, avoiding eye contact gives the impression that you're afraid or intimidated. Same goes for drivers on the roads. Make eye contact with them before you cross the road.

Take the keys. Always carry them with you. Leaving your house or car unlocked or hiding your keys under the car while you run are invitations for theft. Holding your key as you run also allows you to use it as a weapon if you are confronted by an attacker and need to fight back. You can use it to gouge his eyes or jab him in the neck.

THE BEST WAY

Q: What's the best way to stay safe on the roads?

A: Run with a partner. Two people are much less likely to be harassed or attacked than one. Besides, a running partner will serve you well in a scenario where one of you has a simple accident – you might step in a pothole and twist your ankle, for example. Your running partner doesn't have to be another woman. Many men and women who work together or live in the same street have become supportive, encouraging running partners. Here's an alternative: try running with the family dog to see if that works for both of you.

' If you have to run at night, wear reflective gear, go with a friend and stick to populated, well-lit areas.'

Carry ID. Only 26 per cent of respondents to the *Runner's World* poll said they always carry ID while running. Because driving licences can be awkward to carry, try ID Me Kits, identification strips that attach to your running shoe, wrist or ankle. Visit *www.idmekits.co.uk* for more details. Another creative approach: go to a pet shop and make your own 'dog tag', then thread it onto your shoelace.

Carry a mobile phone. Only 6 per cent of poll respondents said they always run with a mobile phone. Not good. These lightweight devices fit easily on a waist clip or in a bum bag. Along with their obvious use, mobile phones can be deterrents to attackers if you have them in plain view on your waist.

Be an alert road runner. Many runners become blasé on the roads, especially if they're on a regular running route. Don't get lazy; remember where you are. Also, look out for hostile drivers. If you encounter one, restrain yourself and move on. Some people – especially men – will challenge the driver. That's a big mistake. In a battle between a car and a runner, the car wins.

Connect with police. Runners don't typically like to hear about crime that goes on in their running locality, but it's important to stay informed. It's a good idea if individuals and running clubs build relationships with their local police force so they can stay updated on crime activity.

Bend one rule at a time. If you must break one safety rule, be extra diligent about following every other one. For example, if you have to run at night, wear reflective gear, go with a friend and stick to populated, well-lit areas.

Be self-reliant. It's fine to take an alarm on a run, but don't be entirely dependent on it. Safety devices often give people a false sense of security – you just depend on them being there. You need to be prepared for them not to work. It's a better idea to invest in yourself. Your body is your best weapon. Which leads to . . .

> '*Making eye contact with other runners or people on your route shows that you are aware of them.*'

Carrying a mobile phone or some change for a phone call when you run could be a lifesaver.

THE FINISH LINE

Three things to remember about this chapter:

1. Be careful on the trails and scenic running paths. Runners often enjoy natural areas that are somewhat off the beaten path. These are great places to escape from cars and exhaust fumes, and to run without worries about fighting off the traffic. But places that are less well-travelled also have fewer people to come to your assistance when you need help. So be especially vigilant when running in these areas.

2. Don't wear headphones. OK, a lot of people prefer to run while listening to their favourite tunes, and who can blame them? But don't run with headphones unless you're in a traffic-free area that's absolutely safe. A treadmill qualifies, but few other places do. Your ears are one of your best alert systems; don't cover them up.

3. Carry a mobile phone. Today's mobiles weigh no more than an energy bar, and one could come in very, very handy if you get injured or have an accident. You'll probably want to turn the ringer off, as your workout time should be free of outside distractions. But you'll be happy to have the mobile phone with you on that rare occasion when you need it.

Learn self-defence. Contrary to popular belief, most programmes focus on reducing your risk of being a target, so you'll never have to employ the groin kick. But you'll learn it just in case, along with other confidence-building moves. Women who complete a self-defence programme can expect to see a change in how they present themselves.

Their body language will say, 'No, don't challenge me.' What's more, in a dangerous situation, you need to react quickly, and an hour-long class once a year won't prepare you to do that. So you need to attend refresher courses regularly. Try your local council or college for classes.

WEBWISE

Many women use running to increase their sense of personal strength and independence, but safety is always an important consideration. The Suzy Lamplugh Trust has lots of advice on personal safety.
www.suzylamplugh.org

CHAPTER 38

Run like
Oprah

Match Her Courage and Commitment Pace for Pace

US chat-show legend Oprah Winfrey lost 32 kg (5 st) and ran a marathon on a training programme just like the one in this book. If she did it, you can too.

Bob Greene was stunned, to say the least, when he received a phone call from Winfrey in the early spring of 1993. At the time, Greene was head of the exercise programme at Telluride Ski Resort in Colorado. He had only met Winfrey 6 months earlier when she was visiting the resort. She wanted to try mountain biking; he took her on several strenuous rides through the surrounding trails, where Winfrey has a home.

Now Winfrey had something other than cycling in mind. She was calling Greene to ask him to move to Chicago to become her personal trainer. Greene hesitated. 'I like to sit down with potential new clients to make sure they're serious,' he recalls. 'With Oprah, that wasn't possible.'

Still, it was Oprah asking, so he eventually agreed. Greene, an exercise physiologist, was fully aware of Oprah and her yo-yoing weight-loss problems. Seven years earlier, in front of a national TV audience, she had told the story of her successful routine on the Slim-Fast programme. But that didn't last long. Within months the weight had crept back on.

A HEALTHY WEIGHT-LOSS APPROACH

Oprah had climbed back up to over 100 kg (around 16 st) and found that she couldn't shift much weight despite her adherence to a low-calorie, low-fat diet (as detailed in the best-selling cookbook *In the Kitchen with Rosie*). Greene naturally wondered about Oprah's commitment to an exercise programme.

However, 5 minutes into their first session, he says he knew that he'd made a good choice. 'I could tell she was completely determined,' he says. 'And she never wavered.' Both Oprah and Greene had the same original goal: healthy weight loss.

But how? 'I made a decision from the very beginning to centre Oprah's exercise programme around running,' Greene says. 'There were other options,' he continues, 'including swimming or cycling. But if you want quick weight-loss results, as Oprah did, running is the best.' At their first training session, Oprah and Greene walked about 2 miles. Slowly. 'I wanted to assess her condition,' Greene says. He found her healthy enough to begin, a few days later, a programme that mixed jogging and walking.

Her initial pace worked out to about 17 minutes per mile. But 2 weeks into her programme, Oprah was running and walking 3 or 4 consecutive miles at that pace. Scheduling these workouts was not easy. Five days a week, Oprah would rise at 5 a.m. to run before taping the *Oprah Winfrey Show*. Each afternoon, she'd climb onto the StairMaster for 45 minutes, followed by half an hour or so of weight training.

ON A ROLL

By early summer, Oprah was on a roll. 'She was achieving a steady, sustainable 3.5- to 4.5-kg (8- to 10-lb) weight loss every month,' Greene says, 'and she didn't have to change her diet.' There was one brief setback. 'About 3 weeks into our programme, Oprah noticed she'd actually gained weight, not lost it, which is a common phenomenon for people who start a serious exercise programme,' Greene says. 'But that weight falls straight off after another week or so. Unfortunately, many people give up exercising as soon as the weight comes on. It's a convenient excuse.'

Oprah did not give up. 'She was so excited, because she soon began seeing dramatic results,' Greene says. 'The body abides by the laws of physics. The more weight you lose, the faster you run. And the faster you run, the more weight you lose.' By July 1993, Oprah was running 5 to 6 miles a day at 10- or 11-minute-per-mile pace. By midsummer, she had lost

Oprah Winfrey with her trainer Bob Greene, whose expertise helped Oprah run her first marathon.

more than 19 kg (3 st). It was time to race. 'I believe in using races as motivators,' Greene says. 'Sometimes it's hard to keep going on an exercise programme if you don't have a goal in sight. You need to focus.'

He had hoped to find a 10-K for Oprah to enter but couldn't locate one that matched her busy weekend schedule. Eventually, he decided to be more ambitious, so in August 1993 he entered Oprah in the America's Finest City Half-Marathon in San Diego. Oprah completed the distance in a respectable 2:16.

With her finisher's medal triumphantly in hand, Oprah began pressing Greene to come up with a new challenge. 'She told me she had always loved watching the Chicago marathon,' he says. 'She'd cheer and think, "I'd like to do that some day".'

A NEW GOAL

Greene downplayed the idea. First, he told her, she should concentrate on reaching her goal weight of 68 kg (10 st 10 lb). She was so close. And on November 10, 1993, she made it. That same morning, for the first time ever, she completed her 5-mile training loop at an 8-minute-per-mile pace. 'I was so proud of her,' Greene recalls. 'Sometimes people will say to me, "Oprah's got it easy because she has a personal chef and a personal trainer". But that's rubbish. No one can run for you. She worked herself as hard as any athlete I've seen. She deserved the results she achieved.'

From that day on, the focus of Oprah's training programme shifted dramatically. She had achieved her weight loss. She'd even run a half-marathon. What was left? 'Obviously, we wanted to maintain the weight loss, first and foremost,' Greene says. 'But we also knew Oprah was ready to begin running more seriously. We decided to move from a weight-loss programme to a training programme. We decided that in 1994 she'd run a marathon.'

So, beginning in January of that year, Oprah stepped up her training. Curiously, she began by running less, but this was part of the plan. 'We stopped the two-a-day workouts,' Greene says. 'I even cut back somewhat on her mileage. Instead, I put her on a much more intensive strength-training regime, because I knew that training for a marathon would

---

THE BEST WAY

Q : What's the best way to find a coach?

A : Oprah Winfrey hired a personal trainer. This has proved to be a very successful path for many beginning exercisers, but you'll probably be happy to find a coach or friend to offer advice and encouragement. While you can find excellent coaches on the Internet these days, the best coach is someone from your community whom you can actually meet, talk to and perhaps run with on occasion. Ask around to see if you can find one. Beginning running classes are starting to appear in more places; you might find one in your town.

'It's just so inspiring to watch someone transform herself, and that's what Oprah has done.'

THE FINISH LINE

Three things to remember about this chapter:

1. Don't expect a miracle a day. Running is without question the simplest, most effective, least-time-consuming exercise. But that doesn't make it a miracle worker. You won't be able to run a mile further every day, and you won't lose a pound a day, and you might never encounter that mystical 'runner's high'. Everyone faces obstacles, whether their name is John Smith or Oprah Winfrey. Just stick with the plan; the progress (and maybe a small miracle) will come.

2. Physics is on your side. Oprah's coach Bob Greene makes this statement, and he's right. As you get in shape and train a little more, you'll probably lose a couple of pounds. Which will enable you to run a little further and faster. Which will help you lose several additional pounds. And so on. This isn't a vicious cycle; it's a virtuous cycle. And you'll become part of it if you stick to your programme.

3. Consider the occasional race. You do not have to race to get in shape, or to lose weight or to call yourself a runner. But races can help. First and foremost, they're motivators, to use Bob Greene's term. They help you train. But races also introduce you to the community of runners and help you see that you are one of millions, and that 99.9 per cent of those other runners are just like you (while 0.1 per cent hopes to go to the Olympics some day).

be hard on her body. I wanted to make sure her joints were strong and healthy.'

A DAILY RENEWAL

By midsummer 1994, Oprah was running as much as 50 miles a week, including longer distances on weekends. At times, she complained. 'This is such a struggle,' she'd say to Greene. To which he answered, 'No, it's not. It's a daily renewal.'

His message took hold, and Oprah stuck to the programme. Three months later she completed the Marine Corps Marathon without walking a single step. 'I'll never forget mile 25 of that race,' Greene says today. 'She was just so pumped. There were tears in her eyes. It was so moving.'

'She could have given up months ago,' he continues. 'She certainly had enough legitimate excuses. But she didn't. I like to think her progress and her commitment will show millions of other people that they can improve their lives, too. Maybe they won't run a marathon. But they can run a 5-K. Or they can lose the weight they've been wanting to get rid of. It's just so inspiring to watch someone transform herself, and that's what Oprah has done. She's a runner now for life.'

WEBWISE

Tawni Gomes, a big Oprah Winfrey fan (who has even appeared on the show several times), has been inspiring other women to lose weight and get fit for a number of years. Her website is simple but effective.
www.connectingconnectors.com

9
THE 8-WEEK
TRAINING PLAN

CHAPTER 39

For the
Already Active

Workouts, Tips and Inspiration

Now it's time to hit the road, literally and figuratively. Whether you've read every word in the preceding 38 chapters or not, you're eager to get started.

Fine. Let's get going then. But please review the following before you dash away from the starting line.

1. Use this plan – the 8-Week Training Plan – if you're under 40, less than 9 kg (20 lb) overweight and a regular participant in some form of physical exercise, such as football, tennis, cycling, swimming or walking. Otherwise, play it safe and turn to the 24-Week Training Plan that begins on page 284.

2. Get your doctor's approval. Unless you have a known health problem or risks, your doctor should encourage you to begin an exercise programme. In fact, consider letting your doctor know about this book, so it can be recommended to others who want to get fit, lose weight and live more healthily.

3. Schedule your workouts. You won't find time for them unless you *make* time for them. Enter them in your diary, computer, daily appointment planner, on the front of your fridge or wherever else you keep your schedule.

4. Expect bad days. Everyone has them, but they pass quickly, and the next workout is often better than the previous one. So stick to the plan.

5. Don't rush. In the fitness world, rushing leads to injuries and discouragement. Be patient, and go slowly. The goal is to reach 30 minutes of running, not to set any records getting there.

Make sure you obtain your doctor's permission before beginning any type of exercise programme.

'*Sit as little as possible. Give no credence to any thought that was not born outdoors while moving about freely.*'

Friedrich Nietzsche

WEEK 1

Day	Workout	Comments
Monday	Run 1 min; Walk 2 min; Repeat 10X	
Tuesday	Walk easy 30 min	
Wednesday	Run 1 min; Walk 2 min; Repeat 10X	
Thursday	Walk easy 30 min	
Friday	Run 1 min; Walk 2 min; Repeat 10X	
Saturday	Run 1 min; Walk 2 min; Repeat 10X	
Sunday	Rest	

TRAINING TIP:

To fuel up for your workout, eat a piece of fruit or an energy bar about 2 hours before you lace up your shoes. An hour later, drink 230 ml (8 fl oz) of a sports drink. The drink will ensure that you are fully hydrated, and also that you have sufficient sodium and potassium for a healthy workout.

'*Don't bother just to be better than your contemporaries or predecessors. Try to be better than yourself.*'

William Faulkner, American writer (1897–1962)

WEEK 2

Day	Workout	Comments
Monday	Run 2 min; Walk 1 min; Repeat 10X	
Tuesday	Walk easy 30 min	
Wednesday	Run 3 min; Walk 1 min; Repeat 7X; Run 2 min	
Thursday	Walk easy 30 min	
Friday	Run 4 min; Walk 1 min; Repeat 6X	
Saturday	Run 4 min; Walk 1 min; Repeat 6X	
Sunday	Rest	

TRAINING TIP:

Always walk 2 to 3 minutes for a warm-up before you begin your workout, and walk another 2 to 3 minutes as a cooldown afterwards. Don't stretch prior to running. Save it for after your workout or in the evening while you're watching TV.

'*Obstacles are those frightening things that become visible when we take our eyes off our goals.*'

Henry Ford

WEEK 3

Day	Workout	Comments
Monday	Run 5 min; Walk 1 min; Repeat 5X	
Tuesday	Walk easy 30 min	
Wednesday	Run 5 min; Walk 1 min; Repeat 5X	
Thursday	Walk easy 30 min	
Friday	Run 6 min; Walk 1 min; Repeat 4X; Run 2 min	
Saturday	Run 6 min; Walk 1 min; Repeat 4X; Run 2 min	
Sunday	Rest	

TRAINING TIP:

Hold your arms comfortably at your sides while running, aiming for maximum relaxation. Bend them 90 degrees at the elbows, and move them forwards and back at your waist. Bend your fingers into a relaxed grasp, and don't let your hands sway back and forth across the middle of your torso.

'When you get to the end of your rope, tie a knot and hang on.'

Theodore Roosevelt

WEEK 4

Day	Workout	Comments
Monday	Run 8 min; Walk 1 min; Repeat 3X; Run 3 min	
Tuesday	Walk easy 30 min	
Wednesday	Run 9 min; Walk 1 min; Repeat 3X	
Thursday	Walk easy 30 min	
Friday	Run 10 min; Walk 1 min; Repeat 2X; Run 8 min	
Saturday	Run 11 min; Walk 1 min; Repeat 2X; Run 6 min	
Sunday	Rest	

TRAINING TIP:

In hot, sunny weather, wear sunscreen, sunglasses (to relax your facial muscles), and a visor or cap to keep the sun off your face. Expect to run more slowly in particularly hot, humid weather, and take more walking breaks as necessary. Run in the early morning or late evening if you can.

'*Sweat cleanses from the inside.
It comes from places a shower
will never reach.*'

Dr George Sheehan, American writer (1918–1993)

WEEK 5

Day	Workout	Comments
Monday	**Run 12 min; Walk 1 min; Repeat 2X; Run 4 min**	
Tuesday	**Walk easy 30 min**	
Wednesday	**Run 13 min; Walk 1 min; Repeat 2X; Run 2 min**	
Thursday	**Walk easy 30 min**	
Friday	**Run 14 min; Walk 1 min; Repeat 2X**	
Saturday	**Run 15 min; Walk 1 min; Run 14 min**	
Sunday	**Rest**	

TRAINING TIP:

On occasion, skip your running and walking workout and do a cross-training workout instead. Cycle for 30 to 40 minutes, try the elliptical trainer in a gym or join a circuit weight-training class. The break from running will refresh you, and you'll learn new skills while developing new muscles.

'*You can have anything you want, if you want it badly enough. You can be anything you want to be, if you hold that desire with singleness of purpose.*'

Abraham Lincoln

WEEK 6

Day	Workout	Comments
Monday	Run 16 min; Walk 1 min; Run 13 min	
Tuesday	Walk easy 30 min	
Wednesday	Run 17 min; Walk 1 min; Run 12 min	
Thursday	Walk easy 30 min	
Friday	Run 18 min; Walk 1 min; Run 11 min	
Saturday	Run 19 min; Walk 1 min; Run 10 min	
Sunday	Rest	

TRAINING TIP:

Running is a great way to build strong bones, but you also need plenty of calcium – 1,000 mg a day and 1,500 mg if you're over 50. Drink a glass or two of low-fat milk per day, or enjoy a pot or two of low-fat yogurt or cottage cheese. Dark green, leafy vegetables are another great calcium source.

> *'Only those who risk going too far can possibly find out how far they can go.'*
>
> T.S. Eliot

WEEK 7

Day	Workout	Comments
Monday	Run 20 min; Walk 1 min; Run 9 min	
Tuesday	Walk easy 30 min	
Wednesday	Run 22 min; Walk 1 min; Run 7 min	
Thursday	Walk easy 30 min	
Friday	Run 24 min; Walk 1 min; Run 5 min	
Saturday	Run 26 min; Walk 1 min; Run 3 min	
Sunday	Rest	

TRAINING TIP:

Beginning runners often develop shinsplints or sore knees. These pains should pass quickly if you treat them immediately with ice packs after your workouts. Put a bag of frozen peas on your shins or knees for 15 minutes. If the pain persists, take several days off before beginning training again.

'*One cannot consent to creep when one feels an impulse to soar.*'

Helen Keller, American writer (1880–1968)

WEEK 8

Day	Workout	Comments
Monday	Run 27 min; Walk 1 min; Run 2 min	
Tuesday	Walk easy 30 min	
Wednesday	Run 28 min; Walk 1 min; Run 1 min	
Thursday	Walk easy 30 min	
Friday	Run 29 min; Walk 1 min	
Saturday	Run 30 min	
Sunday	Rest	

TRAINING TIP:

For clean air and healthy lungs, try not to do your workouts at the side of a busy street or during rush-hour traffic. Find quiet streets where any exhaust will be dispersed quickly. Even better, as often as possible, try to run in green areas – in parks, on bike trails, around lakes and so on.

10
THE 24-WEEK
TRAINING PLAN

CHAPTER 40

Starting
from Scratch

Workouts, Tips and Inspiration

This is the place to begin your training plan if you're over 40, more than 9 kg (20 lb) overweight or starting to exercise for the first time in a long time. Don't try to rush into things by attempting the 8-Week Training Plan. You'll be much happier and more successful taking the slow and gradual approach on the following pages. Please review the following points before you get going.

1. Tell your doctor that you intend to begin a very gradual running and walking plan. You may need a complete physical checkup before you begin this training programme.

2. Don't expect miracles. It took you years to get out of shape, and it will take time to get back in shape. Using this programme, you'll get there, day by day and week by week.

3. Do expect changes. As you work through the programme, you'll find that it gets easier and easier, even though you're running further and further. That's the miracle of the body becoming reacquainted with its natural ability to run and walk.

4. Don't worry when you miss a day . . . or a week. Simply get going again as soon as you can. But don't try to make up for lost time by pushing yourself to exhaustion.

5. Train for life. When you reach the end of the 24-Week Training Plan, don't stop. Keep going. You can run more if you want, or simply continue with the same or a very similar workout plan. But don't surrender your hard-won fitness.

Note: When you see 'Run 1:30 min', this means 'Run for 1 minute and 30 seconds'.

Success may come quickly to you as a beginning runner, but the race is never won. Run for life.

'Our greatest glory is not in never falling,
but in rising every time that we fall.'

Confucius

WEEK 1

Day	Workout	Comments
Monday	Run 30 sec; Walk 2 min; Repeat 12X	
Tuesday	Walk easy 30 min	
Wednesday	Run 30 sec; Walk 2 min; Repeat 12X	
Thursday	Walk easy 30 min	
Friday	Run 30 sec; Walk 2 min; Repeat 12X	
Saturday	Run 30 sec; Walk 2 min; Repeat 12X	
Sunday	Rest	

TRAINING TIP:

Despite the well-known 'runner's high', runners don't feel good every day. In fact, they have good days and bad days. You'll experience the same. Don't let the bad days get you down. Stick to your programme, and it won't be long before you start enjoying the good days again.

> '*I find that the harder I work,
> the more luck I seem to have.*'

Thomas Jefferson

WEEK 2

Day	Workout	Comments
Monday	Run 1 min; Walk 2 min; Repeat 10X	
Tuesday	Walk easy 30 min	
Wednesday	Run 1 min; Walk 2 min; Repeat 10X	
Thursday	Walk easy 30 min	
Friday	Run 1 min; Walk 2 min; Repeat 10X	
Saturday	Run 1 min; Walk 2 min; Repeat 10X	
Sunday	Rest	

TRAINING TIP:

If you need a jolt to get psyched up for your workout, try a modest-sized cup of coffee. Many studies have shown that coffee increases attention and boosts endurance performance. Coffee has very few, if any, health risks and isn't the major diuretic it was once thought to be.

'Bid me run, and I will strive with things impossible.'

Shakespeare, *Julius Caesar*

WEEK 3

Day	Workout	Comments
Monday	Run 1:30 min; Walk 2 min; Repeat 8X; Run 2 min	
Tuesday	Walk easy 30 min	
Wednesday	Run 1:30 min; Walk 2 min; Repeat 8X; Run 2 min	
Thursday	Walk easy 30 min	
Friday	Run 1:30 min; Walk 2 min; Repeat 8X; Run 2 min	
Saturday	Run 1:30 min; Walk 2 min; Repeat 8X; Run 2 min	
Sunday	Rest	

TRAINING TIP:

For sore muscles, have a massage or try self-massage with your own hands or with any number of simple wooden and plastic devices that make it easier to massage yourself. Massage feels good, keeps your muscles loose and supple, and doesn't require any medication.

' The credit belongs to those who are actually in the arena, who strive valiantly; who know the great enthusiasms and spend themselves in a worthy cause.'

Theodore Roosevelt

WEEK 4

Day	Workout	Comments
Monday	Run 2 min; Walk 2 min; Repeat 7X; Run 2 min	
Tuesday	Walk easy 30 min	
Wednesday	Run 2 min; Walk 2 min; Repeat 7X; Run 2 min	
Thursday	Walk easy 30 min	
Friday	Run 2 min; Walk 2 min; Repeat 7X; Run 2 mln	
Saturday	Run 2 min; Walk 2 min; Repeat 7X; Run 2 min	
Sunday	Rest	

TRAINING TIP:

Many beginning runners like to listen to music on their headphones. Fine, but always make safety your primary concern. Don't listen to music if you're running on roads with lots of traffic or in areas where you feel vulnerable. The best place to run and listen to music simultaneously is on a treadmill.

'If you can fill the unforgiving minute with sixty seconds' worth of distance run – yours is the Earth and everything that's in it.'

Rudyard Kipling

WEEK 5

Day	Workout	Comments
Monday	Run 3 min; Walk 2 min; Repeat 6X	
Tuesday	Walk easy 30 min	
Wednesday	Run 3 min; Walk 2 min; Repeat 6X	
Thursday	Walk easy 30 min	
Friday	Run 3 min; Walk 2 min; Repeat 6X	
Saturday	Run 3 min; Walk 2 min; Repeat 6X	
Sunday	Rest	

TRAINING TIP:

Try a sports drink *after* your workout as well as during the workout. A post-run drink will help to restore the energy you've spent, and also to replenish your salt and potassium levels. This will prevent cramps and help you recover fully for your next training session.

> 'Talk to me not of time and place;
> I owe I'm happy in the chase.'

Shakespeare, *Epistle to David Garrick, Esq*

WEEK 6

Day	Workout	Comments
Monday	Run 4 min; Walk 2 min; Repeat 5X	
Tuesday	Walk easy 30 min	
Wednesday	Run 4 min; Walk 2 min; Repeat 5X	
Thursday	Walk easy 30 min	
Friday	Run 4 min; Walk 2 min; Repeat 5X	
Saturday	Run 4 min; Walk 2 min; Repeat 5X	
Sunday	Rest	

TRAINING TIP:

To help you succeed in this training programme, wear a good pair of running shoes. You could use old tennis shoes, cross-trainers or other trainers, but they're much more likely to produce an injury. Besides, running is just easier in a real pair of running shoes.

'*Success is a journey, not a destination. The doing is usually more important than the outcome.*'

Arthur Ashe

WEEK 7

Day	Workout	Comments
Monday	Run 5 min; Walk 2 min; Repeat 4X; Run 2 min	
Tuesday	Walk easy 30 min	
Wednesday	Run 5 min; Walk 2 min; Repeat 4X; Run 2 min	
Thursday	Walk easy 30 min	
Friday	Run 5 min; Walk 2 min; Repeat 4X; Run 2 min	
Saturday	Run 5 min; Walk 2 min; Repeat 4X; Run 2 min	
Sunday	Rest	

TRAINING TIP:

The most efficient runners are those with the least wasted motion, and that should be your goal. Don't take an overly long stride, and don't leap into the air each time you push off with your rear foot. Run with an erect posture, your ears over your shoulders over your hips over your heels.

'*In this age, which believes that there is a shortcut to everything, the greatest lesson to be learned is that the most difficult way is, in the long run, the easiest.*'

Henry Miller, American writer (1891–1980)

WEEK 8

Day	Workout	Comments
Monday	Run 6 min; Walk 2 min; Repeat 3X; Run 6 min	
Tuesday	Walk easy 30 min	
Wednesday	Run 6 min; Walk 2 min; Repeat 3X; Run 6 min	
Thursday	Walk easy 30 min	
Friday	Run 6 min; Walk 2 min; Repeat 3X; Run 6 min	
Saturday	Run 6 min; Walk 2 min; Repeat 3X; Run 6 min	
Sunday	Rest	

TRAINING TIP:

Give treadmills a try. In the last decade, they have improved from clunky old collections of nuts and bolts into sleek, smooth-running machines. Many runners and walkers now do some of their training on treadmills, particularly in the summer heat and winter's cold and darkness.

'*I have fought the good fight, I have finished the race, I have kept the faith.*'

2 Timothy 4:7

WEEK 9

Day	Workout	Comments
Monday	Run 7 min; Walk 2 min; Repeat 3X; Run 3 min	
Tuesday	Walk easy 30 min	
Wednesday	Run 7 min; Walk 2 min; Repeat 3X; Run 3 min	
Thursday	Walk easy 30 min	
Friday	Run 7 min; Walk 2 min; Repeat 3X; Run 3 min	
Saturday	Run 7 min; Walk 2 min; Repeat 3X; Run 3 min	
Sunday	Rest	

TRAINING TIP:

For a great, leg-refreshing cooldown after your workout, walk or run backwards for 60 seconds. Backwards running forces you up onto your toes and stretches the muscles and tendons at the back of the legs that are tightened by forwards running. Strange glances from others? Don't worry about them.

'*The will to win means nothing without the will to prepare.*'

Juma Ikangaa, New York City Marathon winner

WEEK 10

Day	Workout	Comments
Monday	Run 8 min; Walk 2 min; Repeat 3X	
Tuesday	Walk easy 30 min	
Wednesday	Run 8 min; Walk 2 min; Repeat 3X	
Thursday	Walk easy 30 min	
Friday	Run 8 min; Walk 2 min; Repeat 3X	
Saturday	Run 8 min; Walk 2 min; Repeat 3X	
Sunday	Rest	

TRAINING TIP:

Some beginning runners believe that they're supposed to keep their mouth closed and breathe only through the nose. This is a myth. Runners breathe relaxed – and sometimes very deeply – through both the nose and the mouth. Just do what comes naturally, and you'll be fine.

'*Pain is temporary. Pride is for ever.*'

Anonymous

WEEK 11

Day	Workout	Comments
Monday	Run 10 min; Walk 2 min; Repeat 2X; Run 6 min	
Tuesday	Walk easy 30 min	
Wednesday	Run 10 min; Walk 2 min; Repeat 2X; Run 6 min	
Thursday	Walk easy 30 min	
Friday	Run 10 min; Walk 2 min; Repeat 2X; Run 6 min	
Saturday	Run 10 min; Walk 2 min; Repeat 2X; Run 6 min	
Sunday	Rest	

TRAINING TIP:

To control your urge for sugary foods, make sure you eat a small meal every 3 to 4 hours. People who skip meals are much more likely to crave sweets when their blood-sugar level plummets, and then binge on the wrong kinds of foods. Far better to eat many small meals, each of which includes a little protein.

> *'It is a rough road that leads to the heights of greatness.'*
>
> Seneca, Roman playwright

WEEK 12

Day	Workout	Comments
Monday	Run 12 min; Walk 2 min; Repeat 2X; Run 2 min	
Tuesday	Walk easy 30 min	
Wednesday	Run 12 min; Walk 2 min; Repeat 2X; Run 2 min	
Thursday	Walk easy 30 min	
Friday	Run 12 min; Walk 2 min; Repeat 2X; Run 2 min	
Saturday	Run 12 min; Walk 2 min; Repeat 2X; Run 2 min	
Sunday	Rest	

TRAINING TIP:

If you have allergies, you'll probably feel better working out early in the morning when pollen levels are lowest. If you develop itchy eyes, runny nose or other symptoms, ask your doctor about eyedrops or other medication. They've greatly improved in recent years.

'There be some sports are painful, and their labour delight in them sets off.'

Shakespeare, *The Tempest*

WEEK 13

Day	Workout	Comments
Monday	Run 6 min; Walk 1 min; Repeat 4X; Run 2 min	
Tuesday	Walk easy 30 min	
Wednesday	Run 6 min; Walk 1 min; Repeat 4X; Run 2 min	
Thursday	Walk easy 30 min	
Friday	Run 6 min; Walk 1 min; Repeat 4X; Run 2 min	
Saturday	Run 6 min; Walk 1 min; Repeat 4X; Run 2 min	
Sunday	Rest	

TRAINING TIP:

Wear your running shoes for running, and not for other activities. Take good care of them, and they will last for 400 to 500 miles. After 6 months, replace your shoes even if you can't see excessive wear, as the midsoles (the most important part of the shoe) gradually break down.

'*True sport is always a duel: a duel with nature, with one's own fear, with one's own fatigue, a duel in which body and mind are strengthened.*'

Yevgeny Yevtushenko, Russian poet

WEEK 14

Day	Workout	Comments
Monday	Run 8 min; Walk 1 min; Repeat 3X; Run 3 min	
Tuesday	Walk easy 30 min	
Wednesday	Run 8 min; Walk 1 min; Repeat 3X; Run 3 min	
Thursday	Walk easy 30 min	
Friday	Run 8 min; Walk 1 min; Repeat 3X; Run 3 min	
Saturday	Run 8 min; Walk 1 min; Repeat 3X; Run 3 min	
Sunday	Rest	

TRAINING TIP:

You don't need to exercise every day or every week or every month. Over the many years of your life, the important thing is that you make a place for regular running and walking. When you are a beginning runner just getting into the habit of it, consistency is crucial to your success.

'It eluded us then, but that's no matter.
Tomorrow we will run faster . . . Stretch
out our arms farther.'

F. Scott Fitzgerald, American writer (1896–1940)

WEEK 15

Day	Workout	Comments
Monday	Run 10 min; Walk 1 min; Repeat 2X; Run 8 min	
Tuesday	Walk easy 30 min	
Wednesday	Run 10 min; Walk 1 min; Repeat 2X; Run 8 min	
Thursday	Walk easy 30 min	
Friday	Run 10 min; Walk 1 min; Repeat 2X; Run 8 min	
Saturday	Run 10 min; Walk 1 min; Repeat 2X; Run 8 min	
Sunday	Rest	

TRAINING TIP:

Running makes you brighter. One study showed that subjects scored higher on a difficult test after completing a 12-week training programme. Their scores dropped when they stopped working out regularly. The subjects needed at least two 30-minute training sessions a week to maintain their scores.

'Vision without action is a daydream.
Action without vision is a nightmare.'

Japanese proverb

WEEK 16

Day	Workout	Comments
Monday	Run 12 min; Walk 1 min; Repeat 2X; Run 4 min	
Tuesday	Walk easy 30 min	
Wednesday	Run 12 min; Walk 1 min; Repeat 2X; Run 4 min	
Thursday	Walk easy 30 min	
Friday	Run 12 min; Walk 1 min; Repeat 2X; Run 4 min	
Saturday	Run 12 min; Walk 1 min; Repeat 2X; Run 4 min	
Sunday	Rest	

TRAINING TIP:

To shed those unwanted extra kilos, try these three simple strategies: eat a solid, nutritious breakfast to fill your tank; drink water throughout the day instead of soft drinks or high-calorie juices; and skip desserts. If you must have something sweet occasionally, rely on fruit and fruit-flavoured yogurt.

'*Never give in. Never give in. Never give in. Never, never, never.*'

Sir Winston Churchill

WEEK 17

Day	Workout	Comments
Monday	Run 14 min; Walk 1 min; Repeat 2X	
Tuesday	Walk easy 30 min	
Wednesday	Run 14 min; Walk 1 min; Repeat 2X	
Thursday	Walk easy 30 min	
Friday	Run 14 min; Walk 1 min; Repeat 2X	
Saturday	Run 14 min; Walk 1 min; Repeat 2X	
Sunday	Rest	

TRAINING TIP:

Sprinters run on their toes, but distance runners land first on their heels and then roll smoothly to a toe-off from the forefoot. Don't try to run on your toes. That will prove awkward and ultimately fatiguing. Let your heel come down naturally onto the ground under your centre of gravity.

'*Even if you're on the right track, you'll get run over if you just sit there.*'

Will Rogers, American actor and cowboy (1879–1935)

WEEK 18

Day	Workout	Comments
Monday	Run 16 min; Walk 1 min; Run 13 min	
Tuesday	Walk easy 30 min	
Wednesday	Run 16 min; Walk 1 min; Run 13 min	
Thursday	Walk easy 30 min	
Friday	Run 16 min; Walk 1 min; Run 13 min	
Saturday	Run 16 min; Walk 1 min; Run 13 min	
Sunday	Rest	

TRAINING TIP:

A regular training programme demands good sleep habits and about 8 hours a night of shut-eye. That can be hard to achieve for many busy adults, but it pays off. Try to go to sleep and wake up at about the same time every day. Consistency is as good in your approach to sleep as in your approach to training.

'*Sport is not about being wrapped up in cotton wool . . . Sport, like all life, is about taking risks.*'

Sir Roger Bannister

WEEK 19

Day	Workout	Comments
Monday	Run 18 min; Walk 1 min; Run 11 min	
Tuesday	Walk easy 30 min	
Wednesday	Run 18 min; Walk 1 min; Run 11 min	
Thursday	Walk easy 30 min	
Friday	Run 18 min; Walk 1 min; Run 11 min	
Saturday	Run 18 min; Walk 1 min; Run 11 min	
Sunday	Rest	

TRAINING TIP:

A runner's watch will help you complete all your workouts with absolute precision. The watch might appear complicated at first, but you only need to master one or two functions to time all your running and walking intervals. Some watches will even beep when it's time for you to start and stop running.

> *Running is the greatest metaphor for life because you get out of it what you put into it.*
>
> Oprah Winfrey

WEEK 20

Day	Workout	Comments
Monday	Run 20 min; Walk 1 min; Run 9 min	
Tuesday	Walk easy 30 min	
Wednesday	Run 20 min; Walk 1 min; Run 9 min	
Thursday	Walk easy 30 min	
Friday	Run 20 min; Walk 1 min; Run 9 min	
Saturday	Run 20 min; Walk 1 min; Run 9 min	
Sunday	Rest	

TRAINING TIP:

Stinky shoes? There are several things you can do. Some runners sprinkle a little baking powder in their shoes once or twice a week. Others stuff a newspaper in the shoes when they get sweaty-damp, and the newspaper soaks up the dampness. You can also air-dry your shoes in front of a small electric fan.

'*He who fears being conquered is sure of defeat.*'

Napoleon Bonaparte

WEEK 21

Day	Workout	Comments
Monday	Run 23 min; Walk 1 min; Run 6 min	
Tuesday	Walk easy 30 min	
Wednesday	Run 23 min; Walk 1 min; Run 6 min	
Thursday	Walk easy 30 min	
Friday	Run 23 min; Walk 1 min; Run 6 min	
Saturday	Run 23 min; Walk 1 min; Run 6 min	
Sunday	Rest	

TRAINING TIP:

Running and walking get your heart and lungs in great cardiovascular shape. However, they don't do much for your muscle strength. That's why runners should strength train with light dumbbells several times a week. This becomes even more important as you age and begin to lose muscle tone.

'I have not failed 10,000 times. I have successfully found 10,000 ways that will not work.'

Thomas Edison

WEEK 22

Day	Workout	Comments
Monday	Run 26 min; Walk 1 min; Run 3 min	
Tuesday	Walk easy 30 min	
Wednesday	Run 26 min; Walk 1 min; Run 3 min	
Thursday	Walk easy 30 min	
Friday	Run 26 min; Walk 1 min; Run 3 min	
Saturday	Run 26 min; Walk 1 min; Run 3 min	
Sunday	Rest	

TRAINING TIP:

For a food that is high in protein and healthy omega-3 fatty acids, choose tuna. You can now buy it in pouches you don't have to drain (as you do tuna from tins). The tuna from pouches tastes fresher, too. Try it in pitta bread with lettuce and tomato, or in salads.

'*Nothing is particularly hard if you divide it into small steps.*'

Henry Ford

WEEK 23

Day	Workout	Comments
Monday	Run 28 min; Walk 1 min; Run 1 min	
Tuesday	Walk easy 30 min	
Wednesday	Run 28 min; Walk 1 min; Run 1 min	
Thursday	Walk easy 30 min	
Friday	Run 28 min; Walk 1 min; Run 1 min	
Saturday	Run 28 min; Walk 1 min; Run 1 min	
Sunday	Rest	

TRAINING TIP:

If you start to develop any aches and pains in the ankles or knees, try the supplement glucosamine or glucosamine chondroitin. Studies have shown that glucosamine can improve joint health and relieve pain. Best of all, it's relatively inexpensive and has no side effects.

*'Do what you can, with what you have,
where you are.'*

Theodore Roosevelt

WEEK 24

Day	Workout	Comments
Monday	Run 30 min Congratulations!	
Tuesday	Walk easy 30 min	
Wednesday	Run 30 min	
Thursday	Walk easy 30 min	
Friday	Run 30 min	
Saturday	Run 30 min	
Sunday	Rest	

TRAINING TIP:

Studies show that you run most efficiently at a stride rate of about 160 steps per minute. Every time one of your feet hits the ground, that's a step. (A 'stride' includes two steps.) If you're taking fewer than 160 steps per minute, you're probably over-striding. If so, simply relax and lift your knees less.

Credits

Text

'No More Excuses' on page 26 is adapted from 'First Steps' by Tawni Gomes. Copyright 2000 by Tawni Gomes. Reprinted with permission.

'Making Time for Exercise' on page 30 is adapted from 'Fitting It In' by Doug Rennie. Copyright 2002 by Doug Rennie. Reprinted with permission.

'The Best Foods for Runners' on page 99 is adapted from 'Foods You Can Use' by Alisa Bauman. Copyright 1999 by Alisa Bauman. Reprinted with permission.

'Boost Your Consistency' on page 145 is adapted from 'Excuse-Free Running' by Bob Cooper. Copyright 2003 by Bob Cooper. Reprinted with permission.

'Stay Flexible' on page 224 is adapted from 'Make It Routine' by Beryl Bender Birch. Copyright 2001 by Beryl Bender Birch. Reprinted with permission.

'Run like Oprah' on page 270 is adapted from 'The Oprah Winfrey Plan' by Gretchen Reynolds. Copyright 1995 by Gretchen Reynolds. Reprinted with permission.

Photography

John Hamel/Rodale Images: pages 8–13, 16, 25, 38, 88, 93, 94, 99, 162, 184, 208, 211, 217, 259

Ed Landrock/Rodale Images: pages 72, 86, 96, 171, 183, 192, 196, 221, 261

Mitch Mandel/Rodale Images: pages 27, 102 (chocolate), 104 (raisins), 111, 112, 130, 132, 186, 209, 229–231, 252, 276–283, 286–309

Brian Mather/Rodale Images: page 148

Rodale Images: pages 42, 104 (pasta), 116 (carrots), 133, 160, 215

Margaret Skrovanek/Rodale Images: pages 170, 177, 198

Kurt Wilson/Rodale Images: pages 105, 115, 117, 119, 134, 213

Tim de Frisco: page 270

© Mitchell Gerber/Corbis: page 271

© Hilmar: pages 15, 21, 24 (baby), 26, 28, 57, 63, 64, 67, 74, 76, 83, 110, 114, 118 (woman), 121, 128, 140 (runner), 141, 145, 146, 149, 157, 158, 169, 180, 240, 243, 248, 250, 260

Michael Medby Photography: pages 225–227

© Mediadisk: page 91

© PhotoDisc: pages 188, 242, 256, 275

© Photos.com: pages 14, 17, 18, 19, 20, 23, 24 (runner), 30, 32, 34, 40, 41, 44, 46, 48, 49, 51, 52, 54, 55, 59, 60, 62, 68, 70, 71, 73, 78, 79, 80, 81, 82, 84, 89, 98, 100 (bananas), 100 (fruit), 101, 102 (fruit), 103, 106 (fruit), 106 (strawberries), 106 (bread), 108, 109, 116 (fruit), 118 (fruit), 122, 123, 124, 129, 131, 135, 137, 138, 140 (shoes), 143, 147, 151, 153, 155, 156, 164, 165, 166, 168, 176, 179, 182, 189, 191, 199, 205, 206, 212, 214, 219, 222, 224, 228, 232, 234, 236, 237, 238, 244 (man – fade image), 244 (bicycles), 246, 249, 254, 255, 262, 266, 268, 274, 284, 285

Index

Underlined page references indicate boxed text.

Boldface references indicate illustrations.